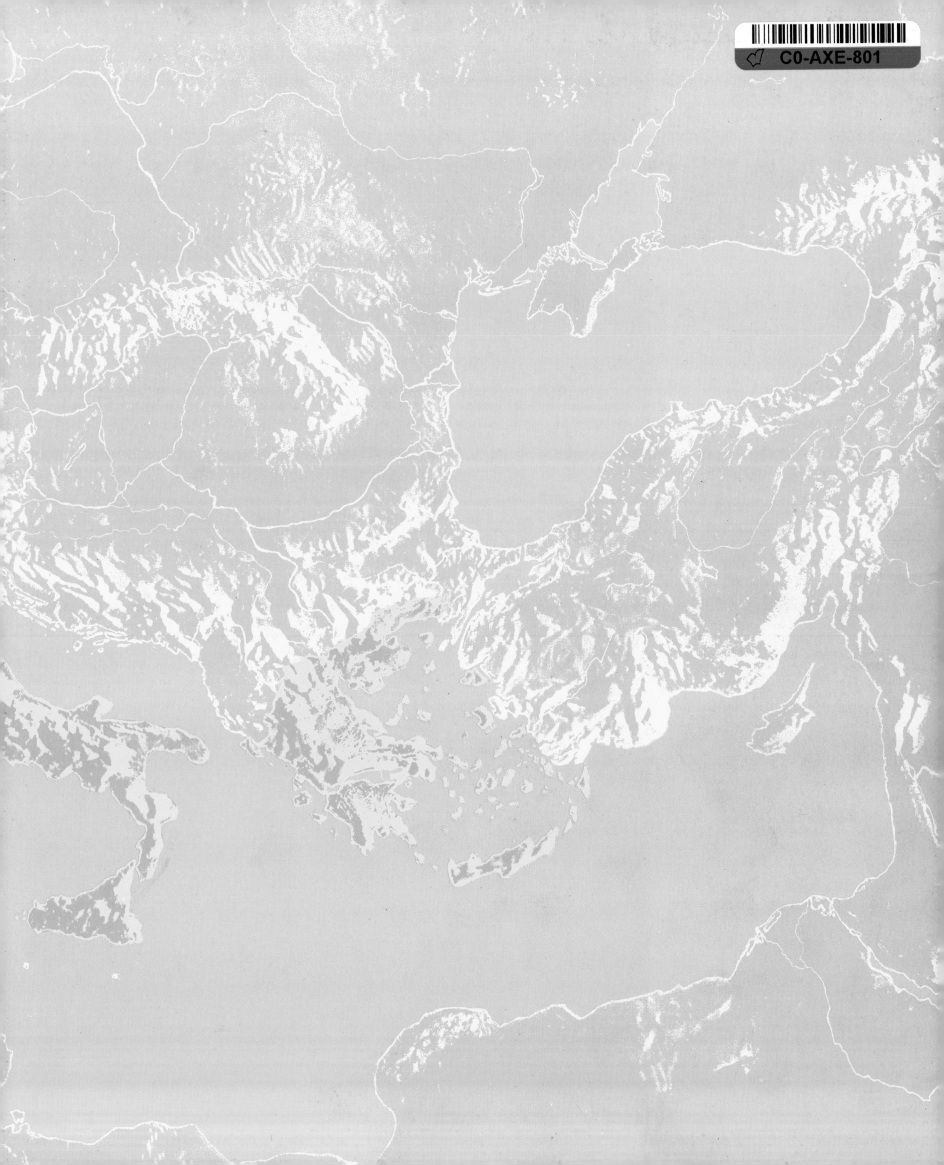

Europe, a bird's eye view

Europa i fugle flugt
Europa aus der Luft
Europa a vista de pájaro
L'Europe vue du ciel
Europa vista dal cielo
Europa in vogelvlucht]
Europa à vista de pássaro
Η Ευροπα σε πανοραμική άποψη

Published by   Euredition bv, Den Haag

Edited by   Dick van Koten and
                Guido Peeters, additional texts

Aerial Photographs supplied by
                Luftbild Klammet & Aberl, München,
                except those for Belgium and
                The Netherlands which are supplied by
                Daniel Philippe, Airprint Bruxelles and
                Dick Sellenraad, AirView Rotterdam
                and others

Produced by   Kopub bv / Buro AD, Dirk van Wikselaar
                Typesetting: EPS, Amsterdam
                Colour separations:
                ACI-van Tijn & Zack, Amsterdam
                Printing and binding: Brepols, Turnhout

© MCMXC   ILLUSTRA
                P.O. Box 9511, NL 3007 AM Rotterdam

ISBN and distribution:
UK   1 85422 102 7
                Harvey Sales / Magna Books, Leicester

D   3-7658-0672-2

F   2-73-820333-7

I   88-239-0178-2
                Orsa Maggiore / Stock Libri, Torriana (FO)

NL   90 6113 413 7
                Atrium / ICOB cv, Alphen aan den Rijn

EUROPA–EUROPE
L'EUROPE–Η ΕΥΡΩΠΗ

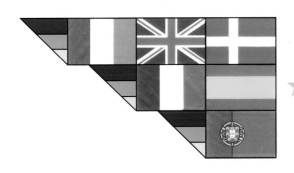
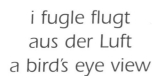
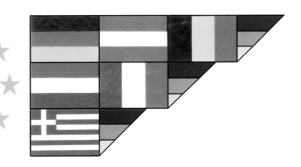

i fugle flugt
aus der Luft
a bird's eye view

a vista de pájaro
vue du ciel
vista dal cielo

in vogelvlucht
à vista de pássaro
σε πανοραμική άποψη

Jacques DELORS
Président de la
Commission Européenne

Med fantasi og intelligens, men frem for alt gennem en uafladelig iver har europærne bearbejdet deres jord – gjort naturen nyttig – og bygget deres byer. Disse drivfjedre finder vi tilbage i de smukke fotografier, der viser De Europæiske Fællesskaber i fugleflugt.

Luftfotografierne i denne bog vidner ikke blot om historiens fremskridt, men også om den nye fremgang i de lande, der tilhører vort fællesskab.

Hvor er Europa, vort fælles fæadreland, dog smukt: det er inspirationen for vore anstrengelser, kilden til vore rigdomme.

Det er forlæggerens fortjeneste, at han med denne fotoserie erindre os herom, og han støttes heri fuldt og helt af Den Europæiske Kommission.

Denne bog bidrager således på sin egen måde til de gradvise, politiske og økonomiske, forsøg på at samle de europæiske folk og forene dem til gavn for freden, uafhængigheden og udfoldelsen, mæn også i samklang med andre.

Til alle dem, der til vor store glæade har været med til at skabe dette værk, retter vi en varm tak.

Jacques DELORS
Formand for
Den Europæiske Kommission

Die Europäer haben mit Kreativität und Klugheit, vor allem aber mit unermüdlichem Fleiß ihren Boden bearbeitet, sich die Gaben der Natur zunutze gemacht und ihre Städte errichtet. Die eindrucksvollen Luftaufnahmen aus den Mitgliedsstaaten der Gemeinschaft gewähren einen faszinierenden Blick auf die Leistungen dieser schöpferischen Kräfte.

Die Luftaufnahmen in diesem Buch zeugen nicht nur vom geschichtlichen Fortschritt, sondern auch vom neuen Elan in den Ländern unserer Gemeinschaft.

Wie schön ist doch dieses Europa, unser gemeinsames Vaterland! Es beseelt unsere Anstrengungen, es ist Quelle unserer Reichtümer.

Verdienst des Herausgebers ist es, uns – übrigens mit voller Unterstützung seitens der Europäischen Kommission – mit dieser Fotosammlung daran zu erinnern.

Bas Buch trägt also auf seine ganz besondere Weise zu den schrittweisen politischen und wirtschaftlichen Bemühungen bei, die europäischen Völker friedlich und mit dem Ziel der Unabhängigkeit, der Entfaltung, aber auch der Verbundenheit mit Außenstehenden zu vereinen.

Allen, die zu unserer großen Freude an der Realisierung dieser Ausgabe mitgewirkt haben, sei an dieser Stelle unser Dank ausgesprochen.

Jacques DELORS
Vorsitzender der
Europäischen Kommission

The creativity and ingenuity, but above all, the diligence with which we Europeans have cultivated our land, sustained the naturel environment, and built our cities, is expressed in the splendid series of photographs contained in this bird's eye view of the Member States of the European Community.

The aerial photographs in this book not only bear witness to historical progress, but also to new developments taking place in the countries of our Community.

How beautifel Europe is – our common inheritance! It's an inspiration for our efforts and the source of our wealth!

The publisher has produced a successful reminder of this with this collection of photographs, published with the close support of the European Commission.

Thus, in its own way, this book contributes to the gradual, political and economic attempts to unify and unite the European Community for the benefit of peace, independence and development, but also to achieve solidarity with other countries.

We should like to express our deepest appreciation and gratitude to all those who have contributed to the publication of this book.

Jacques DELORS
President of the
European Commission

6

Con creatividad y genialidad, pero sobre todo con continuo esfuerzo, lo europeos han cultivado la tierra, sirviéndose de la naturaleza, y han construido sus ciudades. Esto es lo que refleja esta hermosa serie de fotos a vista de pájaro de los países miembros de la Comunidad Europea.

Las fotos aéreas de este libro muestran no sólo el desarrollo de la historia sino también los nuevos desarrollos en los países de la Comunidad.

Qué hermosa es nuestra Europa, nuestra patria común: inspiración de nuestros esfuerzos, fuente de nuestras riquezas.

Es un mérito del editor que no los vuelva a recordar mediante esta colección de fotos en la que también ha colaborado la Comunidad Europea.

Este libro contribuye por tanto de una manera muy particular en los continuos intentos políticos y económicos de unir los pueblos europeos en favor de la paz, la independencia y el desarrollo, pero también la solidaridad respecto a terceros.

A todos los que han contribuido en la realización de este libro les hacemos llegar nuestro más sincero agradecimiento.

Jacques DELORS
Presidente de la
Comisión Europea

La créativité, le génie, mais surtout le travail inlassable des Européens pour cultiver leur sol, pour domestiquer les éléments et pour bâtir leurs cités, sont les impressions fortes que suscitent l'observation de ces belles photos des différents Etats de la Communauté Européenne vue du ciel.

Les photographies aériennes contenues dans cet ouvrage témoignent à la fois de la permanence de l'Histoire mais aussi du renouveau entrepris dans les Etats de notre Communauté.

Qu'elle est belle cette Europe, notre patrimoine commun, l'inspiratrice de nos efforts, la source de nos richesses!

L'éditeur a la mérite de nous le rappeler en rassemblant ces photos dans un seul volume, publié sous l'égide de la Commission Européenne.

Cet ouvrage contribue ainsi à sa manière, aux efforts menés sur les plans politique et économique pour rapprocher et unir les peuples européens dans un but de paix, d'indépendance, et de développement, mais aussi de solidarité vis-à-vis des autres.

Que tous ceux qui ont contribué à la réalisation de ce livre, pour notre plus grand plaisir, trouvent ici l'expression de nos remerciements.

Jacques DELORS
Président de la
Commission Européenne

Con molta creatività e genio, ma sopratutto con tanto lavoro incessante, gli Europei hanno coltivato il loro suolo per assoggettare la natura ed hanno costruito le loro città. Queste loro innate capacità le ritroviamo in una meravigliosa serie di foto degli Stati soci della Comunità Europea.

Le foto panoramiche aeree in codesto libro dimostrano non solo lo sviluppo storico ma anche il nuovo progresso nei paesi della nostra Comunità.

Qunat'è bella questa nostra Europa, nostra patria comune, ispiratrice dei nostri sforzi, fonte della nostra ricchezza!

E merito dell'editore di farcelo ricordare con l'aiuto di queste bellissime foto, pubblicate sotto l'auspicio della Commissione Europea.

Codesto testo contribuisce perciò a modo suo, ai tentativi progressivi sul piano politico ed economico, di avvicinare i popoli europei e di unirli a favore della pace, dell'indipendenza e dello sviluppo, ma anche in armonia con altri.

A tutti colore che hanno collaborato alla realizzazione di questo testo, desideriamo esprimere la nostra gratitudine.

Jacques DELORS
Presidente della
Commissione Europea

Met beeldende en verstandelijke vermogens maar vooral met niet aflatende ijver hebben de Europeanen hun grond bewerkt – de natuur dienstbaar gemaakt – en hun steden gebouwd. Deze drijfveren vinden we terug in de schitterende reeks foto's van de lidstaten van de Europese Gemeenschap in vogelvlucht.

De luchtfoto's in dit boek getuigen niet alleen van de voortgang van de Geschiedenis maar ook van de nieuwe vooruitgang in de landen van onze Gemeenschap.

Wat is Europa, ons gemeenschappelijk vaderland, toch mooi: bezieling voor onze inspanningen, bron van onze rijkdommen!

Het is de verdienste van de uitgever om ons met deze verzameling foto's hieraan te herinneren, daarin volgaarne bijgestaan door de Europese Commissie.

Dit boek draagt aldus op zijn eigen wijze bij aan de geleidelijke, politieke en economische, pogingen om de Europese volkeren bijeen te brengen en te verenigen ten bate van de vrede, de onafhankelijkheid en de ontplooiing, maar ook in saamhorigheid met derden.

Aan allen die, tot ons grote genoegen, aan de totstandkoming van deze uitgave meegewerkt hebben gaat hierbij onze dank uit.

Jacques DELORS
Voorzitter van de
Europese Commissie

A criatividade, o génio, mas sobretudo o trabalho infatigável dos Europeus para cultivar o seu solo, para dominar os elementos e para construir as suas cidades, são as fortes impressões que se suscitam ao observar estas belas fotografias dos diferentes Estados da Comunidade Europeia, em vista aérea.

As fotografias aéreas contidas nesta obra testemunham não só a permanência da História, mas também da renovação empreendida nos Estados da nossa Comunidade.

Como é bela esta Europa, o nosso património comum, inspiradora dos nossos esforços, manancial da nossa riqueza!

O editor tem o mérito de nos trazer isto à lembrança, juntando estas fotografias num só volume, publicado sob a égide da Comunidade Europeia.

Esta obra contribui assim, na sua própria maneira, aos esforços empreendidos no plano político e económico para aproximar e unir os povos europeus com um alvo de paz, de independência e de desenvolvimento, mas também de solidariedade mútua.

Que todos aqueles que contribuiram para a realização deste livro, para nosso grande prazer, sintam aqui a expressão do nosso agradecimento.

Jacques DELORS
Presidente da
Comissão Europeia

Με δημιουργικότητα και πνευματικές ικανότητες, αλλά προπαντώς με αδιάλειπτη εργατικότητα οι Ευρωπαίοι έχουν καλλιεργήσει τη γη, χαλιναγωγήσει τη φύση και οικοδομήσει τις πόλεις τους. Είναι τα κίνητρα αυτά που βρίσκουμε στις θαυμάσιες αεπωφωτογραφίες από τα κράτη μέλη της Ευρωπαϊκής Κοινότητας.

Οι αεροφωτογραφίες στο βιβλίο αυτό δε μάς δείχνουν μόνο τη συνέχεια της Ιστορίας, αλλά και τη νέα πρόοδο στις χώρες της Κοινότητάς μας.

Τι ωραία που είναι η Ευρώπη, η κοινή μας πατρίδα: έμπνευση για τα έργα μας και η πηγή των πλούτων μας.

Είναι η αξία του εκδότη που με τις φωτογραφίες αυτές μάς τα θυμίζει όλα αυτά κι 'η Ευρωπαϊκή Επιτροπή με ικανοποίηση υποστηρίζει το σκοπό αυτό.

Το βιβλίο αυτό δίνει με το δικό του τρόπο συνεισφορές στις βαθμιαίες, πολιτικές και οικονομικές προσπάθειες για να συγκεντρωθούν και ενωθούν οι ευρωπαϊκοί λαοί για χάρη της ειρήνης, της ανεξαρτησίας και της ανάπτυξης, αλλά επίσης σε αλληλεγγύη με τρίτους.

Με μεγάλη μας ικανοποίηση εκφράζουμε την ευχαρίστησή μας σ'όλους που συμμετείχαν στην πραγματοποίηση της έκδοσης αυτής.

Jacques DELORS
Πρόεδρος της
Ευρωπαϊκής Επιτροπής

Fra Schumanplanen til Europa uden grænser

Muren i Berlin, der forsvinder, det er Europa; statuen af Mannekenpis i Bruxelles, det er Europa, Den lille Havfrue i København, Palma, ferieparadiset, Eiffeltårnet, Kreta og dens mytologi, det grønne Irland, Venedig med kanalerne, Radio-Luxemburg, ost fra Gouda, vinen fra Porto, Shetlandsøerne, der får os til at tænke på trøjer af fin uld, det er altsamen Europa.

I denne gamle verdensdel, der gennem tiderne har gennemgået så mange indgribende forandringer, findes der 12 lande og 325 millioner europæere, der nu gennem to generationer prøver at danne et fælleskab i fred, frihed og solidaritet.

De Europæiske Fællesskabers fødselsdag kan fastsættes til d. 9 maj 1950, kl. seks om aftenen. Det var den dag da den franske udenrigsminister Robert Schuman formulerede de mål og betingelser i en plan, der skulle komme til at bære hans navn.

I 1951 skulle E.K.S., Den Europæiske Kul og Stål Union, komme til at leve op til det centrale mål i denne plan: fælles styring af de råstoffer, der både er uundværlige for freden som for krigen. Gennem Parisaftalen blev Belgiens, Frankrigs, Den Tyske Forbundsrepubliks, Italiens, Luxemburgs og Hollands interesser samlet i en traktat.

Nogle få år efter oprettelsen af E.K.S. nås i 1957 en anden afgørende fase i samensmeltningen af de europæiske økonomier. Med underskrivelsen af Romtraktaten er EF født, De Europæiske Fællesskaber, også kendt som Euro-marked, samt Euratom, Det europæiske fællesskab for atomenergi, oprettet far den fælles udvikling af kerneenergi til fredelige formål.

De tre fællesskaber ledes af fælles organer, hvorved der ved summen af delene da også for første gang er tale om et europæisk fællesskab.

I 1973 slutter Danmark, Irland og Storbritannien sig til de oprindelige seks medlemsstater.

I 1981 udvides Fællesskabet med Grækenland.

Og med Spaniens og Portugals tiltræaden i januar 1986 kommer antallet af medlemsstater endelig op på 12.

En ny afgørende fase ringes ind i 1987 med en ny traktat: Det Fælles Marked. Fællesskabet løfter sig op og går i aktion med henblik på fra 1992 at skabe et Europa uden grænser, hvor mennesker, varer, tjenesteydelser og kapital kan bevæge sig frit.

I endnu højere grad end disse fire fundamentale friheder bør Europas enhed i 1992 også opnå en plads i dets indbyggeres hjerter. Med værdige sociale forhold, et Europa med undervisning, kreativitet og uddannelse med nye teknikker, et Europa for videnskabelig undersøgelse og højteknologi, et Europa der beskytter naturen.

Det skal være et fællesskab, der spiller ind på forandringerne i Østeuropa, men som samtidigt har øje for et mere ligevægtigt økonomisk nord-syd forhold.

Som verdens største eksportør og verdens næststørste importør kan Fællesskabet ikke trække sig tilbage i sig selv. Man har da også afsluttet økonomiske og handelsmæssige traktater med de fleste lande i verden.

Det er Fællesskabets ansigt, rigt på fortiden og åbent overfor impulser uden fra. Denne bog har til formål at lade Dem opdage dette.

Vom Schuman-Plan zum Europa ohne Grenzen

Die Mauer in Berlin verschwindet – das ist Europa; das Männeken-Pis in Brüssel – das ist Europa; die Seejungfrau in Kopenhagen, Palma, das Ferienparadies, der Eiffelturm, Kreta und seine Mythologie, das Grüne Irland, Venedig mit seinen Kanälen, Radio Luxemburg, Goudakäse, der Wein aus Porto, die Shetlandinseln, die uns an feinwollene Pullover denken lassen – das alles ist Europa.

In diesem alten Kontinent, der im Laufe der Jahrhunderte so viele tiefgreifende Veränderungen über sich ergehen lassen mußte, sind zwölf Länder mit zusammen 325 Millionen Europäerinnen und Europäern bereits seit zwei Generationen damit beschäftigt, eine Gemeinschaft in Frieden, Freiheit und Solidarität zu bilden.

Das Geburtsdatum der Europäischen Gemeinschaft läßt sich auf den 9. Mai 1950, um sechs Uhr abends festlegen, und zwar als Robert Schuman, der französiche Außenminister, die Zielsetzungen und Bedingungen eines Plans darlegte, der seinen Namen tragen sollte.

Im Jahre 1951 gibt die EGKS, die Europäische Gemeinschaft für Kohle und Stahl, kurz Montanunion genannt, eine Antwort auf die zentralen Zielsetzungen dieses Plans. Nach ihm müssen die Mitglieder gemeinsam die sowohl im Krieg, als auch in Friedenszeiten unentbehrlichen Grundstoffe verwalten. Im Vertrag von Paris werden damit die Interessen der Länder Belgien, Frankreich, der Bundesrepublik Deutschland, Italiens, Luxemburgs und der Niederlande auf einen Nenner gebracht.

Einige Jahre nach der Errichtung der Montanunion wird ein weiteres entscheidendes Stadium in Zusammenwachsen der Wirtschaftsysteme der europäischen Länder erreicht. Die Unterzeichnung des Römischen Vertrags ist die Geburtsstunde der EWG, der Europäischen Wirtschaftsgemeinschaft, auch Euromarkt genannt.

Gleichzeitig wird die Euratom gegründet, die europäische Gemeinschaft für Atomenergie zur gemeinsamen Entwicklung der friedlichen Nutzung der Kernenergie.

Im Jahre 1973 treten die Länder Dänemark, Irland und Großbritanienen der Gemeinschaft der sechs Gründerstaaten bei.

Im Jahre 1981 schließt sich Griechenland an und im Jahre 1986 schließlich wächst mit dem Eintritt Spaniens und Portugals die Zahl der Mitgliedstaaten auf zwölf.

Eine neue entscheidende Phase bricht mit der Unterzeichnung eines neunen Vertrags an: Der Gemeinsame Markt wird beschlossen. Die Gemeinschaft ergreift konkrete Maßnahmen, damit 1992 in Europa alle Zollschranken fallen und so der freie Verkehr und der Austausch von Arbeitskräften, Waren, Dienstleistungen und Kapital ermöglicht werden kann.

Über diese vier Grundfreiheiten hinaus muß die Einheit von Europa im Jahre 1992 auch einen Platz im Herzen seiner Einwohner einnehmen. Ein Europa mit gerechten sozialen Verhältnissen, mit Ausbildung, Bildung und Erziehung mit Hilfe neuer technischer Mittel, ein Europa in dem wissenschaftliche Forschung betrieben und hochwertige Technologie entwickelt werden, ein Europa zum Schutze der Umwelt.

Die Gemeinschaft wird sich auch auf die Veränderungen im Osten Europas einstellen, ohne dabei das Ziel eines wirtschaftlichen Gleichgewichts zwischen Nord und Süd aus den Augen zu verlieren.

In erster Linie im Export, aber auch im Import, kann sich die Gemeinschaft im Welthandelsverkehr nicht auf sich selbst beschränken. Daher wurden auch Wirtschaft- und Handelsverträge mit den meisten anderen Ländern der Welt abgeschlossen.

Das ist das Gesicht der Gemeinschaft, mit reicher Vergangenheit, offen für Einflüsse van außen. Dieses Buch wird Ihnen helfen, dieses, unser Europa, selbst zu entdecken.

From the Schuman Plan to a Europe without borders

The disappearing Berlin Wall, the little statute of the Mannekenpis in Brussels, the mermaid in Copenhagen, Palma, the holiday paradise, the Eiffel Tower, Crete and its mythology, emerald green Ireland, Venice and its canals, Radio Luxembourg, Gouda cheese, the wine from Porto, the Shetland Islands which remind us of finely knitted sweaters - all these are Europe.

In this old continent, which has been through so many farreaching changes in the course of the centuries, there are 12 countries and 325 million Europeans who have been trying to establish a community in peace, freedom and solidarity for two generations.

It could be said that the European Community was born on 9 May 1950 at 6 o'clock in the evening, when Robert Schuman, the French Minister of Foreign Affairs, formulated the objectives and conditions of a plan that was to bear his name.

In 1951 the E.C.S.C., the European Coal and Steel Community, complied with the central objective of this plan for the joint management of raw materials which are essential both in war and peace time. The Treaty of Paris was to co-ordinate the interests of Belgium, France, the Federal Republic of Germany, Italy, Luxembourg and the Netherlands for this purpose.

Some years after the creation of the ECSC a decisive stage was achieved in the co-ordination of European economies in 1957. The signing of the Treaty of Rome saw the creation of the EEC, the European Economic Community, also known as the Common Market, as well as Euratom, the European Community for atomic energy, set up for the joint development of the peaceful use of neclear energy.

The three communities are led by joint organs, and for the first time the sum of the parts can be said to form a European community.

In 1973, Denmark, Ireland and the United Kingdom joined the original six countries.

In January 1981, the Community expanded to include Greece.

Finally, in January 1986, Spain and Portugal joined to bring the number of Member States up to a total of twelve.

A new decisive stage was reached in 1987 with a new convention: the single market. The Community set into motion the steps which would enable a Europe without borders to be created from 1992, with unlimited free movement of people, goods, services and capital.

Even more than these four fundamental freedoms, the unification of Europe in 1992 will also have a place in the heart of its inhabitants. With worthy social interrelations, a Europe of education, training and understanding of new techniques, a Europe for scientific research and high quality technology, a Europe for the protection of the environment.

This will be a Community which adapts to and takes advantage of the changes in Eastern Europe, but at the same time takes into account a better economic balance in North-South relations.

As the first exporter and the second importer of world trade, the Community will not be able to withdraw into itself. In fact, economic and trade agreements have been concluded with most countries in the world.

This is the face of the Community, rich in the past and open to outside influences. This book will help you to discover all this.

Del plan Schuman a una Europa sin fronteras

El muro de Berlín desaparece, eso es Europa, la estatuilla del Manneken Pis en Bruselas, eso es Europa, la sirena en Copenhague, Palma el paraíso veraniego, la Torre de Eiffel, Creta y su mitología, la verde Irlanda, Venecia y sus canales, Radio Luxemburgo, el queso de Gouda, el vino de Oporto, las islas Shetland, todo es Europa.

En el Viejo Continente, que con al paso de los años ha sufrido tantos cambios, hay doce países y 325 millón europeos, que desde hace dos generaciones intentan formar una Comunidad basada en paz, libertad y solidaridad.

La fecha de nacimiento de la Comunidad Europea puede decirse que es el 9 de mayo de 1950, a las seis de la tarde. En ese momento Robert Schuman, el ministro francés de asuntos exteriores, expone los fines y condiciones de un plan que va a llevar su nombre.

En 1951 la C.E.C.A., la Comunidad Europea del Carbón y del Acero, responderá a los fines principales de ese plan: administrar juntos las materias primas que son imprescindibles tanto para la guerra como para la paz. El tratado de París aunará los intereses de Bélgica, Francia, la R.F. de Alemania, Italia, Luxemburgo y los Países Bajos.

Pocos años después de la institución de la C.E.C.A., en 1957, se logra la fase decisiva en la fusión de las economías europeas. Por el Tratado de Roma se crea la C.E.E., la Comunidad Económica Europea, también conocida por Mercado Común, así como EURATOM (o C.E.E.A), la Comunidad Europea de Energía Atómica, que tiene por objeto trabajar mancomunadamente en el desarrollo pacífico de la energía atómica.

Las tres comunidades son dirigidas por organismos supranacionales y al sumar todo ello podemos hablar por primera vez de una Comunidad Europea.

En 1973 se adhieren Dinamarca, Irlanda y el Reino Unido a los primeros seis países miembros.

En enero de 1981 la Comunidad se amplia con Grecia.

Y, por último, en enero de 1986 se adhieren España y Portugal con lo que los países miembros suman doce.

Una nueva fase decisiva se inicia en 1987 con un nuevo tratado: el mercado único. La Comunidad pretende y trabaja para lograr en 1992 una Europa sin fronteras, con un tráfico ilimitado de personas, bienes, services y capital.

La unidad, más que en esas cuatro libertades fundamentales, tendrá que reinar en los corazones de los habitantes. Con relaciones sociales dignas, una Europa de educación, formación y enseñanza con nuevas técnicas, una Europa para investigaciones científicas y de alta tecnología, una Europa en defensa del medio ambiente.

Esa será una Comunidad que sable adaptarse a los cambios en la Europa Oriental pero que, al mismo tiempo, sabe solucionar el desequilibrio económico entre el Sur y el Norte.

Como primer exportador y segundo importador en el tráfico comercial mundial, la Comunidad no se cerrará en sí misma. Ya se han firmado acuerdos económicos y comerciales con la mayoría de los países del mundo.

Esta es la imagen de esta Comunidad, rica en su pasado y abierta a las influencias externas. Este libro se lo quiere hacer descubrir.

Du plan Schuman à l'Europe sans frontières

Le mur de Berlin qui tombe, c'est l'Europe, la statue du Mannekenpis à Bruxelles, c'est l'Europe, la petite sirène de Copenhague, Palma, paradis de vacances, la tour Eiffel, la Crête et sa mythologie, la verte Irlande, Venise et ses canaux, Radio-Luxembourg, le fromage de Gouda, le vin de Porto, les îles Shetland qui nous font penser aux pullovers de fine laine, c'est aussi et toujours l'Europe.

Sur cette vieille terre d'Europe, qui a connu tant de bouleversements au cours des siècles, ce sont 12 pays, 325 millions d'Européens, qui depuis deux générations construisent une Communauté de paix, de liberté, de solidarité.

L'acte de naissance de la Communauté européenne peut être daté du 9 mai 1950, à 18 heures, quand Robert Schuman, ministre français des Affaires Etrangères, a défini les objectifs et les modalités du plan qui porte son nom.

En 1951, la création de la CECA, Communauté européenne du charbon et de l'acier, répondait à l'objectif central du plan : mettre en commun ces ressources de base, indispensables pour la guerre comme pour la paix. Le traité de Paris associait à cet effet la Belgique, la France, la République fédérale d'Allemagne, l'Italie, le Luxembourg et les Pays-Bas.

Quelques années après la création de la CECA, en 1957, une autre étape décisive était franchie dans l'intégration des économies européennes. La signature du traité de Rome a donné naissance à la CEE, la Communauté économique européenne, plus connue sous le nom de Marché commun, ainsi qu'à l'Euratom, la Communauté européenne de l'énergie atomique, destinée à développer la coopération dans l'utilisation pacifique de l'énergie nucléaire.

Les trois Communautés sont dirigées par

des institutions communes, si bien que l'on peut parler, globalement, d'une Communauté européenne.

En 1973, le Danemark, l'Irlande et le Royaume Uni se joignent aux six Etats fondateurs.

En janvier 1981, la Communauté s'élargit à la Grèce.

En janvier 1986, enfin, l'adhésion de l'Espagne et du Portugal porte a douze le nombre des Etats membres.

Nouvelle étape décisive en 1987, lorsque par un nouveau traité, 'l'Acte Unique', la Communauté précise ses objectifs et moyens d'action en vue de permettre la création, d'ici à 1992, d'une Europe sans frontières, où la circulation des hommes, des marchandises, des services et des capitaux sera totalement libre.

Au delà de ces quatre libertés fondamentales, le Marché unique de 1992, ce sera aussi une Europe du coeur, où la dimension sociale aura la place qui lui revient, une Europe de l'éducation et de la formation aux nouvelles techniques, une Europe de la recherche scientifique et du développement des nouvelles technologies de pointe, une Europe de la protection de l'environnement.

Ce sera une Communauté sensible aux bouleversements qui se produisent à l'Est, mais soucieuse également d'un développement économique plus équilibré entre le Nord et le Sud.

Premier exportateur et deuxième importateur du monde, la Communaté ne vit pas repliée sur elle-même. Elle a conclu des accords économiques et commerciaux avec la plupart des pays du monde.

Ce sont des images de cette Communauté, riche de son passé et ouverte sur l'extérieur que le lecteur va découvrir avec plaisir.

Dal piano Schuman all'Europa senza confini

Il muro di Berlino che cade, questa è l'Europa. La statuetta del bambino che fa la pipì a Bruxelles. Questa è l'Europa. La sirenetta a Copenaghen, Palma, il paradiso delle vacanze. la torre Eiffel, Creta e la sua mitoligia, l'Irlanda verdissima, Venezia e i suoi canali, Radio Lussemburgo, il formaggio di Gouda, il vino di Porto, le isole dello Shetland che ci fanno ricordare le magliette di lana finissima. Tutto questo è Europa.

In questo vecchio Continente, che nel corso dei secoli ha sopportato dei profondi mutamenti, si trovano 12 Paesi e 325 milioni di europei che già da due generazioni tentano di creare una Comunità in pace, libertà e solidarietà.

La data di nascita della Comunità Europea può essere stabilita il 9 maggio 1950, alle ore sei di sera, quando il ministro degli esteri francese Robert Schuman ha esposto le condizioni e uzi scopi di un piano che avrebbe portato il suo nome.

Nel 1951 la Comunità Europea del Carbone e dell'Acciaio amministra le materie prime, tanto importanti sia in tempo di pace che in quello di guerra. La convenzione di Parigi ha unito gli interessi del Belgio, della Francia, della Repubblica Federale tedesca, dell'Italia, del Lussemburgo e dei Paesi Bassi.

Alcuni anni dopo la fondazione della Comunità Europea del Carbone e dell'Acciaio, venne realizzata (nel 1957) una successiva fase che fu determinante pe l'economia Europea.

La firma dell'Accordo di Roma rappresenta la fondazione della Comunità Economica Europea, nota anche con il nome di Mercato Comune Europeo. L'Euratom fu fondata per lo sviluppo comune dell'uso pacifico dell'energia atomica.

Nel 1973 si sono aggiunti ai sei Paesi originari l'Irlanda, la Danimarca e la Gran Bretagne.

Nel gennaio 1981 la Comunità viene allargata con l'entrata della Grecia.

Nel gennaio 1986 infine il numero degli Stati soci della Comunità sale a dodici con l'entrata della Spagna e del Portogallo.

Una nuova fase decisiva è iniziata nel 1987 con una nuova Convenzione: il Mercato comune.
Si è create la Comunità che inizierà i lavori che condurranno per 1992, a un'Europa senza confini, con liberta circolazione di persone, merci, servizi e capitali.

Prima nelle esportazioni e seconda nelle importazioni nell'ambito del comercio mondiale, la Comunità non potrà isolarsi in se stessa. Accordi economici e commerciali con la maggior parte dei Paesi del mondo sono stati già conclusi.

Questo è l'aspetto della Comunità Europea, ricca di un glorioso passato e aperta al futuro.

Van het plan Schuman naar Europa zonder grenzen

De muur in Berlijn die verdwijnt, dat is Europa, het beeldje van Mannekenpis in Brussel, dat is Europa, de zeemeermin in Kopenhagen, Palma, het vakantieparadijs, de Eiffeltoren, Kreta en zijn mythologie, het groene Ierland, Venetië en zijn kanalen, Radio-Luxemburg, Goudse kaas, de wijn uit Porto, de Shetlandeilanden die ons doen denken aan fijnwollen truitjes, dat is allemaal Europa.

In dit oude werelddeel, dat in de loop der eeuwen zoveel ingrijpende vanderingen gekend heeft, zijn er 12 landen en 325 miljoen Europeanen, die al twee generaties lang een Gemeenschap proberen te vormen in vrede, vrijheid en solidariteit.

De geboortedatum van de Europese gemeenschap kan op 9 mei 1950, om zes uur 's avonds, bepaald worden. Als Robert Schuman, de Franse minister van Buitenlandse Zaken, de doelstellingen en voorwaarden verwoord heeft van een plan dat zijn naam zal gaan dragen.

In 1951 zal de E.G.K.S. , de Europese gemeenschap voor kolen en staal, beantwoorden aan de centrale doelstelling van dat plan: gezamenlijk de grondstoffen te beheren, die zowel voor de oorlog als ook voor de vrede onontbeerlijk zijn. Het verdrag van Parijs zal daartoe de belangen van België, Frankrijk, de Duitse bondsrepubliek, Italië, Luxemburg en Nederland bij elkaar brengen.

Enkele jaren na de totstandkoming van de E.G.K.S. wordt in 1957 een andere beslissende fase in de samensmelting van de Europese economieën bereikt. Het tekenen van het Verdrag van Rome brengt de E.E.G. tot stand, de Europees economische gemeenschap, ook wel bekend onder de naam Euromarkt, alsmede Euratom, de Europese gemeenschap voor atoomenergie, opgericht voor de gezamelijke ontwikkeling van het vreedzaam gebruik van kernenergie.

Aan de drie gemeenschappen wordt leiding gegeven door gemeenschappelijke organen en bij de som van de delen is er dan ook voor het eerst sprake is van een Europese gemeenschap.

In 1973 voegen Denemarken, Ierland en het Verenigd Koninkrijk zich bij de zes oorspronkelijke lidstaten.

In januari 1981 wordt de Gemeenschap uitgebreid met Griekenland.

En januari 1986 tenslotte brengt met de toetreding van Spanje en Portugal het aantal lidstaten op een totaal van twaalf.

Een nieuwe beslissende fase wordt ingeluid in 1987 met een nieuw verdrag: De gezamelijke Markt. De Gemeenschap onderneemt aktie die het mogelijk moet maken om vanaf 1992 een Europa zonder grenzen tot stand te brengen, met een onbeperkt vrij verkeer van mensen, goederen, diensten en kapitaal.

Meer nog dan deze vier fundamentale vrijheden zal de éénheid in 1992 aan Europa ook een plaats in het hart van zijn bewoners moeten krijgen. Met waardige sociale verhoudingen, een Europa van onderwijs, vorming en opleiding met nieuwe technieken, een Europa voor wetenschappelijk onderzoek en hoogwaardige technologie, een Europa ter bescherming van het milieu.

Dat zal een Gemeenschap zijn die inspeelt op de veranderingen in Oost-Europa, maar tegelijkertijd oog zal hebben voor een meer evenwichtige economische Noord-Zuid relatie.

Als eerste in de uitvoer en de tweede in de invoer van het werelshandelsverkeer zal de Gemeenschap zich niet op zichzelf kunnen terugtrekken. Economische en handelsakkoorden met de meeste landen ter wereld zijn dan ook gesloten.

Dat is het gezicht van deze Gemeenschap, rijk aan het verleden en open voor invloeden van buiten. Dit boek zal u dat graag laten ontdekken.

Do plano Schuman para uma Europa sem fronteiras

A Europa é o muro de Berlim que desaparece, a estátua do Menino a fazer xixi em Bruxelas, a Sereia em Copenhaga, o paraíso de férias em Palma, a Torre Eifel, a mitologia de Creta, a Irlanda verde, os canais de Veneza, a Rádio Luxemburgo, o queijo de Gouda, o vinho do Porto, as ilhas de Shetland que nos fazem lembrar camisolas de lã fina; tudo isto é a Europa.

Neste velho continente que sofreu tantas mudanças ao longo dos séculos, há 12 países e 325 milhões de habitantes que desde há duas gerações tentam formar uma Comunidade em paz, liberdade e solidariedade.

A data de nascimento da Comunidade europeia pode ser fixa a 9 de Maio de 1950, às seis horas da tarde, hora a que Robert Schuman, o ministro francês dos Negócios Estrangeiros, proferiu os objectivos e condições dum plano que veio a ficar com o seu nome.

Em 1951 a C.E.C.A., ou seja a Comunidade Europeia de Carvão e Aço, vai satisfazer o objectivo central desse plano: gerir em conjunto as matérias primas tão indispensáveis tanto em tempo de guerra como em tempo de paz. Este acordo reune assim os interesses da Bélgica, França, República Federal da Alemanha, Itália, Luxemburgo e Países Baixos.

Algungs após a formação desta C.E.C.A. atinge-se outra fase decisiva na coligação das economias europeias: é assinado o Acordo de Roma que vem dar origem à C.E.E., a Comunidade Económica Europeia. Esta também é conhecida por Euromercado, assim como Euratom, a Comunidade Europeia de energia atómica, fundada com o objectivo de desenvolver e utilizar em conjunto e pacificamente a energia nuclear.

A gerência destas três comunidades é realizada por órgãos comuns, e fazendo a soma dos componentes existentes diz-se então pela primeira vez que se trata duma Comunidade Europeia.

Em 1973 junta-se a Dinamarca, a Irlanda e o Reino Unido aos seis países já membros.

Em Janeiro de 1981 a Comunidade enriquece com a adição da Grécia.

Em Janeiro de 1986, finalmente com a entrada da Espanha e de Portugal o número de membros aumenta par um total de doze.

Em 1987 inicia-se outra fase decisiva com novo acordo: o Mercado Comum. A Comunidade visa então e empreende medidas para que seja possível a partir de 1992 a existência de uma Europa sem fronteiras. Isto implica assim um tráfego livre e ilimitado de indivíduos, de mercadorias, serviços e capital.

No entanto, além destas quatro liberdades fundamentais, a unidade da Europa em 1992 também terá de tomar um lugar no coração dos seus habitantes. Por meio de relações sociais dignas, uma Europa de ensino, educação e formação com novas técnicas, uma Europa para investigação científica e alta tecnologia, uma Europa para a proteção de meio ambiente.

Será uma Comunidade que segue as mudanças da Europa do Leste mas que ao mesmo tempo não perderá de vista uma relação Notre-Sul de maior quilíbrio económico.

Como primeira na exportação e segunda na importação respeitante ao movimento comercial mundial, a Comunidade não se pode isolar do resto. Por isso se assinaram acordos comerciais com a maioria das nações no mundo.

E esta a face da Comunidade tão rica de passado histórico e aberta as influênias influências do exterior. Este livro via ajudá-lo a descobri-la.

Από το σχέδιο Σούμαν σε μια Ευρώπη χωρίς σύνορα

Το τείχος του Βερολίνου που τώρα καταρρέει, αυτό είναι η Ευρώπη, το μικρό άγαλμα Μαννεκενπίς στις Βρυξέλλες, αυτό είναι η Ευρώπη, η γοργόνα στην Κοπεγχάγη, ο θερινός μαράδεισος Πάλμα, ο πύργος του Άϊφελ, η Κρήτη κι΄η μυθολογία της, το πράσινο νησί Ιρλανδία, η Βενετία με τα κανάλια της, το Ράδιο Λουξεμβούργο, το τυρί Γκαούντα, το κρασί από το Πόρτο, τα νησιά Σέτλαντ που μάς θυμίζουν ψιλομάλλινα πουλόβερ, όλα αυτά είναι η Ευρώπη.

Σ΄αυτή τη γηραία ήπειρο που κατά την πάροδο των αιώνων γνώρισε πολλές ριζικές αλλαγές, υπάρχουν 12 χώρες με 325 εκατομμύρια Ευρωπαίους που ήδη εδώ και δυο γεννεές προσπαθούν να δημιουργήσουν μια Κοινότητα με ειρήνη, ελευθερία και αλληλεγγύη.

Η Ευρωπαϊκή Κοινότητα γεννήθηκε στις 9 Μαϊου 1950 στις 6 η ώρα το βράδυ, όταν ο Ρομπέρ Σούμαν, ο Γάλλος υπουργός εξωτερικών, εξέφρασε τους σκοπούς και τις συνθήκες του σχεδίου που θα έπαιρνε το δικό του όνομα.

Το 1951 θα ανταποκρινόταν η Ε.Κ.Α.Χ., η Ευρωπαϊκή Κοινότητα Άνθρακος και Χάλυβος στον κύριο σκοπό του σχεδίου εκείνου: η κοινή εκμετάλλευση των πρώτων ύλων που είναι απαραίτητες τόσο για τον πόλεμο όσο και για την ειρήνη. Η Συνθήκη του Παρισιού θα ένωνε τα συμφέροντα του Βελγίου, της Γαλλίας, της Ομοσπονδιακής Δημοκρατίας της Γερμανίας, της Ιταλίας, του Λουξεμβούργου και της Ολλανδίας.

Λίγα χρόνια μετά την πραγματοποίηση της Ε.Κ.Α.Χ., το 1957, φτάνουν τα μέλη σε άλλο αποφασιστικό στάδιο για τη συγχώνευση των ευρωπαϊκών οικονομιών. Με την υπογραφή της Συνθήκης της Ρώμης γεννήθηκε η Ε.Ο.Κ., η Ευρωπαϊκή Οικονομική Κοινότητα, που είναι γνωστή σαν Ευρωαγορά, όπως και η Euratom, η Ευρωπαϊκή Κοινότητα Ατομικής Ενέργειας που ιδρύθηκε για την κοινή ανάπτυξη

ειρηνικής χρησιμοποίησης της ατομικής ενέργειας.

Κοινοτικά όργανα διευθύνουν τις τρείς κοινότητες αυτές και για πρωτή φορά πρόκειται για Ευρωπαϊκη Κοινότητα.

Το 1973 προστέθηκαν η Δανία, η Ιρλανδία και το Ηνωμένο Βασίλειο της Μεγάλης Βρετανίας στα αρχικά κράτη μέλη .

Τον Ιανουάριο 1981 με την εισχώριση της Ελλάδας μεγάλωσε η Κοινότητα.

Και τελικά από τον Ιανουάριο 1986, μετά την εισχώριση της Ισπανίας και Πορτογαλίας, αποτελείται η Κοινότητα από δώδεκα κράτη μέλη.

Το 1987 αρχίζει ένα νέο αποφασιστικό στάδιο με νέα συνθήκη: η κοινή Αγορά. Η Κοινότητα δίνει την προσοχή της και παίρνει αποφασιστικά μέτρα για να πραγματοποιηθεί από το 1992 μια Ευρώπη χωρίς σύνορα με απεριόριστη ελεύθερη διακίνηση ανθρώπων, αγαθών, υπηρεσιών και κεφαλαίων.

Η ενιαία Ευρώπη, εκτός από τις τέσσερις βασικές ελευθερίες αυτές, θα πρέπει το 1992 να κερδίσει πάνω από όλα μια θέση στην καρδιά των κατοίκων της με αξιοπρεπές κοινωνικές σχέσεις, μια Ευρώπη παιδείας, εκπαίδευσης και μόρφωσης με νέες μεθόδους, μια Ευρώπη για επιστημονική έρευνα και εξαίρετες τεχνολογίες, μια Ευρώπη για την προστασία του περιβάλλοντος.

Αυτή θα είναι μια Κοινότητα που θα αντιδρά αμέσως στις αλλαγές στην Ανατολική Ευρώπη, αλλά που ταυτόχρονα θα βλέπει πιο ισορροπημένα οικονομική σχέση ανάμεσα στο Βοριά και στο Νότο.

Η Κοινότητα, πρώτη στην εξαγωγή και δεύτερη στην εισαγωγή του παγκόσμιου εμπορίου, δε θα μπορέσει να κλειστεί στον εαυτό της και γι΄αυτό συνάφτηκαν οικονομικές κι΄εμπορικές συμβάσεις με τις περισσότερες χώρες στον κόσμο.

Αυτό είναι το πρόσωπο της Κοινότητας, πλούσια σε ιστορία και ανοιχτή στις επιρροές που έρχονται από έξω. Διαβάζοντας το βιβλίο αυτό θα το ανακαλύψετε κι΄εσείς.

Indledning

På en flyvetur hen over alle EF-lande fra nord til syd og fra øst til vest tegnes et billede af de forskellige landskaber og byer. Billeder af gamle stæder og landsbyer og af nye udviklingscentre og industriområder veksler med typiske natur- og landskabsoptagelser. Alt sammen præsenteret med en næsten endeløs variering af kontraster eller sammenkædning af paraleller, både i oversigter og i detaljer. I teksterne til fotografierne er økonomi, råstoffer og indkomstkilder vigtige stikord. Vanskeligere er det at lægge historiske og kulturelle forbindelser. Men også dette aspekt er klart tilgodeset, specielt i de forbindende tekster.

Danmark

Vi begynder vor flyvetur i Danmark. Det land, hvorfra vikingerne allerede for længe siden sejlede rundt om det område, der nu udgør EF. Normanner-domkirken i Cefalu på Sicilien giver os et helt andet billede af vikingerne end det om de berygtede, rå og blodtørstige søulke. Men naturligvis har et land, der blandt sine sønner tæller Hans Christian Andersen, også et andet ansigt.

Nordsøen og Skotland

Højt over Nordsøen, olie, gas og sild, flyver vi til det skotske højlands vældige natur. Når vi fra havet ser ind mod Skotlands rå kyst, huskes vi på, hvorledes den mægtige spanske armada i en af de første europæiske konflikter her måtte tage tælling, hvormed Spaniens verdensmagt blev brudt og de nordeuropæiske lande overtog føringen. Men vi erindres også om den sidste store og tragiske europæiske konflikt, idet det var herfra, at skibskonvoyerne til Murmansk sejlede ud under den anden verdenskrig.

Irland

Kongen og statholderen Willem d. III's sejr ved Boyne i Irland over sin svoger Karl d. II, den afsatte katolske konge af England, havde store følger. Kelternes grønne ø kom herved ind i den britiske magtsfære, og det var først og fremmest skotske kolonister, der kom til at befolke øen nordfra. Den nuværende konflikt i Nord-Irland er en direkte følge heraf. Men allerede tidligere i historien spillede troen her en væsentlig rolle. For det var irske munke, der bragte kristendommen til en stor del af nordvesteuropa. Derfor går vi i St. Brendaans fodspor over Wales og England til Nederlandene og de tyske lande.

Storbritannien

Britannien, England og Wales, var romerske provinser, der forsøgte at beskytte sig mod angreb fra skotterne i nord ved at bygge den såkaldte Hadrians mur. Romerne blev slået af anglerne og sakserne, der kom fra det nordtyske lavland, og som blev optaget i befolkningen, som var det de oprindelige keltere. Længe var begrebet Europa for England synonymt med kontinentet, og man foretrak i højere grad at koncentrere sig om imperiet. Den anden verdenskrig gjorde det klart, at kontinentet geografisk ikke lå så langt borte, og selvfølgelig er denne fornemmelse blevet styrket yderligere. efter medlemskabet af EF. Det britiske rige har givet Europa et universalsprog. En stor fordel både for William Shakespeare og The Beatles. Penge fra hele verden strømmer stadig til klodens finansielle centrum: London. En tunnel til Europa vil om kort tid give England en direkte forbindelse til kontinentets hjerte.

Benelux

Ulden fra de engelske får var engang råstof for lagenindustrien, der igen var ansvarlig for det mægtige Brugges fremvækst, det første europæiske kulturcentrum nord for Alperne. Da det flamske Brugges stjerne begyndte at dale begyndte det brabantske Antwerpens netop at stige. Men Antwerpen blev som hovedstad i datidens verden igen afløst af det hollandske Amsterdam. Mellem Rubens Antwerpen og Rembrandts Amsterdam rasede de religionskrige, der delte Europa og især Nederlandene. Deltaet, der dannes af Rhinen, Maas og Schelde, har allerede i århundreder været et vigtigt europæisk handelscentrum. Rotterdams havn, i centrum af deltaet, kan stolt kalde sig den største i verden. I Benelux, hvor flere europæiske kulturer mødes, finder vi også Bruxelles og Luxemburg, værdige europæiske hovedstæder, hvor forskellige EF-instanser har fået sæde.

Forbundsrepublikken Tyskland

Flyver man fra Holland ind over Forbundsrepublikken Tyskland er der landskabsmæssigt næsten ingen forskel at se. Især på grænsen mellem land og vand løber det danske, tyske og hollandske vadehav umærkeligt over i hinanden. Og også udenfor Forbundsrepublikkens grænser, bag Elben, fortsætter det nordtyske lavland gennem DDR og Polen. Lübeck er nu en grænseby, men engang var det den centralt beliggende og den vigtigste af alle Hansestæderne, der lå spredt i lavlandet fra Nederlandene til Den Botniske Bugt. Sammen med Bremen og Hamburg kalder Lübeck sig stadig: Hansestad.

Fra det nordlige flyver vi ikke direkte mod syd, men tager først en tur langs Rhinen. Rhinen var romerriget nordlige grænse, og den er stadig Nordvest-Europas pulsåre, hvor det industrielle hjerte, Rhin-Ruhrområdet, banker kraftigt. Via floden Main og Rhin-Donaukanalen vil Donaufloden inden længe blive forbundet med Rhinen, og det gamle romerske ønske om at kunne sejle fra Sorte-havet til Nordsøen vil da i vore dage gå i opfyldelse. Bag Frankfurt am Main bliver landskabet stadigt mere bakket, indtil vi i den sydlige del af fristaten Bayeren kommer til Alperne, Europas tag.

Frankrig

Gemmen flere tiår danner Rhinen nu igen grænse mellem Frankrig og Tyskland, og en gammel konflikt er nu forhåbentlig for altid ude af verden. Konflikten begyndte i Verdun, da Karolingerriget blev delt i tre dele. I den vestlige del opstod Frankrig, og i øst lagdes grunden til Tyskland. Områderne herimellem var gennem århundreder indsatsen i en lang række europæiske konflikter. Det fransk-tyske samarbejde efter den anden verdenskrig var også begyndelsen til det europæiske samarbejde. Valget af Straatsburg som sæde for Europaparlamentet kan uden videre siges at være symbolsk og historisk korrekt. Det stærkt centraliserende Frankrigs ubestridte hovedstad er naturligvis Paris, omgivet af et stort antal historiske og moderne forstæder. Frankrig indtager en central position i Europa. Ikke alene geografisk, men også i kulturel og åndelig henseende. Vincent van Gogh tog til Frankrig for at male og mellem de to verdenskrige fandt den såkaldte 'lost generation' af amerikanere et hjem i Paris.

Den Iberiske Halvø

Vi flyver over Pyrenæerne til den Iberiske Halvø. Rom rystede i sin grundvold, da Hannibal forlod Spanien og drog over Alperne med sin hær og sine elefanter. Senere blev Spanien en romersk provins, og en ny arabisk periode tog først sin begyndelse i middelalderen. Tilbagetrængningen af den arabiske indflydelsessfære og Spaniens og Portugals fremvækst skulle komme til at foregå gradvist. I det år da det sidste arabiske bolværk, Granada, faldt, opdagede Columbus, der kom fra Genua, og som netop havde byttet sine portugisiske herre for spanske, den nye verden: Amerika. Portugal og Spanien havde ikke alene delt den Iberiske Halvø, men for nemheds skyd delte de også verden mellem sig. I øvrigt kun for en kort periode, idet de nordlige landes opblomstring hurtigt gjorde en ende på aspirationerne om det delte verdensherredømme. Relativt isoleret udøvedes her kunst og videnskab. Men ud af dette isolement voksede der sig regelmæssigt fra Velazques til Picasso videnskabsmænd og kunstnere i verdensklasse. Den spanske borgerkrig styrkede i længere tid denne isolationsfølelse. Både Portugal og Spanien fremviser i den allernyeste historie en stærk demokratisk indstilling, og med deres medlemskab af EF ser man i disse lande med stor forventning Europa og fremtiden imøde.

Italien

Italienerne har god grund til at være stolte. Intet land i Europa kan berømme sig af ikke mindre end to gange i historien at have stået i spidsen. Naturligvis allerførst Romerriget, der omfattede et betydeligt større område end det nuværende EF. Men måske har middelalderens bystater været af meget større betydning for vor tids vestlige kultur. I Florens kan man endnu mærke renæssancens indflydelse. Fra dogerepublikken Venedig drog Marco Polo ud på sine rejser til det fjerne østen. De varer, der skulle nord på over land, ankom til Genua. Rom bliver naturligvis ved med at være den Evige Stad og Neapel bør De have set, før De dør. Sicilien var i hænderne på både grækere, romere, vikinger og spaniere og øen var kun lige blevet herre i eget hus, da Garibaldi indlemmede den i den nye italienske enhedsstat.

Grækenland

Det var uomtvisteligt her den europæiske civilisation blev født. Men det er også et land, der ligesom Italien, kun har eksisteret i ca. hundrede år i sin moderne statsretslige form. Det klassiske Grækenlands bidrag til verdenskulturen er så talrige og utællelige, at vi kun nævner enkelte løse navne og begivenheder. Gudernes opholdssted på bjerget Olympen, hvorefter de moderne olympiske lege er opkaldt. Delphi med sit orakel og naturligvis Athen med Akropolis og Parthenon.

Senere fik den bysantiske kultur stor indflydelse her, og også korsfarerne har her sat deres fodspor og efterladt sig deres mindesmærker. Vi slutter vor flyvetur hen over Europa ved øen Kretas mest østliche punkt. Det eneste sted i Europa, hvor der naturligt vokser palmer og også det sted, hvor tyren ifølge myten fra havet gik i land med Europa på ryggen. Den Europa, der gav sit eget navn til det nye land.

Mit diesem Band ermöglichen wir Ihnen eine Flugreise, die Sie von Nord nach Süd und von West nach Ost über die zwölf Mitgliedsstaaten der Europäischen Gemeinschaft führt. Auf dieser Reise werden Sie einige der interessantesten Ansichten der überflogenen Länder kennenlernen, charakteristische Landschaften ebenso wie traditionsreiche Städte und moderne Industriegebiete. Sie werden erkennen, daß die Europäische Gemeinschaft nicht nur ein wirtschaftlicher und politischer Zusammenschluß von zwölf Staaten ist, sondern auch ein durch eine gemeinsame Geschichte zusammengeschweißter Kulturraum, der sich von der Nordsee bis zum Mittelmeer, vom Atlantik bis zur Ägäis erstreckt. Deshalb finden sich trotz aller Gegensätze auch zahlreiche Ähnlichkeiten – Zeugnisse traditioneller Wechselwirkungen, die das zusammengefügt haben, was man als das Abendland zu bezeichnen pflegt. Der europäische Einigungsprozeß hat uns die Möglichkeit eröffnet, nach verheerenden Kriegen, zu dieser Gemeinsamkeit zurückzufinden und sie noch enger zu gestalten.

Dänemark

Ausgangspunkt unserer Reise ist Dänemark, die Heimat jener Wikinger, die schon vor über tausend Jahren das ganze Gebiet umsegelten, das heute die EG bildet. Einst als blutrünstige Seeräuber verschrien, haben sie sich jedoch auch als tüchtige Kolonisten hervorgetan und eine eigenständige Kultur entwickelt, von der noch heute ihre eindrucksvollen Palast- und Kirchenbauten im fernen Sizilien Zeugnis ablegen.

Die Nordsee und Schottland

Seit alters als Fischfanggrund wichtig, hat die Nordsee durch Erdöl- und Erdgasfunde neue wirtschaftliche Bedeutung erlangt. Wir erreichen Schottland mit seiner wunderschönen Hauptstadt Edinburgh und überfliegen die wilde Natur der schottischen Hochlande mit ihren sagenumwobenen Seen und tief ins Land einschneidenden Fjorden. Vor der Küste Schottlands fand die mächtige spanische Armada ein klägliches Ende – ein Ereignis von welthistorischer Bedeutung, ging doch dadurch die Vormachtstellung von der Iberischen Halbinsel auf den nordwesteuropäischen Raum über: die Niederlande und England wurden zu den neuen 'Herren der Meere'.

Irland

Die Bewohner Irlands unterhielten in vorrömischer Zeit Handelsbeziehungen mit dem Mittelmeerraum, und nach der Christianisierung waren es irische Mönche, die die britischen Inseln und das Festland missionierten. Trotz seiner vorgeschobenen Lage im Atlantik war Irland stets dem europäischen Kontinent zugewandt. Bis 1171 ein vereintes Königreich, wurde Irland nach der Eroberung durch Heinrich II. immer mehr in englischen Machtbereich einbezogen, was zu politischer und wirtschaftlicher Unterdrückung führte. Die noch heute in Nordirland andauernden Unruhen sind nichts anderes als eine Fortsetzung der jahrhundertelangen irischen Bemühungen um Abschüttlung der englischen Herrschaft. Der Süden der Insel wurde 1922 Freistaat, erlangte erst 1949 die vollständige politische Unabhängigkeit von Großbritannien.

England und Wales

Der Südteil der von Kelten bewohnten britischen Insel, also England und Wales, wurde durch Cäsars Eroberungsfeldzug zur römischen Provinz, die sich durch den Hadrianswall der Einfälle der schottischen Pikten zu erwehren versuchte. Die Römer wurden von Pikten und Skoten vertrieben, die ihrerseits den aus Norddeutschland eindringenden Angeln und Sachsen weichen mußten. Danach kam das Land in dänische und normannische Hand, doch vermischten sich die Eroberer jeweils stark mit der einheimischen Bevölkerung, so daß Keltisches und Germanisches eine enge Verbindung eingingen. Mit der Entstehung des britischen Kolonialreichs zog sich Großbritannien immer mehr aus Europa zurück, um seine Weltmacht auszubauen, auch wenn es immer wieder in kontinentale Kriege eingriff. Wie nahe man dennoch dem Kontinent blieb, machten nicht zuletzt die beiden Weltkriege den Inselbewohnern deutlich. Dem europäischen Einigungsgedanken stand man zunächst abwartend gegenüber, und erst 1972 trat Großbritannien der Europäischen Gemeinschaft bei. Der Tunnel unter dem Ärmelkanal wird die Beziehungen zum Festland in Zukunft sicherlich noch enger werden lassen.

Benelux

Als Beneluxstaaten bezeichnet man die drei Länder Belgien, Niederlande und Luxemburg, die sich 1958 zu einer Wirtschaftsunion zusammenschlossen. Heute sind Brüssel, die Hauptstadt Belgiens, und Luxemburg die wichtigsten Schaltstellen der Europäischen Gemeinschaft. Einst war es die Wolle englischer Schafe, die Brügge dank seiner Tuchindustrie zum nordwesteuropäischen Wirtschafts- und Kulturzentrum werden ließ. Bald wurde Brügge vom Brabanter Antwerpen und dieses wiederum vom holländischen Amsterdam abgelöst. Nach der Reformation wüteten zwischen dem Antwerpen eines Rubens und dem Amsterdam eines Rembrandt Religionskriege. Ein bedeutender europäischer Wirtschaftsschwerpunkt ist seit Jahrhunderten das Mündungsgebiet von Rhein, Maas und Schelde. In seinem Zentrum liegt Rotterdam, dessen Hafen zum größten der Welt geworden ist. Diesen Aufschwung verdankt er nicht zuletzt dem Erdöl, das in riesigen Raffinerien verarbeitet wird. Brüssel und Luxemburg sind sehenswerte Hauptstädte, zu deren historischen Stadtkernen sich supermoderne Neubauviertel für die EG-Behörden gesellt haben.

Bundesrepublik Deutschland

Die Bundesrepublik entstand 1949 aus den von den drei Westalliierten besetzten Zonen des 1945 besiegten Deutschen Reiches; 1957 wurde auch das zunächst mit Frankreich verbundene Saarland rückgegliedert. Früh schon erwachte hier der Europagedanke, der zu immer stärkerer wirtschaftlichen und politischen Anbindung an die westlichen Demokratien führte, während die Aussöhnung mit dem Osten erst in den siebziger Jahren eingeleitet wurde. Heute ist die Bundesrepublik die stärkste wirtschaftliche Kraft der Europäischen Gemeinschaft. Im Herzen des Kontinents gelegen, hat die Bundesrepublik mehr Nachbarn als jedes andere Land Europas: Dänemark im Norden, die Schweiz und Österreich im Süden, die Niederlande, Belgien, Luxemburg und Frankreich im Westen, die DDR und die Tschechoslowakei im Osten. Schon aufgrund dieser zentralen Lage ergeben sich für die Bundesrepublik intensive wirtschaftliche und politische Wechselwirkungen mit dem gesamten europäischen Kontinent. Unser Flug über Deutschland führt uns von Helgoland, der Insel in der Deutschen Bucht, zu den Hafenstädten an Nord- und Ostsee, einst Mitglied der mächtigen Hanse, über Niedersachsen und Westfalen zum Rhein, dem wir flußaufwärts folgen. Vom Ruhrgebiet, einem traditionellen wirtschaftlichen Kerngebiet, gelangen wir über Bonn und Köln nach Frankfurt, der Bankenmetropole, und weiter über Bayern und den Bodensee bis nach Baden-Württemberg, dem exportorientierten Bundesland mit der stärksten Wirtschaftskraft.

Frankreich

Jahrhundertelang war die Rheingrenze ein Zankapfel zwischen Deutschland und Frankreich. Das hat zur verhängnisvollen Ideologie der 'Erbfeindschaft' zwischen den beiden Völkern geführt, die ihren Anfang schon mit der Teilung des Reichs Karls des Großen im Vertrag von Verdun (843) nahm und zu zahlreichen kriegerischen Auseinandersetzungen führte. Erst durch die Aussöhnung nach dem Zweiten Weltkrieg ist dieser Konflikt endgültig aus der Welt geschafft worden. Ein Symbol dafür ist die Wahl Straßburgs zum Sitz des Europarats: Die Staatsgrenzen sollen nicht mehr trennen, sondern verbinden. Paris ist im zentralistisch verwalteten Frankreich nicht nur die Hauptstadt, sondern seit Jahrhunderten auch der wirtschaftliche und geistige Mittelpunkt des Landes, der auf das gesamte europäischen Kulturleben ausstrahlt. Reich an Kulturzeugnissen ist freilich auch das übrige Land, wie prächtige Kathedralen und Klöster, stolze Schlösser und geschichtsträchtige Städte bezeugen. Nicht weniger sehenswert sind die Landschaften Frankreichs, vom Montblanc, dem höchsten Berg Europas, bis zur sonnigen Mittelmeerküste mit der wilden Camargue und der vielbesuchten Côte d'Azur. Dor finden wir das Fürstentum Monaco, das eng mit Frankreich verflochten, aber politisch unabhängig ist.

Die Iberische Halbinsel

Von Frankreich aus gelangen wir über die Pyrenäen auf die Iberische Halbinsel. Von hier brach Hannibal mit einem mächtigen Heer samt Kriegselefanten auf, um die Alpen zu überqueren und das Römerreich aus den Angeln zu heben. Später wurde die Halbinsel römische Provinz und Westgotenreich. Ab 711 n.Chr. wurde sie von den islamischen Mauren erobert, die eine hohe kulturelle und wirtschaftliche Blüte herbeiführen. Während der Rückeroberung durch die Christen (Reconquista) bildeten sich zwei neue Staaten heraus: Spanien und Portugal. Im gleichen Jahr, in dem Granada als letzte maurische Bastion fiel, entdeckte Kolumbus in spanischen Diensten die Neue Welt und legte damit den Grundstein für die Weltgeltung der Iberischen Halbinsel: Spanien und Portugal teilten die Welt unter sich auf. Dies wurde ihnen freilich von Niederländern und Engländern streitig gemacht, und mit Spaniens Armada ging auch das Iberische Weltreich unter. Ab dem 18. Jahrhundert und erst recht nach den Napoleonischen Kriegen wurden die iberischen Staaten immer mehr isoliert. Dennoch gingen aus dieser Abgeschlossenheit zahlreiche Wissenschaftler und Künstler von Weltruf hervor. Im 20. Jahrhundert etablierten sich in Spanien und Portugal Diktaturen, doch seit deren Ablösung hat eine demokratische Entwicklung eingesetzt, die schließlich zum Beitritt zu den Europäischen Gemeinschaften führte. Einen Eindruck von der Vielfalt und der reichen Geschichte der Iberischen Halbinsel vermitteln unsere Abbildungen.

Italien

Mit Recht sind die Italiener stolz auf ihr Land, das als einziges in Europa zweimal im Lauf seiner Geschichte von überragender Bedeutung war: Einst war die Apenninenhalbinsel politisches und wirtschaftliches Zentrum des Römischen Reiches, eines Gebiets, das weit größer war als die heutige EG, und die italienischen Stadtstaaten in Mittelalter und Neuzeit waren kulturelle und wirtschaftliche Schwerpunkte des gesamten Abendlandes. Rom, die Ewige Stadt, wahrte als Sitz der Päpste auch nach dem Untergang des Römerreichs Weltgeltung. Von der Dogenrepublik Venedig brach Marco Polo in den Fernen Osten auf, und jahrhundertelang beherrschten Venedig und Genua Europas Handel mit dem Osten. Florenz wurde zur Wiege der Renaissance, die das Stadtbild und die gesamteuropäischen Künste entscheidend geprägt hat. Immer noch ist Neapel die Stadt, die man auch einem alten Spruch vor seinem Tod unbedingt gesehen haben muß. Uraltes Kulturland ist schließlich Sizilien, eine Insel, die zum Schnittpunkt vieler Kulturkreise wurde; nach fortwährender Fremdherrschaft kam sie erst im ausgehenden 19. Jahrhundert an das geeinte Italien.

Griechenland

Dieses Land ist unangefochten die Wiege der abendländischen Kultur, doch seine staatliche Einheit hat es erst im 19. Jahrhundert erlangt. In der Antike zerfiel es in rivalisierende Stadtstaaten, die sich erbittert bekriegten, so daß es vor der Zeitenwende eine leichte Beute der Römer wurde. Auf die byzantinische Herrschaft folgten ab dem 15. Jahrhundert die Türken, die die einheimische Bevölkerung unterjochten, bis das Land dank der Intervention europäischer Mächte 1832 seine Selbständigkeit erlangte. Trotz aller Wechselfälle der Geschichte sind noch zahlreiche Zeugnisse einer glanzvollen Vergangenheit erhalten – Heiligtümer und Paläste, Theater und zahlreiche Kunstwerke. Unser Flug über Europa endet auf Kreta. Auf dieser Insel betrat Zeus in Stiergestalt mit der asiatischen Königstochter Europa den Boden jenes Kontinents, der, wie die griechische Mythologie zu berichten weiß, der wunderschönen Geliebten des obersten Griechengotts seinen Namen verdankt.

A flight over the 12 European Community (EC) Member States, from North to South and from East to West, reveals a tapestry of different landscapes and settlements. Old cities and villages, newly laid out centres of growth and industrial areas, alternate with the natural scenery and landscapes that are characteristic of each region. In the text that accompanies the photographs an attempt has been made to give an idea of the economic, social and cultural histories that have made the areas so diverse.

Denmark

Our aerial tour begins in Denmark. In ancient times the Vikings had already, sailed around the whole area which forms today's EC. As far away as Sicily, the Cathedral of Céfalu bears witness to a side of this early Danish exploration not in tune with their reputation as a bloodthirsty and savage bunch of seafarers. The nation that produced Hans Christian Andersen, whose little mermaid has become the symbol of Copenhagen, is of course bound to have another aspect to its character.

The North Sea and Scotland

Moving across the North Sea with its oil, gas and fishing industries, to the mighty grandeur of the Scottish Highlands. It was against these shores that part of the Spanish Armada (literally "invincible fleet") came to grief. That destruction in July 1588 initiated the decline and ultimately the destruction of the Spanish Empire, as well as causing a shift of power to the Northern countries. In more recent times these seas have once more seen maritime tragedy. It was from here that the convoys set out for Murmansk during the Second World War.

Ireland

The victory of King (Stadtholder) William III in Ireland at the river Boyne, over his brother-in-law James II, the dethroned Catholic King of England, had tremendous consequences for Ireland. The green island of the Celts fell under the influence of the British in particular; with Scottish colonists penetrating the island from the North. The present conflict in Northern Ireland can, in part, be attributed to that historical event, after the Battle of the Boyne Irish Catholics were stripped of almost every right, including that of education. However, religion had played an important role in Ireland even earlier, as it was Celtic Monks who brought Christianity to a large part of Northwest Europe. Following the path of St. Brendan, we will now head for the Low Countries and Germany, by way of England and Wales.

England and Wales

By 122AD, England and Wales were already part of the Roman Empire, which was defending itself in the North by starting to build Hadrian's Wall against the raids of the Scots. Roman power was replaced by the Danes, who were succeeded in turn by the Angles and Saxons coming from the Northern German lowland plain, and who absorbed, as it were, the original Celts. In more recent times the concept of "Europe" to the British became synonymous with "the Continent", and they preferred to devote their attention to their own Empire. The two World Wars made them realise that "the Continent" was not so very far away after all, and this has become even more evident since joining the EC. The British Empire has provided Europe with a universal language, with possibly Shakespeare as its greatest exponent. In our own times pop music has spread English to all corners of the world, making it a truly international language. In business London is still one of the great financial centres. The building of the Channel Tunnel will bring Great Britain and Europe closer to each other.

The Benelux countries

In the 13th century wool from English sheep was the raw material for the trade in cloth and, consequently, for the rise to influence of Bruges, the first European cultural centre North of the Alps. When the importance of Flemish Bruges declined it was replaced by the star of Brabantine Antwerp. Antwerp was in its turn ousted by Amsterdam as the centre of the world of trade. The years between the Antwerp of Rubens and the Amsterdam of Rembrandt saw religious warfare that divided Europe and, more particularly, the Low Countries. The Rhine-Meuse-Scheldt estuary has been an important European centre for centuries, and Rotterdam, situated in the middle of it, may justifiably call itself the world's number one port. Here, at the crossroads of different European cultures, we also find Brussels and Luxembourg, the capitals in which are the seats for several EC institutions.

The German Federal Republic

When entering the Federal Republic of Germany from Holland by air, it is difficult to notice any real difference in the landscape of the two countries. Along the coast the Danish, German and Dutch tidal shallows – German "Watten" and Dutch "Wadden" – merge unobtrusively into each other. The picture is similar in the North German lowland plain, stretching far beyond the River Elbe into the German Democratic Republic and Poland. Lübeck is a frontier town today, but there was a time when it was the centre and principal seat of the Hanseatic League, the members of which were to be found in that same lowland plain stretching from the Low Countries up to the Finnish Gulf. Even now Bremen and Hamburg proudly use the prefix "Hansestadt". Rather than heading immediately South, let us first fly along the Rhine. In early Roman times this river was the Northern border of the Roman Empire; now it is the artery of Northwest Europe, with the Rhine-Ruhr area as its industrial heart. Now that the Rhine is connected with the Danube through the River Main and the Rhine-Danube Canal it is possible to fulfil the old Roman wish to travel from the Black Sea to the North Sea by water. Beyond Frankfurt am Main the hills gradually become steeper until we get to the Alps, the roof of Europe, in the South of the Federal State of Bavaria.

France

For several decades the Rhine has formed the border between France and Germany, finally eliminating a territorial conflict which is centuries old. This conflict began at Verdun, when the Carolingian Empire was divided into three parts. To the West were the beginnings of France, and to the East those of Germany. For hundreds of years the countries in between were the scene of many wars. The Franco-German co-operation which followed the Second World War marked the beginning of the European collaboration: Strasbourg, on the border between these two countries, is rightly the choice for the seat of the European Parliament. Paris, the undisputed capital of France, is encircled by a number of satellite towns. As far as Europe is concerned, France is the centre, not only in terms of territory, but also culturally and intellectually. Vincent Van Gogh went there to paint, and the "lost generation" found a home there.

The Iberian Peninsula

Flying across the Pyrenees we come to the Iberian Peninsula. It was from here that Hannibal's army made its famous march with elephants across the Alps towards Rome. Later on, Spain became a province of the Roman Empire, and in the Middle Ages a new Arabic era began. The rise of Portugal and Spain took place simultaneously with the demise of Arabic influence. When Granada its last bastion fell Columbus was setting off to discover America. Columbus, who came from Genoa, had just changed allegiance from his old Portuguese masters to the Spanish. Not only had Portugal and Spain divided the Iberian Peninsula, but they were also planning to divide up the rest of the world. However, the rise of the Northern European countries put an end to this plan. The arts and sciences flourished in comparative isolation in this area. From Velasquez to Picasso, there have been world famous artists and scientists here. Spain's isolation was underlined by its tragic Civil War, but recently the country has surprised the rest of Europe by adapting itself so quickly to the changing Europe. Together with Portugal, it recently joined the EC and looks to a future within Europe with high hopes.

Italy

The Italians have good reason to be proud of their achievements. It was, of course, from here that the Roman Empire was controlled. In terms of territory, that Empire was far larger than the present EC. But it is possible that the mediaeval city states had a greater cultural importance. In Florence the impact of the Renaissance can still be felt, and it was from the Doge Republic of Venice that Marco Polo set off for the Far East. Despite the claims of Napels, it is still Rome that remains the eternal city. In Genoa, merchandise was unloaded to be transported overland to Northern Europe. Sicily was successively in the hands of the Greeks, Romans, Vikings and Spaniards; it finally became independent, running its own affairs before merging into Garibaldi's united Italy in 1860.

Greece

Greece is the unchallenged birthplace of European civilization, but like Italy, it is a country that has only existed for about a hundred years in its present form. The contribution of classical Greece to world culture is so great and varied that only a few names can be mentioned here. Olympia, after which the Olympic Games are named; Delphi with its Oracle, and of course, Athens with the Parthenon. The Byzantine civilization was also influential here and the numerous Crusaders left behind traces of their passing. Our aerial tour over Europe will end at the historic spot where, according to Greek mythology, the history of Europe began. On the Eastern most point of Crete, the only place on Europe where there are non-cultivated, purely natural palm trees, is the place where Zeus as a bull, with the maiden Europa on his back, came ashore. That land was called Europe.

Introducción

Por medio de un viaje aéreo por los doce países de la Comunidad Europea, de norte a sur, de este a oeste, se le da un esbozo de los diversos paisajes y asentamientos. Imágenes de ciudades, pueblos antiguos, de nuevos polos de crecimiento y terrenos industriales se van alternándo con tomas características de los paisajes y de la naturaleza. Y todo ello en una variedad sin fin de constrastes o serie de paralelismos, tanto en su visión de conjunto como en detalles. En el texto que acompaña a las fotografías hay palabras claves: economía, materias primas y fuentes de ingresos. Más difícil es hacer relaciones culturales e históricas. Pero también este aspecto, sobre todo en los textos de enlace, está claramente presente.

Dinamarca

Iniciamos nuestro viaje aéreo en Dinamarca. El país de los vikingos que en tiempos antaños comprendía lo que ahora es la CEE. El asentamiento Céfalu en Sicilia nos muestra una cara muy distinta que la famosa de aquellos rudos y sangrientos marineros. Pero, naturalmente, un país que ha criado a Christian Andersen tiene que tener una cara muy distinta.

Mar del Norte y Escocia

Sobrevolando el Mar del Norte, petróleo, aceite y arenques, hacia la majestuosa naturaleza de las Highlands escocesas. Si miramos desde el mar la rugosa costa escocesa tenemos que pensar en la poderosa Armada española que una vez llevo aquí las de perder y con ello comenzaría el hundimiento del poder mundial español y el surgimiento de los países nórdicos. Pero también pensamos en el último, trágico gran conflicto pues de aquí salieron en la Segunda Guerra Mundial los convoyes a Murmansk.

Irlanda

La victoria del Rey-Estatúder Guillermo III a Boyne en Irlanda sobre su cuñado Jacobo II, el rey inglés católico que fue destronado, tuvo grandes consecuencias. La verde isla de los Celtas entró así en la influencia inglesa y sobre todo los colonistas escoceses irían a habitar la isla entrando por el norte. El actual conflicto en Irlanda del Norte es una consecuencia directa de este hecho. Pero ya antes la fe desempeñó un papel muy importante. Pues fueron los monjes irlandeses los que llevaron la fe cristiana al noroeste de Europa. Por ello seguimos los pasos de Sint-Brendaan, por Gales e Inglaterra, hacia los Países Bajos y Alemania.

Gran Bretaña

Bretaña, Inglaterra y Gales, eran provincias romanas que intentaban defenderse de los ataques de los escoceses del norte con la Hadrianus Wall, los romanos fueron derrotados por los daneses que a su vez fueron derrotaros por los anglos y los sajones, que procedían de la zonas bajas del norte de Alemania, y que aceptados entre la población llegaron a hacerse prácticamente originarios celtas. El término Europa ha sido para Inglaterra durante mucho tiempo un sinónimo del continente y se prefería dedicarse más a su propio imperio. La Segunda Guerra Mundial mostró que el continente geográficamente no está tan lejos y, por supuesto, este sentimiento ha crecido desde el ingreso en la CEE. El Reino Británico ha dado e Europa un idioma universal. Una gran ventaja para tanto William Shakespeare como para los Beatles. El dinero del mundo pasa todavía por el corazón financiero del mundo: Londres. Y el túnel a Europa unirá Inglaterra con el corazón del continente.

Benelux

La lana de las ovejas inglesas fue en su tiempo la materia prima de la industria pañera, que a su vez fue responsable del surgimiento de la poderosa Brujas, el primer centro cultural al norte de los Alpes. Cuando la estrella de Brujas en Flandes declinaba, ascendía la de Amberes, en Brabante. Pero Amberes fue seguida como capital del mundo a la sazón por Amsterdam, en Holanda. Entre la Amberes de Rubens y el Amsterdam de Rembrandt hubo guerras religiosas que dividieron a Europa y, en especial, a los Países Bajos. El delte del Rin, Mosa y Escalda es ya desde hace siglos un centro importante de comercio en Europa. El puerto de Rotterdam, en el centro, puede decir con orgullo que es el puerto mayor del mundo. En el Benelux, en la encruijada de diversas culturas, encontramos también Bruselas y Luxemburgo, dignas capitales en las que residen instancias de la CEE.

República Federal de Alemania

Si volamos desde Holanda a Alemania apenas vemos diferencias en el paisaje. Sobre todo en la frontera de tierra y mar las islas Frisias pasan de Dinamarca a Alemania y a Holanda sin que se note. Y también fuera de las fronteras de la República Federal Alemana, detrás del Elba, vemos la llanura del norte de Alemania pasar a Alemania Oriental y Polonia. Lübeck es ahora una ciudad fronteriza, pero en su tiempo fue una ciudad central y la más importante de las ciudades del Ansa que extendidas por la llanura llegaban desde los Países Bajos hasta el Golfo de Finlandia. Junto a Brema y Hamburgo sigue utilizando con orgullo el prefijo: Hanzestad (Ciudad del Ansa).

Desde el norte na vamos directamente al sur sino que primero sobrevolamos el Rin. En la época romana este río significó la frontera más septentrional y ahora el Rin sigue siendo la arteria de la Europa del noroeste, en la que late fuertemente el corazón industrial, la región de Rin-Ruhr. Por el Main y el canal Rin-Danubio, el Danubio estará algún día vinculado con el Rin, el sueño de los romanos: poder ir del Mar Negro al Mar del Norte navegando. Después Francfort am Main el paisaje es cada vez más accidentado hasta que llegamos en el sur al estado Libre de Baviera en los Alpes, el techo de Europa.

Francia

Ya desde varia décadas el Rin señala la frontera entre Francia y Alemania y un antiguo conflicto ha sido, esperemos, superado. Este conflicto empezó en Verdún, cuando en tiempos del reino carolingio éste se dividió en tres. Al oeste significó el nacimiento de Francia y al este el comienzo de Alemania. Los territorios entre ellos fueron durante siglos la causa numerosos conflictos europeos. La colaboración franco-germana tras la Segunda Guerra Mundial ha significado también el inicio de la colaboración europea. La elección de Estrasburgo como sede del Parlamento Europea puede ser calificada sin más como un hecho simbólico e histórico. La indiscutida capital de la muy centralizada Francia es naturalmente París con su multitud de circundantes ciudades modernas e históricas. En Europa Francia tiene una posición central. No sólo geográficamente sino también desde el punto de vista cultural y espiritual.

Vincent van Gogh vino a Francia para pintar y entre las dos guerras mundiales la así llamada 'lost generation' de americanos encontró su casa en París.

Península Ibérica

Volamos sobre los Pirineos hacia la Península Ibérica. Los fundamentos de Roma se tambalearon cuando Aníbal partió de España y pasó los Alpes con sus ejércitos y elefantes. Más tarde España se convirtió en una Provincia del imperio romano; en la Edad Media conocería una época árabe. Luego poco a poco se eliminó la influencia árabe y surgieron España y Portugal. El año en que caía el último baluarte árabe, Granada, descubría Colón, que procedía de Génova y que había dejado a sus amos portugueses por los españoles, el Nuevo Mundo: América. Portugal y España no sólo habían dividido la Península Ibérica, sino también por comodidad el Mundo entero. No por mucho tiempo pues el surgimiento de los países nórdicos hundío rápidamente estas aspiraciones de dividir la hegemonía mundial. En un cierto aislamiento se ejercitaron aquí las artes y las ciencias. Pero desde Velázquez a Picasso surgieron de este aislamiento artistas y científicos de gran nivel. La Guerra Civil en España fortaleció aún más esos sentimientos por bastante tiempo. Tanto España como Portugal han mostrado en la historia reciente una fuerte actitud democrática y con su ingreso en la CEE se mira con muchas expectativas a Europa y el futuro.

Italia

Los italianos tienen el derecho de estar orgullosos. Ningún país puede decir que ha estado en primer plano dos veces en la historia. Naturalmente, primero con el Imperio Romano que superaba la superficie de la actual Europa. Pero quizás los estados-ciudades de la Edad Media han sido de mayor importancia para la actual cultura occidental. En Florencia aún se puede probar la influencia del Renacimiento. De la República de Venecia partió Marco Polo para sus viajes al Lejano Oriente. A Genova llegaban las mercancías que habían de ser transportadas por tierra hacia el norte. Roma sigue siendo la Ciudad Esterna y usted ha de ver Nápoles antes de morir. Sicilia estuvo en manos de griegos, romanos, vikingos y españoles y fue independiente haste que Garibaldi la unió al nuevo estado unido de Italia.

Grecia

La indiscutida cuna de la civilización europea. Pero también un país, al igual que Italia, que en su versieon estatal moderna tan sólo existe unos cien años. Las contribuciones de la Grecia clásica a la cultura mundial son tan numerosas, tan incontables que sólo podemos mencionar unos nombres y datos sueltos. La residencia de los dioses en el Olimpo que daría su nombre a los modernos Juegos Olímpicos. Delfi con su oráculo y naturalmente Atenas con su Acrópolis y Partenón. La civilización bizantina tuvo aquí mucha influencia y también los cruzados han dejado aquí sus huellas y recuerdos. Finalizamos nuestro vuelo sobre Europa en el punto más oriental de la isla Creta. El único lugar en Europa donde crecen palmeras no cultivados y también el lugar donde según el mito llegó a tierra el toro desde el mar con Europa a su espalda la cual daría su nombre a estas nuevas tierras.

Introduction

Un voyage aérien au-dessus des 12 Etats-membres de la CEE, du Nord au Sud et de l'Est à l'Ouest, illustrera pour nous la diversité des paysages et des établissements humains. Les images des villes et des villages anciens, des nouveaux centres de développement et des zones industrielles alternent avec celles de beautés naturelles et de paysages qui sont caractéristiques de la région. Le tout dans une variété presque incessante de contrastes et de parallèles, qu'il s'agisse de vues d'ensemble ou de détails.

En regardant les illustrations, vous vous apercevrez que dans les textes, des mots tels que: économie, matières premières, sources de revenus constituent des mots-clefs importants. Mais les choses deviennent beaucoup plus difficiles lorsqu'on en arrive à l'histoire culturelle. Toutefois, une tentative a été faite dans ce sens, principalement dans les textes qui constituent des éléments de liaison.

Danemark

Commençons notre survol des pays d'Europe par le Danemark, avec les Vikings, qui aux époques anciennes déjà, longèrent les côtes de tous les territoires qui forment la CEE aujourd'hui. Dans la lointaine Sicile, la cathédrale de Cefalu témoigne d'une autre réalité que celle qui veut que les Vikings n'aient été qu'une bande de pirates sauvages assoiffés de sang. Car une nation qui a donné naissance à Hans Christian Andersen dont la petite Sirène est devenue le symbole de Copenhague, doit, bien sûr, présenter un autre visage également.

Mer du Nord et Écosse

Traversons la Mer du Nord (pétrole, gaz et harengs) en direction des majestueux paysages naturels des Highlands écossais. Si nous regardons les côtes d'Ecosse depuis l'Atlantique, c'est alors l'image de l'Armada espagnole (la flotte invincible) qui surgit à l'esprit. Une flotte totalement détruite au cours de l'un des tout premiers conflits européens, sonnant ainsi le début du déclin et de la destruction finale de l'Empire espagnol, ainsi que la modification du rapport des forces dans les pays nord-européens. Mais nous penserons également aux navires du dernier conflit gigantesque et tragique quia secoué l'Europe parce que c'est ici, au cours de la Deuxième Guerre mondiale, que les convois partaient pour Mourmansk.

Irlande

La victoire du roi-stathouder Guillaume III sur la Boyne, en Irlande, au détriment de son beau-frère, le roi d'Angleterre catholique détrôné Jacques II eut des conséquences énormes. L'île verte des Celtes se retrouva alors dans la sphère d'influence britannique et ce furent surtout les colons écossais qui allaient investir l'île par le nord. Le conflit actuel qui agite l'Irlande du Nord est le résidu de cet événement historique. Mais auparavant déjà, la religion avait joué un rôle important en Irlande car ce furent des moines celtiques qui christianisèrent une grande partie de l'Europe du Nord-Ouest. C'est pourquoi, sur les traces de saint Brendan, nous mettrons le cap sur les Pays-Bas et les pays germaniques via le pays de Galles et l'Angleterre.

Grande-Bretagne

La Grande-Bretagne, c'est-à-dire ici l'Angleterre et le pays de Galles, était déjà une province romaine qui se défendait au Nord contre les raids des écossais grâce au mur d'Hadrien. Les Romains furent suivis par les Danois, qui à leur tour, cédèrent la place aux Angles et aux Saxons qui venaient des basses plaines du nord de l'Allemagne et qui absorbèrent les Celtes d'origine. Pour les Britanniques, le concept d'Europe fut, pendant des siècles synonyme, de continent et ils ont préféré se concentrer sur leur propre Empire. Les guerres mondiales de ce siècle les ramenèrent au continent qui n'était, après tout, pas tellement éloigné, et ceci est devenu d'autant plus évident depuis qu'ils ont rejoint la CEE. L'Empire Britannique a donné à l'Europe une langue universelle. Un avantage énorme pour William Shakespeare et les Beatles. L'argent du monde contemporain passe toujours par le centre financier du monde: Londres. A propos, ce tunnel que l'on creuse vers l'Europe, amènera la Grande-Bretagne au cœur du continent!

Benelux

A une certaine époque, la laine des moutons anglais était la matière première du commerce des draps et, par conséquent, du développement et de la grandeur de Bruges, le premier centre culturel européen au nord des Alpes. Lorsque l'importance de Bruges la flamande déclina, l'étoile d'Anvers la brabançonne commença à monter. Mais Anvers, en tant que capitale mondiale, fut à son tour supplantée par Amsterdam la hollandaise. Entre l'Anvers de Rubens et l'Amsterdam de Rembrandt, il y eut les guerres de religion qui portèrent une rude atteinte à l'Europe et, plus particulièrement, aux Pays-Bas. L'estuaire du Rhin, de la Meuse et de l'Escaut a constitué un centre européen important pendant des siècles et le port de Rotterdam, situé au cœur de cet estuaire, peut s'appeler fièrement le plus grand port de mer du monde. Ici, au carrefour des différentes cultures européennes, nous trouvons également Bruxelles et Luxembourg, des capitales européennes dignes d'estime, où plusieurs institutions de la CEE ont trouvé des installations adéquates.

République Fédérale d'Allemagne

Lorsqu'on aborde la République Fédérale depuis la Hollande par avion, c'est à peine si l'on peut percevoir une différence dans le paysage de ces deux pays. Les terres faiblement émergées du Danemark, de l'Allemagne et des Pays-Bas, en allemand 'Watten' et en néerlandais 'Wadden', qui bordent la côte, se fondent insensiblement l'une dans l'autre. Et à l'intérieur du pays, nous apercevons le même phénomène pour la basse plaine du nord de l'Allemagne qui s'étend loin au delà de l'Elbe en République Démocratique d'Allemagne et en Pologne. Aujourd'hui, Lübeck est une ville frontière, mais il fut un temps où c'était le centre et le siège principal de la Ligue hanséatique, dont les membres se retrouvaient dans cette même plaine basse qui s'étend des Pays-Bas jusqu'au golfe de Finlande. Brême et Hambourg continuent d'ailleurs toujours à se prévaloir fièrement du préfixe de "Hansestadt" (ville de la Hanse).

Nous ne descendrons pas immédiatement vers le sud, mais survolerons d'abord le Rhin. A l'époque romaine, ce fleuve formait la frontière septentrionale de l'Empire romain; aujourd'hui, c'est l'artère du nord-ouest de l'Europe dont le cœur industriel, c'est-à-dire la région Rhin-Ruhr, continue à battre nerveusement. Par le Main et le canal du Rhin au Danube le vieux désir romain de voyager depuis la mer Noire jusqu'à la mer du Nord est réalisé. Au delà de Francfort-sur-le-Main, les coteaux s'élèvait progressivement jusqu'aux Alpes, le toit de l'Europe, dans la partie sud de l'état fédéral de Bavière.

France

Depuis plusieurs décades, le Rhin forme la frontière entre la France et l'Allemagne et ceci a fini par éliminer un vieux conflit. Ce conflit fut entamé à Verdun, lorsque l'Empire carolingien fut scindé en trois parties. A l'Ouest, nous trouvons les rudiments de la France et, à l'Est, ceux de l'Allemagne. Pendant des siècles, les pays qui se trouvaient entre ces deux entités ont été la proie de nombreux actes de guerre européens. La coopération franco-allemande après la Seconde Guerre mondiale a coïncidé avec le début de la coopération européenne. Strasbourg peut donc être qualifié de bon choix, s'agissant du siège du Parlement Européen.

Capitale indiscutable d'une France fortement centralisée, Paris, bien sûr, qui est encerclé par toute une série de villes satellites. En Europe également, la France est au centre non seulement sur le plan territorial, mais aussi sur le double plan de la culture et de l'esprit. Vincent van Gogh y est venu pour peindre et ce que l'on a appelé 'la génération perdue' a également trouvé un asile ici.

Péninsule ibérique

Nous franchissons maintenant les Pyrénées pour aborder la péninsule ibérique. Rome trembla lorsque Hannibal et son armée quittèrent l'Espagne pour leur célèbre traversée des Alpes. Après avoir été une province de l'Empire romain, avec la conquête arabe une nouvelle ère commençait. Le déclin de l'influence arabe et la montée du Portugal et de l'Espagne eurent lieu en même temps et lorsque le dernier bastion arabe (Grenade) tomba, Colomb obtint ses navires pour découvrir l'Amérique. Colomb, originaire de Gênes, venait d'échanger ses maîtres portugais contre de nouveaux maîtres, espagnols cette fois.

Le Portugal et l'Espagne s'étaient non seulement partagé la péninsule ibérique, mais songeaient également à se partager l'hégémonie mondiale. Mais il ne fallut pas attendre longtemps avant que la montée des pays du Nord mette fin à ce plan. C'est dans un isolement relatif, que les arts et les sciences fleurirent ici. De Velasquez à Picasso, il est arrivé à maintes reprises que des artistes et des scientifiques auréolés d'une gloire mondiale se manifestent ici. La tragique guerre civile d'Espagne renforça encore le sentiment d'isolement si besoin était. Mais à l'époque moderne, la nation espagnole a de nouveau surpris le monde en s'adaptant à celui-ci d'une manière extrêmement rapide. Avec le Portugal, l'Espagne est devenue récemment membre de la CEE et affronte, avec de grands espoirs, l'avenir et l'Europe.

Italie

Les Italiens peuvent être fiers à bon droit de ce qu'ils ont réalisé. En Europe, aucune autre nation ne peut se vanter d'avoir été deux fois aux avant-postes de l'Histoire. Naturellement, il y eut l'Empire romain qui surpassait la CEE actuelle de loin si l'on pense par exemple à l'étendue de son territoire. Mais peut-être que les Villes-Etats du Moyen Age eurent un impact beaucoup plus direct sur la culture du monde occidental actuel. A Florence, l'influence de la Renaissance se fait toujours sentir et c'est depuis la République des Doges à Venise que Marco Polo partit pour l'Extrême-Orient. A Gênes, on débarquait des marchandises qui devaient être transportées par terre jusqu'aux lointaines contrées du Nord. Bien sûr, Rome reste la Ville éternelle et Naples est un endroit qu'il faut avoir vu avant de mourir. La Sicile tomba entre les mains des Grecs, des Romains, des Vikings et des Espagnoles et régla elle-même ses propres affaires avant d'émerger dans ce qui allait devenir l'état italien unifié de Garibaldi.

Grèce

Le berceau sans pareil de la civilisation européenne, mais aussi, comme l'Italie, un pays qui, dans sa version moderne et actuelle, n'existe que depuis une bonne centaine d'années seulement. Les contributions de la Grèce classique à la culture universelle sont si immenses et nombreuses que la simple mention de quelques noms et de quelques faits ne peut être faite qu'au hasard. Aussi ne mentionnerons-nous qu'Olympie qui donna son nom aux modernes Jeux Olympiques, Delphes, avec son oracle, et bien sûr Athènes, avec son Parthenon. La civilisation byzantine a eu une grande influence également et les nombreux croisés ont laissé derrière eux certaines structures. Notre survol de l'Europe se terminera à l'endroit historique où, selon la mythologie grecque, commença l'histoire de l'Europe. Sur la pointe extrême-orientale de la Crète, le seul endroit d'Europe où l'on puisse voir des palmiers absolument naturels, c'est-à-dire non cultivés, se trouve l'endroit où le taureau avec Europe sur son dos aborda au rivage crétois. Et ce fut ce pays qui fut appelé Europe.

Introduzione

Sorvolando i dodici paesi membri della Comunità Europea, da Nord a Sud, da Est a Ovest, potremo avere un'immagine della diversità dei paesaggi e degli insediamenti urbani.

Le immagini delle antiche città e villaggi, dei nuovi centri abitati e delle zone industriali si alternano a magnifici paesaggi naturali propri di ogni paese. Tutto ciò in un'infinita varietà di contrasti e di similitudini, sia che si tratti di sguardi d'insieme che di dettagli. Nelle didascalie che illustrano le fotografie ritroveremo sovente parole chiave quali: economia, materie prime, fonti di ricchezza. Resta tuttavia difficile dare una descrizione esauriente della storia culturale di questi paesi. Nei testi che rappresentato degli elementi di collegamento è stato fatto tuttavia un tentativo in questo senso.

Danimarca
Iniziamo il nostro viaggio in Danimarca, paese dei Vichinghi che in passato navigarono lungo tutte le coste dei paesi che costituiscono oggi la Comunità Europea. Nella lontana Sicilia, il Duomo di Cefalù rende testimonianza del fatto che i Vichinghi furono ben altro che non i selvaggi pirati noti solamente per la loro ferocia. In effetti, il paese che ha dato i natali a Hans Christian Andersen, la cui Sirenetta è divenuta il simbolo di Copenaghen, deve presentare anche un altro aspetto.

Mar del Nord e Scozia
Attraversiamo il Mar del Nord (petrollo, gas e aringhe) e dirigiamoci verso i maestosi paesaggi naturali degli Highlands scozzesi. Guardando le coste della Scozia dall'Oceano Atlantico viene fatto di pensare alla leggendaria Armada Spagnola (la flotta invincibile) completamente distrutta nel corso di uno dei primi conflitti europei: ciò segnò l'inizio del declino e della distruzione totale dell'Impero spagnolo e il conseguente cambiamento del rapporto di forze nei paesi della Europa del Nord. Rammenteremo ugualmente le navi nell'ultimo tragico conflitto mondiale, poichè proprio di qui, nel corso della Seconda Guerra mondiale, partirono i convogli per Murmansk.

Irlanda
La vittoria del Re Stadtholder, Guglielmo III, sulla Boyne, in Irlanda, contro suo cognato, lo spodestato re cattolico d'Inghilterra, Enrico II, ha avuto profonde conseguenze. La verde isola dei Celti si ritrovò allora nella sfera di influenza degli inglesi e furono soprattutto i coloni scozzesi che si recarono dal Nord a popolare quella zona. L'attuale conflitto che interessa l'Irlanda del Nord è una diretta conseguenza di questo avvenimento storico.

D'altronde, già in passato, la religione aveva svolto un ruolo importante in Irlanda, poichè furono dei monaci celti che portarono il Cristianesimo in una vasta parte dell'Europa Nord-occidentale. E per questa ragione che, sulle orme di San Brendano, ci sposteremo ora verso i Paesi Bassi e quelli tedeschi, passando attraverso il Galles e l'Inghilterra.

Gran Bretagna
La Gran Bretagna, vale a dire l'Inghilterra e il Galles, era anticamente una Provincia Romana, che si difendeva a Nord, dagli attacchi degli scozzesi, per mezzo del Muro di Adriano. I Romani furono soppiantati dai Danesi, a cui successero gli Angli e i Sassoni che provenivano dalle pianure del Nord della Germania e che assorbirono i Celti d'origine. Per lungo tempo l'Europa fu, per l'Inghilterra, sinonimo di 'continente' e gli inglesi preferirono interessarsi al proprio impero. La Seconda Guerra Mondiale ha dimostrato che il continente non è poi così lontano geograficamente e questa idea è stata rafforzata dalla partecipazione dell'Inghilterra alla Comunità Europea. L'Impero Britannico ha dato all'Europa una lingua universale e ciò ha costituito un vantaggio sia per Shakespeare che per i Beatles.

Tutto il denaro del mondo contemporaneo passa sempre attraverso il centro finanziario del mondo: Londra. Il tunnel che attraversa la Manica congiungerà tra breve l'Inghilterra al continente.

Benelux
Un tempo, la lana delle pecore inglesi costituiva la materia prima per l'industria tessile ed era all'origine della ricchezza di Bruges, il primo centro culturale europeo a Nord delle Alpi. Quando la potenza di Bruges cominciò a declinare, la città di Anversa assurse a maggior importanza. Tuttavia Anversa, come capitale del mondo, venne a sua volta sostituita da Amsterdam. Fra l'Anversa di Rubens e l'Amsterdam di Rembrandt, ci furono guerre di religione che crearono gravi problemi all'Europa, e in particolare ai Paesi Bassi. L'estuario del Reno, della Mosa e della Schelda ha costituito nell'antichità un importante centro europeo e il porto di Rotterdam, al centro di questo estuario, è ora il più grande porto commerciale del mondo. Nel Benelux, punto di convergenza di numerose culture europee, troviamo anche Bruxelles e Lussemburgo, capitali europee in cui hanno sede varie istituzioni della Comunità Europea.

Repubblica Federale Tedesca

Quando si raggiunge la Germania Occidentale, provenendo in aereo dall'Olanda, è difficile percepire le differenze di paesaggio fra i due paesi. Sulla costa del Mar del Nord confluiscono i confini della Germania, della Danimarca e della Olanda, senza notevoli differenze. Si può notare che il paesaggio pianeggiante, si estende anche oltre i confini della Germania Occidentale, fino alla Repubblica Democratica Tedesca e alla Polonia. Lubecca, attualmente città di confine, fu un tempo centro e sede principale della Lega Anseatica, i cui membri si ritrovavano in questa stessa pianura che va dai Paesi Bassi al Golfo di Finlandia. Brema ed Amburgo continuano a fregiarsi con orgoglio del titolo di 'Hansestadt' (= città della Hnase). Non scendiamo direttamente da Nord a Sud, ma sorvoliamo ora il Reno.

In epoca romana, questo fiume costituiva la frontiera settentrionale dell'impero romano; oggi esso è una via di comunicazione verso l'Europa nord-occidentale, in cui si trova anche il grande centro industriale della Ruhr. Attraverso il Meno e il canale dal Reno al Danubio, il Reno è oggi collegato con il Danubio, e ciò realizza un vecchio sogno dei Romani, quello di giungere navigando dal Mar Nero al Mar del Nord. Dopo Francoforte, il paesaggio diventa sempre più accidentato, fino a che non raggiungiamo le Alpi, il tetto dell'Europa.

Francia

Da molti decenni, il Reno segna il confine fra la Francia e la Germania e ciò è servito ad eliminare un vecchio conflitto iniziatosi a Verdun, quando l'Impero Carolingio fu diviso in tre parti. Ad occidente si costituì la Francia mentre ad oriente ebbe inizio la storia della Germania. Per secoli le zone che si trovano fra questi due grandi paesi furono oggetto di conflitti a livello europeo. La collaborazione franco-tedesca, dopo la seconda guerra mondiale, ha coinciso con l'inizio della cooperazione europea. La scelta di Strasburgo come sede del Parlamento Europeo, può essere definita una buona scelta storica. Parigi, capitale di un paese fortemente centralizzato, è circondata da un gran numero di città satelliti. La Francia, in Europa, costituisce un centro non solo geografico, ma anche spirituale e culturale. Vincent van Gogh si era recato in Francia per dipingere e la colonia americana della 'Lost Generation' trovò a Parigi la sua patria ideale.

Penisola Iberica

Attraversiamo ora i Pirenei e raggiungiamo la Penisola Iberica. Roma tremò quando Annibale e il suo esercito lasciarono la Spagna ed attraversarono le Alpi. Più tardi la Spagna divenne una provincia romana e solo nel Medio Evo essa conobbe una nuova era araba. L'allontanamento dall'influenza araba e il sorgere della potenze spagnola e portoghese avvennero contemporaneamente e quando l'ultimo baluardo arabo (Granada) cadde, Colombo potè ottenere le navi per scoprire l'America. Colombo, originario di Genova, sostituì i suoi padroni portoghesi con quelli spagnoli. Il Portogallo e la Spagna si erano divisi la penisola iberica e progettavano di dividersi anche l'egemonia mondiale. Tuttavia l'ascesa dei paesi del Nord pose fine a questo progetto e le arti e la scienze si svilupparono qui in un relativo isolamento. Nonostante ciò da Velasquez a Picasso si manifestarono artisti e uomini di scienza conosciuti a livello mondiale. La tragica guerra civile spagnola contribuì ad accrescere questo senso di isolamento che si è spezzato in epoca recente con la entrata della Spagna e del Portogallo nella Comunità Europea.

Italia

Gli italiani hanno molte buone ragioni per essere fieri del loro paese. Nessuna nazione in Europa può vantarsi di essere stata per due volte ai massimi livelli della storia. Ricordiamo prima di tutto l'Impero romano il cui territorio era molto più vasto di quello dell'attuale Comunità Europea. Ma furono forse soprattutto le Città-stato del Medioevo ad esercitare una maggior influenza sulla cultura del mondo occidentale europeo. A Firenze possiamo percepire l'influsso del Rinascimento ed è dalla Repubblica di Venezia che Marco Polo partì per i suoi viaggi in Estremo Oriente.

A Genova venivano sbarcate le merci che dovevano poi essere trasportate via terra fino ai lontani paesi del Nord. Roma resta per noi la città eterna e non si può morire senza avere visto Napoli. La Sicilia fu preda dei Greci, dei Romani, dei Vichinghi e degli Spagnoli e divenne indipendente prima di essere annessa da Garibaldi all'Italia.

Grecia

Culla della civiltà europea, la Grecia è un paese che, come l'Italia, esiste nella sua veste moderna e attuale solo da un centinaio d'anni. Il contributo della Grecia classica alla cultura universale si è manifestato in maniera così vasta e ricca che è impossibile menzionarne tutti i nomi e gli avvenimenti.

Ricordiamo soltanto l'Olimpo che diede il nome ai moderni Giochi Olimpici, l'Oracolo di Delfi, e naturalmente Atene e il Partenone. Anche la civiltà bizantina ha avuto qui largo influsso e i numerosi crociati hanno lasciato vaste tracce. Il nostro viaggio aereo sull'Europa termina nel luogo storico, in cui, secondo la mitologia greca, iniziò la storia d'Europa. Sull'estrema punta orientale dell'isola di Creta, l'unica zona in Europa in cui crescono palme allo stato naturale, si trova il luogo in cui il toro con Europa sulla schiena approdò alla riva di Creta. Questo paese fu chiamato Europa.

Inleiding

Op een luchtreis langs de twaalf lidstaten van de Europese Gemeenschap, van noord naar zuid en van oost naar west, wordt een beeld geschetst van de verschillende landschappen en nederzettingen. Beelden van oude steden en dorpen en van nieuwe groeikernen en industriegebieden worden afgewisseld met typerende natuur- en landschapsopnamen. En dat alles in een vrijwel eindeloze variëteit van contrasten of aaneenschakeling van parallellen, zowel in overzichten als in details.

In de begeleidende tekst bij de foto's zijn belangrijke sleutelwoorden: economie, grondstoffen en bronnen van inkomsten. Moeilijker is het om culturele en historische verbanden te leggen. Maar ook dit aspect is, vooral in verbindende teksten, duidelijk aanwezig.

Denemarken

We starten onze luchtreis in Denemarken. Het land van de Vikingen die al lang geleden het gehele gebied omzeilden dat thans de EG vormt. De Noormannendom van Céfalu in Sicilië geeft ons een heel ander beeld dan dat van die beruchte, ruwe bloeddorstige zeeschuimers. Maar natuurlijk heeft een land dat Hans Christian Andersen heeft voortgebracht, ook een heel ander gezicht.

Noordzee en Schotland

Hoog over de Noordzee, olie, gas en haring, vliegen we naar de machtige natuur van de Schotse Hooglanden. Als we vanaf zee naar de ruwe kust van Schotland kijken, dan moeten we denken aan de machtige Spaanse Armada die hier in één van de eerste Europese conflicten het onderspit moest delven en daarmee de ondergang van de Spaanse wereldmacht en de opkomst van de noordelijke landen markeerde. Maar we denken ook aan dat laatste grote en tragische Europese conflict, want hiervandaan vertrokken in de Tweede Wereldoorlog de scheepsconvooien naar Murmansk.

Ierland

De overwinning van de Koning-Stadhouder Willem III aan de Boyne in Ierland op zijn zwager James II, de onttroonde katholieke Koning van Engeland, had grote gevolgen. Het groene eiland van de Kelten kwam hierdoor binnen de Britse invloedssfeer en vooral Schotse kolonisten zouden het eiland vanuit het noorden gaan bevolken. Het huidige conflict in Noord-Ierland is hiervan het rechtstreekse gevolg. Maar al eerder in de geschiedenis speelde het geloof hier een belangrijke rol. Want het waren Ierse monniken die in een groot gedeelte van Noordwest-Europa het christendom brachten. Daarom gaan we in het spoor van Sint-Brendaan, over Wales en Engeland, naar de Lage en Duitse landen.

Groot-Brittannië

Engeland en Wales, Brittannië, waren Romeinse provincies die zich tegen de aanvallen van de Schotten uit het noorden trachten te beschermen met de Hadrianus Wall. De Romeinen werden verslagen door de Denen, die op hun beurt weer verslagen werden door de Angelen en de Saksen, die uit de Noordduitse laagvlakte kwamen, en in de bevolking opgenomen werden als waren het de oorspronkelijke Kelten. Lange tijd was voor Engeland het begrip Europa synoniem met het continent en men gaf er de voorkeur aan om zich sterker te richten op het eigen wereldrijk. De Tweede Wereldoorlog leerde dat het continent geografisch niet zover weg lag en vanzelfsprekend is dit gevoel nog veel meer versterkt sinds de toetreding tot de EG. Het Britse rijk heeft Europa een universele taal geleverd. Een groot voordeel zowel voor William Shakespeare als voor de Beatles. Het geld van de wereld stroomt nog steeds naar het financiële hart van de wereld: Londen. En de tunnel naar Europa zal Engeland straks ook rechtstreeks verbinden met het hart van het continent.

Benelux

De wol van de Engelse schapen was eens de grondstof voor de lakenindustrie, die op zijn beurt weer verantwoordelijk was voor de opkomst van het machtige Brugge, het eerste Europese culturele centrum ten noorden van de Alpen. Toen de ster van het Vlaamse Brugge begon te dalen kwam die van het Brabantse Antwerpen juist omhoog. Maar Antwerpen werd als hoofdstad van de toenmalige wereld op zijn beurt weer opgevolgd door het Hollandse Amsterdam. Tussen het Antwerpen van Rubens en het Amsterdam van Rembrandt woedden de godsdienstoorlogen die Europa, en de Lage Landen in het bijzonder, verdeelden. De Delta van Rijn, Maas en Schelde is al sedert eeuwen een belangrijk Europees handelscentrum. De haven van Rotterdam, in het centrum hiervan, mag zich trots de grootste haven ter wereld noemen. In de Benelux, op het kruispunt van verschillende Europese culturen, vinden we ook Brussel en Luxemburg, waardige Europese hoofdsteden waar verschillende EG-instituten hun plaats vonden.

Bondsrepubliek Duitsland

Als we de Bondsrepubliek Duitsland vanuit Nederland per vliegtuig binnenvliegen is er landschappelijk nauwelijks verschil te zien. Vooral op de grens van land en water lopen de Deense, Duitse en Nederlandse Wadden ongemerkt in elkaar over. En ook buiten de grenzen van de Bondsrepubliek, achter de Elbe, zien we de Noordduitse laagvlakte doorlopen tot over de DDR en Polen. Lübeck is nu een grensstad, maar het was eens de centraal gelegen en meest belangrijke van alle Hanzesteden die verspreid in die vlakte lagen vanaf de Lage Landen tot aan de Finse Golf. Met Bremen en Hamburg bedient het zich nog steeds van het trotse voorzetsel: Hanzestad.

Vanuit het noorden gaan we niet rechtstreeks naar het zuiden maar eerst vliegen we langs de Rijn. In de Romeinse tijd was deze rivier de noordelijke grens en nu is de Rijn nog steeds de slagader van Noordwest-Europa, waarin het industriële hart, het Rijn-Ruhrgebied, fel klopt. Via de Main en het Rijn-Donaukanaal zal de Donau eerdaags verbonden zijn met de Rijn en de oude Romeinse wens om te varen van de Zwarte Zee tot de Noordzee zal dan in onze dagen in vervulling zijn gegaan. Achter Frankfurt am Main wordt het landschap steeds meer geaccidenteerd totdat we in het zuiden van de Vrijstaat Beieren bij de Alpen komen, het dak van Europa.

Frankrijk

Alweer enkele tientallen jaren vormt de Rijn weer de grens tussen Frankrijk en Duitsland en een oud conflict zal nu hopelijk voorgoed uit de wereld zijn. Dit conflict begon in Verdun, toen het Karolingische rijk werd opgesplitst in drie delen. In het westen werd dit de bakermat van Frankrijk en in het oosten het begin van Duitsland. De gebieden ertussen waren eeuwenlang de inzet van tal van Europese conflicten. De Duits-Franse samenwerking na de Tweede Wereldoorlog betekende ook het begin van de Europese samenwerking. De keuze van Straatsburg als zetel van het Europese Parlement kan zonder meer symbolisch en historisch juist genoemd worden.

De onbetwiste hoofdstad van het sterk gecentraliseerde Frankrijk is natuurlijk Parijs, omringd door een groot aantal historische en moderne voorsteden. In Europa neemt Frankrijk een centrale positie in. Niet alleen geografisch, maar ook in cultureel en geestelijk opzicht. Vincent van Gogh kwam naar Frankrijk om te schilderen en tussen de Twee Wereldoorlogen vond de zogenaamde 'lost generation' van Amerikanen in Parijs hun huis.

Iberisch schiereiland

We vliegen over de Pyreneeën naar het Iberische schiereiland. Rome schudde op zijn grondvesten toen Hannibal Spanje verliet en met zijn leger en olifanten de Alpen overstak. Later werd Spanje een provincie van het Romeinse rijk en een nieuwe Arabisch tijdperk zou weer eerst beginnen in de Middeleeuwen. Het terugdringen van de Arabische invloedssfeer en de opkomst van Spanje en Portugal zou zich geleidelijk aan voltrekken. In het jaar dat het laatste Arabische bolwerk viel, Granada, ontdekte Columbus, die uit Genua kwam en zijn Portugese broodheren juist voor Spaanse had ingeruild, de Nieuwe Wereld: Amerika. Portugal en Spanje hadden niet alleen het Iberisch schiereiland verdeeld, maar de wereld werd voor het gemak ook maar verdeeld. Niet voor lang overigens want de opkomst van de Noordelijke landen maakte spoedig een einde aan de aspiraties van de verdeelde wereldhegemonie. In een betrekkelijke isolatie werden hier kunsten en wetenschappen beoefend. Maar van Velazques tot aan Picasso groeiden uit dit isolement regelmatig kunstenaars en wetenschappers van wereldformaat. De Burgeroorlog in Spanje versterkte nog de gevoelens van het isolement voor een lange tijd. Zowel Spanje als Portugal vertoonden in de recente geschiedenis een sterke democratische instelling en met de toetreding tot de EG wordt er hier met hoge verwachtingen naar Europa en de toekomst uitgekeken.

Italië

De Italianen hebben recht van reden om trots te zijn. Geen land in Europa kan er zich op beroemen maar liefst tweemaal in de geschiedenis vooraan gestaan te hebben. Natuurlijk allereerst het Romeinse Rijk dat het grondgebied van de huidige EG nog verre overtrof. Maar misschien zijn de middeleeuwse stadstaten nog wel van veel groter belang geweest voor de huidige westelijke cultuur. In Florence kun je de invloed van de Renaissance nog ondergaan. Vanuit de Dogerepubliek Venetië vertrok Marco Polo voor zijn reizen naar het Verre Oosten. In Genua werden de goederen aangevoerd die overland naar het Noorden vervoerd werden. Rome blijft natuurlijk de Eeuwige Stad en Napels moet u gezien hebben voordat u sterft. Sicilië was in de handen van Grieken, Romeinen, Vikingen en Spanjaarden en het was nog even eigen baas in eigen huis voordat Garibaldi het bij de nieuwe Italiaanse eenheidsstaat voegde.

Griekenland

De onbetwiste geboorteplaats van de Europese beschaving. Maar ook een land, evenals Italië, dat in zijn moderne staatkundige versie nog maar zo'n honderd jaar bestaat. De bijdragen van het klassieke Griekenland aan de wereldcultuur zijn zo talrijk, zo ontelbaar dat we enkel wat losse namen en feiten kunnen noemen. De verblijfplaats van de Goden op de berg Olympia, waar de moderne Olympische Spelen naar genoemd zijn. Delphi met zijn orakel en natuurlijk Athene met zijn Acropolis en Parthenon. De Bijzantijnse beschaving had hier later een grote invloed en ook de Kruisvaarders hebben hier hun voetsporen en herinneringen achtergelaten. We eindigen onze vlucht boven Europa op de meest oostelijke punt van het eiland Kreta. De enige plek in Europa waar niet gecultiveerde palmen groeien en ook de plaats waar volgens de mythe de stier uit zee aan land kwam. Met op zijn rug Europa, die haar naam aan dat nieuwe land gaf!

Introduçao

Numa viagem aérea ao longo dos doze estados membros de Comunidade Europeia, de norte para sul e de oriente para ocidente, é dada uma imagem das diferentes paisagens e povoações. Imagens de cidades e aldeias antigas e de novos centros de desenvolvimento e de regiões industriais são intercaladas com vistas de natureza e de paisagens típicas. E tudo numa quase infinita variedade de contrastes ou de paralelos enlançados, tanto numa vista geral como em pormenor.

Nos textos que acompanham as fotografias encontram-se palavras-chaves de grande significado: economia, matérias prima e fundos de receita. O mais difícil é fazer as ligações culturais e históricas. Mas tambem esta aspecto está presente, em especial nos textos de sequência.

Dinamarca

Iniciamos a nossa viagem aérea na Dinamarca. O pais dos viquinges, os quais há já muito tempo navegaram pelas regiões, que formam hoje a CEE. A influência dos Normandos de Céfalu, na Sicilia dá-nos uma ideia diferente da de piratas dos mares, de má fama, grosseiros e sanguíneos. Mas, como é natural, o país que criou Hans Christian Andersen, tem ainda outro aspecto diferente.

Mar do Norte e Escócia

Alto por cima do Mar do Norte – petróleo, gás e arenques – voamos em direcção à natureza esmagadora dos planaltos escoceses. Se observarmos a costa rude de escócia, do lado do mar, pensamos logo na potente Armada espanhola, que aqui sofreu uma derrota, num dos primeiros conflitos europeus e assim marcou o desmonoramento da potência mundial espanhola e o desenvolvimento dos países nórdicos. Mas nós pensamos tambem no último grande e trágico conflito europeu, porque daqui partiramos navios para Murmansk, durante e Segunda Guerra Mundial.

Irlanda

A victória do Rei-Governador Guilhermo III, junto ao Boyne, na Irlanda sobre o seu cunhado James II, o Rei da Inglaterra católico, descoroado, teve grandes consequências. A ilha verde dos celtas passou assim ao dominio britânico e foram os colonistas escoceses que passariam a habitar a ilha vindos do norte. O conflito actual na Irlanda do Norte é uma consequência directa disto. mas já antes disso, na história, a religião desenpenhou aqui um papel importante. Porque foram monges irlandeses que numa grande parte da Europa do noroeste introduziram o cristianismo. Por isso seguimos as pegadas do São Brandão, através da Gália, na Inglaterra, para os Países Baixos e os Germânicos.

Grã-Bretanha

Bretanha, Inglaterra e Gália foram províncias romanas, que tentaram defender-se dos ataques dos escoceses vindos do norte por meio da Hadrianus Wall. Os romanos foram derrotados pelos dinamarqueses, os quais foram por sua vez derrotados pelos anglos e os saxões, que vieram da planície do norte da Alemanha e que foram aceites no seio da povoação como se fossem os celtas de origem. Durante muito tempo a Europa foi para a Inglaterra o sinónimo de o continente e lá dava-se a preferência de se dirigir com mais vigor ao seu próprio reino mundial. A Segunda Guerra Mundial mostrou que o continente geograficamente não estava tão longe e, como é natural, este sentimento foi reforçado pela entrada na CEE. O reino britânico forneceu à Europa uma língua universal. Uma grande vantagem, tanto para William Shakespeare, como para os Beatles. O dinheiro de mundo continua a fluir para o centro financeiro do mundo: Londres. E o tunel para a Europa ligará brevemente a Inglaterra com o centro da continente.

Benelux

A lã dos carneiros ingleses fori em tempos a matéria prima para a indústria de panos, a qual por sua vez causou o desenvolvimento da poderosa Brugge, o primeiro centro cultural da Europa, ao norte dos Alpes. Quando a estrela da Brugge flamenga começou a descair, elevou-se precisamente a da Antuérpia brabançona. Mas Antuérpia, como capital do mundo de então, foi sucessida por Amesterdão da olanda. Entre a Antuérpia de Rubens e a Amesterdão de Rembrandt ardeu a guerra das religiões que dividiu a Europa e os Países Baixos, em especial. O delta do Reno, do Mosa e do Escalda é já à séculos um imporante centro comercial europeu.

O porto de Roterdão, no centro desta, pode-se orgulhar de ser o maior porto do mundo. Na Benelux, no cruzamento de diversas culturas europeias, encontramos tambem Bruxelas e Luxemburgo, dignas capitais europeias, onde diversas institutos da CEE se alojaram.

República Federal da Alemanha

Se entrarmos na Alemanha, pelo ar, vindos da Holanda, pouca diferença se nota na paisagem. Sobretudo nos límites da terra e da água os baixíos da Dinamarca, da Alemanha e da Holanda ligam-se despercebidamente. E mesmo fora da fronteira da República Federal, atrás do Elba, vemos os baixíos do norte da Alemanha continuarem até alem da RDA e da Polónia. Lübeck é agora uma cidade fronteiriça, mas foi em tempos central e a mais importante de todas as cidades anseáticas, distribuídas naquela planície desde os Países Baixos até ao Golfo da Finlândia. Com Bremmen e Hamburgo, usa ainda o cognome Cidade Anseática.

Do norte não vamos directamente para o sul, mas primeiro voamos ao longo do Reno. No tempo romano era este rio a fronteira nórdica e presentemente é o Reno a artéria do noroeste da Europa, no qual bate o coração industrial, a Região do Reno e do Rur. Via o Meno e o canal do Reno-Danúbio será realizada brevemente a ligação entre o Danúbio e o Reno; o antigo sonho dos romanos para navegar do Mar Negro até ao Mar do Norte será nos nossos dias uma realidade. Alem de Franqueforte ao Meno a paisagem torna-se mais acidentada até que no sul dos Estados Livres da Bavária, chegamos aos Alpes, o teto da Europa.

França

Há já dezenas de anos forma o Reno, novamente, a fronteira entre a França e a Alemanha e o velho conflito desapareceu, esperamos, do mundo. Este conflito começou em Verdun, quando o reino Carolíngio foi dividido em três partes. No ocidente foi ele o berço da França, no oriente o início da Alemanha. A região intercalada foi durante muitos séculos a razão de imensos conflitos europeus. A colaboração franco-alemã, a seguir à Segunda Guerra Mundial significou tambem o início da colaboração Europeia. A escolha de Estrasburgo, como a sede do Parlamento Europeu pode ser considerada, sem mais, uma decisão simbólica e histórica.

A incontestável capital da França fortemente centralizada é, naturalmente, Paris, cerqueada por uma grande quantidade de subúrbios históricos e modernos. A França ocupa na Europa uma posição central. Não só geograficamente, mas tambem no ponto de vista cultural e espiritual. Vincent van Gogh veio para a França para pintar e entre as duas Guerras Mundiais a chamada 'lost generation' dos americanos encontrou domicílio em Paris.

A Península Ibérica

Voamos sobre os Pirinéus para a península Ibérica. Roma tremeu nos seus fundamentos, quando Anibal deixou a Espanha e com e seu exército e os elefantes atravessou os Alpes. Mais tarde a Espanha passou a ser uma província do reino romano e uma nova época árabe iniciava-se novamente na Idade Média. O repelir da influência árabe e o florescimento da Espanha e Portugal realizaram-se progressivamente. No ano, em que o último bastião árabe, Granada, caiu, descobriu Colombo, vindo de Génova, e que tinha acabado de trocar os seus mestres portugueses pelos espanhois, o Novo Mundo: a América. Portugal e a Espanha tinham não só dividido a península Ibérica, mas o mundo, por comodidade, foi tambem dividido entre eles. Não por muito tempo, aliás, porque o desenvolvimento dos países nórdicos acabaram brevemente com as aspirações de hegemonia mundial dividida. Num isolamento relativo foram practicadas aqui as artes e as ciências. Mas de Valazquez até Picasso saíram deste isolamento, regularmente, artistas e cientistas de formato mundial. A Guerra Civil na Espanha fortificou ainda mais a sensação do isolamento num longo período. Tanto a Espanha como Portugal demonstraram, na história recente, uma forte atitude democrática e com a entrada na CEE têm-se grandes esperanças na Europa e no futuro.

Itália

Os italianos têm razão para se sentirem orgulhosos. Nenhum outro país na Europa se pode gloriar de ter estado à cabeça duas vezes na história. É claro, em primeiro lugar o Império Romano que superou a superfície da actual CEE. Mas talvez os estados citadinos da idade média tenham sido de muito mais importância do que a cultura ocidental actual. Em Florência observa-se ainda a influência da Renascênca. Da República dos Doges Veneza partiu Marco Polo para a sua viagem para o Extremo Oriente. Em Génova eram desembarcadas as mercadorias que eram transportadas por terra para o Norte. Roma continua, naturalmente a ser a Cidade Eterna e Nápoles deve-se ter visto antes de se falecer. Sicília esteve em mãos dos gregos, dos romanos, dos viquinges e dos espanhois e ainda autónoma antes de Garibaldi a ter incluído no novo estado unitário italiano.

Grécia

O incontestável lugar de nasicmento da civilização da Europa. Mas tambem um país, assim como a Itália, que na sua moderna versão política existe apenas uns cem anos. A contribuição da Grécia clássica à cultura mundial foi imensa; foi tão ampla que podemos citar apenas uns quantos nomes e factos. O domicílio dos Deuses no monte Olimpia, o qual deu o nome aos modernos jogos olímpicos. Delfi com o seu oráculo e naturalmente Atenas com o seu Acropolis e o seu Parthenon. A civilização bizantina teve aqui, mais tarde, uma grande influência e tambem os Cruzados deixaram aqui os seus vestígios e recordações. Terminamos esta voo por cima da Europa, no ponto mais oriental da ilha de Creta. O único lugar na Europa, onde crescem palmeiras não cultivadas e tambem o lugar, onde segundo o mito, o boi veio à terra vindo do mar. Com às costas a Europa, a qual deu o seu nome a essa terra nova!

Με αεροπορικό ταξίδι στα δώδεκα μέλη-κράτη της Ευρωπαϊκής Κοινότητας, από το βορρά μέχρι τη δύση, εικονογράφονται διάφορα τοπία και οικισμοί. Εικόνες από αρχαίες πόλεις και χωριά, από νέα κέντρα αστικής ανάπτυξης και βιομηχανικές περιοχές ανταλλάσσονται με χαρακτηριζόμενες φωτογραφίες από φύση και τοπίο. Αυτό γίνεται σε περίπου απέραντη ποικιλία αντιθέσεων ή σειρά αναλογιών, τόσο στις επισκοπήσεις όσο και σε λεπτομέρειες. Οι κεντρικές ιδέες στο συνοδευόμενο κείμενο των φωτογραφιών είναι; οικονομία, πρώτες ύλες και πηγές εισοδήματος. Είναι κάπως δύσκολο να συνδεθούν πολιτιστικές και ιστορικές σχέσεις. Αλλά και αυτή η πλευρά δείχνεται καθαρά, ιδίως στα συνοδευόμενα κείμενα.

Δανία

Αρχίζουμε το αεροπορικό μας ταξίδι από τη Δανία. Η χώρα των Βίκιγκ που πρίν από αιώνες όργωναν όλη την περιοχή που σήμερα αποτελεί την ΕΟΚ. Το ιερό των Βίκιγκ στο Κεφαλού της Σικελίας μας δείχνει εντελώς άλλη εικόνα από αυτή των διαβόητων, βάναυσων και αιμοδιψών πειρατών. Αλλά οπωσδήποτε η χώρα που γέννησε ένα Χανς Χρίστιαν Άντερσεν έχει εντελώς άλλη μορφή.

Βόρειος Θάλασσα και Σκωτία

Ψηλά πάνω από τη Βόρειο Θάλασσα, πετρέλαιο, φυσικό αέριο και ρέγγα, πετάμε στην ισχυρή φύση της Ορεινής Σκωτίας. Αν από τη θάλασσα κοιτάζουμε την άγρια ακτή της Σκωτίας, θα πρέπει να σκεφτούμε την ισχυρή ισπανική Αρμάντα που νικήθηκε σε μια από τις πρώτες ευρωπαϊκές συγκρούσεις και έτσι κατέρρευσε η ισπανική παγκόσμια δύναμη και άρχισε η ακμή των βόρειων χωρών. Αλλά επίσης θα πρέπει να σκεφτούμε την τελευταία, μεγάλη και τραγική ευρωπαϊκή σύγκρουση, γιατί από εδώ απόπλευσαν κατά το δεύτερο παγκόσμιο πόλεμο νηοπομπές για το Μούρμανσκ.

Ιρλανδία

Η νίκη του βασιλιά-κυβερνήτη Γουλιέλμου Γ' στο Μπόυνε στην Ιρλανδία κατά του γαμπρού του, Ιακώβου Β', του εκθρονισμένου καθολικού βασιλιά της Αγγλίας, είχε μεγάλες συνέπειες. Το πράσινο νησί των Κέλτων εξαιτίας αυτού ήρθε στη βρεταννική σφαίρα επιρροής και προπαντός οι Σκωτσέζοι άποικοι θα οίκιζαν το νησί από το βορρά. Η σημερινή σύγκρουση στη Βόρεια Ιρλανδία είναι η άμεση συνέπεια αυτού. Αλλά ήδη προγενέστερα στην ιστορία είχε παίξει εδώ η θρησκεία σημαντικό ρόλο. Ήταν οι Ιρλανδοί μοναχοί που έφεραν το χριστιανισμό σε μεγάλο μέρος της Βορειοδυτικής Ευρώπης. Γι' αυτό βαδίζουμε στα ίχνη του Αγίου Μπρενταάν, πάνω από την Ουαλία και την Αγγλία, στις Κάτω και Γερμανικές Χώρες.

Μεγάλη Βρεταννία

Η Βρεταννία, η Αγγλία και η Ουαλία, ήταν ρωμαϊκοί νομοί που προσπαθούσαν να αμυνθούν κατά των επιθέσεων των Σκωτσέζων από το βορρά με το τείχος Αδριανού. Οι Ρωμαίοι νικήθηκαν από τους Αγγλοσαξόνες που προήρθαν από τη γερμανική βαθύπεδο και αναμείχτηκαν με το λαό σαν να ήταν πρωτογενείς Κέλτοι. Για πολύ καιρό ήταν για την Αγγλία η Ευρώπη συνώνυμος με την ήπειρο και η Αγγλία προτιμούσε να αφοσιωθεί δυνατά στη δική της αυτοκρατορία. Ο δεύτερος παγκόσμιος πόλεμος έμαθε ότι η ήπειρος, γεωγραφικά, δε βρισκόταν τόσο μακρυά και οπωσδήποτε αυτό το αίσθημα δυνάμωσε κι άλλο από την είσοδο στην ΕΟΚ. Η βρεταννική αυτοκρατορία χάρισε στην Ευρώπη μια παγκόσμια γλώσσα. Μεγάλο πλεονέκτημα τόσο για το Σαίξπηρ όσο και για τους Μπήτλς. Τα χρήματα του κόσμου ρέουν ακόμα στην οικονομική καρδιά της γής; Λονδίνο. Και το τουνέλ στην Ευρώπη θα συνδέσει την Αγγλία απευθείας με την καρδιά της ηπείρου.

Βενελούξ

Το μαλλί των αγγλικών προβάτων ήταν κάποτε η πρώτη ύλη για τη βιομηχανία υφασμάτων, που με τη σειρά της ήταν υπεύθυνη για την άνοδο της δυναμικής Μπρυζ που δημιούργησε το πρώτο ευρωπαϊκό πολιτιστικό κέντρο της Ευρώπης βορινά των Άλπεων. Όταν το άστρο της φλαμανδικής Μπρυζ άρχισε να σβήνει, τότε άρχισε να ανεβαίνει το άστρο της βραβαντινής Αμβέρσας. Αλλά και την Αμβέρσα, την πρωτεύουσα του τότε κόσμου, τη διαδέχτηκε με τη σειρά του το ολλανδικό Άμστερνταμ. Μεταξύ της Αμβέρσας του Ρούμπενς και του Άμστερνταμ του Ρέμπραντ λυσσομανούσαν οι θρησκευτικοί πόλεμοι που διαχώρισαν την Ευρώπη και ιδίως τις Κάτω Χώρες. Το Δέλτα των Ρήνου, Μόζα και Σκάλδη είναι εδώ και αιώνες σημαντικό ευρωπαϊκό εμπορικό κέντρο. Το λιμάνι του Ρόττερνταμ που βρίσκεται στο κέντρο του Δέλτα αυτού μπορεί να ονομάζεται με υπερηφάνεια το μεγαλύτερο διεθνές λιμάνι στον κόσμο. Στο Βενελούξ, στο σταυροδρόμι διαφόρων ευρωπαϊκών πολιτισμών, βρίσκουμε τις Βρυξέλλες και το Λουξεμβούργο, άξιες ευρωπαϊκές πρωτεύουσες όπου διάφορα ινστιτούτα της ΕΟΚ βρήκαν τη θέση τους.

Ομοσπονδιακή Δημοκρατία της Γερμανίας

Πετώντας από την Ολλανδία στη Γερμανία βλέπουμε ότι δεν υπάρχει περίπου καμία διαφορά των τοπίων. Ιδίως στα σύνορα νερού και ξηράς συμμειγνύονται απαρατήρητα τα Φρεισικά νησιά της Δανίας, Ολλανδίας και Γερμανίας. Ακόμα πέρα από τα σύνορα της Ομοσπονδιακής Δημοκρατίας, πίσω από τον Έλβα, βλέπουμε να συνεχίζεται το βορειογερμανικό βαθύπεδο μέχρι και την Ανατολική Γερμανία και την Πολωνία. Η Λυβέκκη τώρα είναι συνοριακή πόλη αλλά κάποτε ήταν το κέντρο και η σημαντικότερη πόλη όλων των χανσεατικών συνεταίρων που σκορπισμένα βρίσκονταν στο βαθύπεδο αυτό, από τις Κάτω Χώρες μέχρι το Φιννικό Κόλπο. Μαζί με τη Βρέμη και το Αμβούργο χρησιμοποιεί ακόμα υπερήφανα το επίθετο; Χανσεατική πόλη.

Από το βορρά δεν πηγαίνουμε απευθείας στο νότο. Πρώτα πετάμε κατά μήκος του Ρήνου που στη ρωμαϊκή εποχή ήταν το βορινό σύνορο του κράτους και τώρα ακόμα αποτελεί ο Ρήνος την αρτηρία της Βορειοδυτικής Ευρώπης όπου η βιομηχανική καρδιά της, η περιοχή του Ρήνου και Ρουρ, χτυπάει δυνατά. Μέσω του Μάιν και του καναλιού Ρήνου-Δουνάβη ο Δουνάβης θα είναι δεμένος με το Ρήνο και η παλαιά ρωμαϊκή επιθυμία για να πλεύσουν από τον Εύξεινο Πόντο στη Βόρειο Θάλασσα θα πραγματοποιηθεί στις δικές μας μέρες.

Πίσω από τη Φραγκφούρτη αμ Μάιν το τοπίο δείχνει όλο και περισσότερο ανάγλυφο μέχρι που θα φτάσουμε στο νότο του ελεύθερου κράτους Βαυαρίας στις Άλπεις, τη στέγη της Ευρώπης.

Γαλλία

Εδώ και δεκάδες χρόνια αποτελεί ο Ρήνος το σύνορο μεταξύ της Γαλλίας και της Γερμανίας και ας ελπίσουμε ότι μια παλαιά σύγκρουση θα έχει εξαφανιστεί για πάντα από τον κόσμο. Η σύγκρουση αυτή άρχισε με τη συνθήκη του Βερντέν όταν το κράτος του Καρόλου του Μεγάλου διαλύθηκε και μοιράστηκε σε τρία μέρη. Η δύση έγινε η κοιτίδα της Γαλλίας και η ανατολή έγινε η αρχή της Γερμανίας. Οι περιοχές ανάμεσα για αιώνες ήταν η διακύβευση πολλών ευρωπαϊκών συγκρούσεων. Η γερμανο-γαλλική συνεργασία, μετά το δεύτερο παγκόσμιο πόλεμο, σήμαινε επίσης η αρχή της ευρωπαϊκής συνεργασίας. Η επιλογή του Στρασβούργου ως έδρα της ευρωπαϊκής Βουλής μπορεί να ονομαστεί χωρίς άλλο συμβολικά

και ιστορικά σωστή.

Η αναμφισβήτητη πρωτεύουσα της έντονα συγκεντρωτικής Γαλλίας είναι ασφαλώς το Παρίσι, τριγυρισμένο από ένα μεγάλο αριθμό ιστορικών και μοντέρνων προάστιων. Στην Ευρώπη η Γαλλία κατέχει κεντρική θέση. Όχι μόνο από γεωγραφική άποψη αλλά επίσης από πολιτιστική και πνευματική άποψη. Ο Βινσέντ βαν Γογκ ήρθε στη Γαλλία να ζωγραφήσει και ανάμεσα στους δύο παγκόσμιους πολέμους βρήκε η λεγόμενη 'lost generation' των Αμερικανών στο Παρίσι το σπίτι της.

Ιβηρική Χερσόνησος

Πετάμε πάνω από τα Πυρηναία στην Ιβηρική χερσόνησο. Η Ρώμη σείστηκε από τα θεμέλια όταν ο Αννίβας ξεκίνησε από την Ισπανία και πέρασε με το στρατό του και τους ελέφαντες από τις Άλπεις. Μετά έγινε η Ισπανία νομός της Ρωμαϊκής αυτοκρατορίας και μια νέα εποχή, η αραβική, θα άρχιζε πάλι στο Μεσαίωνα. Η απώθηση της αραβικής σφαίρας επιρροής και η άνοδος της Ισπανίας και Πορτογαλίας θα γίνονταν βαθμιαία. Το έτος που έπεσε η τελευταία αραβική έπαλξη, η Γρανάδα, ανακάλυψε ο Κολόμβος που προήρθε απο τη Γένουα και που είχε ανταλλάξει τους Πορτογάλους αφέντες με τους Ισπανούς, το Νέο Κόσμο, την Αμερική. Η Πορτογαλία και η Ισπανία δεν είχαν διαμοιράσει μόνο την Ιβηρική Χερσόνησο αλλά επίσης, χάρη ευκολίας, όλη τη γη. Όχι για πολύ καιρό όμως, γιατί η άνοδος των βόρειων κρατών γρήγορα έδωσε τέλος στις φιλοδοξίες της μοιρασμένης παγκόσμιας ηγεμονίας. Σε σχετική απομόνωση εξασκήθηκαν εδώ τέχνες και επιστήμες. Αλλά από τον απομονωτισμό αυτό τακτικά ξεχώρισαν καλλιτέχνες και επιστήμονες διεθνών διαστάσεων, από το Βελάσκεθ μέχρι τον Πικάσσο. Ο εμφύλιος πόλεμος στην Ισπανία δυνάμωνε ακόμα τα αισθήματα απομονωτισμού για πολύ καιρό. Τόσο η Ισπανία όσο κι η Πορτογαλία έδειχναν στην πρόσφατη ιστορία εντατικά δημοκρατική νοοτροπία και με την είσοδό τους στην ΕΟΚ οι κάτοικοι περιμένουν με μεγάλες προσδοκίες την Ευρώπη και το μέλλον.

Ιταλία

Οι Ιταλοί έχουν κάθε δικαίωμα να καμαρώνουν, γιατί κανένα κράτος στην Ευρώπη δε μπορεί να υπερηφανευτεί για το γεγονός ότι ήταν δυο φορές πρώτο στην ιστορία. Φυσικά πρώτ' από όλα η ρωμαϊκή αυτοκρατορία που το έδαφός της υπέρβαινε ασυζητητί το έδαφος της τωρινής ΕΟΚ. Αλλά για το σημερινό πολιτισμό μπορεί να είναι πιο σημαντικές οι μεσαιωνικές πόλεις. Στη Φλωρεντία υφίσταται κανείς ακόμα την επιρροή της αναγέννησης. Από τη δημοκρατία Δόγηδων Βενετία ξεκίνησε ο Μάρκο Πόλο για τα μακρινά του ταξίδια στην Άπω Ανατολή. Στη Γένουα έφταναν τα εμπορεύματα που μεταφέρονταν δια ξηράς στο βορρά. Η Ρώμη ασφαλώς εξακολουθεί να είναι η αιώνια Πόλη και τη Νεάπολη πρέπει να δείτε πρίν πεθάνετε. Η Σικελία ήταν στα χέρια των Ελλήνων, Ρωμαίων, Βίκιγκ και Ισπανών. Για λίγο ήταν αφεντικό του εαυτού της πριν προστεθεί από τον Γκαριμπάλδι στη νέα ιταλική ηνωμένη πολιτεία.

Ελλάδα

Η αναμφισβήτητη γένεση του ευρωπαϊκού πολιτισμού. Αλλά επίσης μια χώρα, όπως η Ιταλία, με μοντέρνα πολιτική μορφή υπάρχουσα μόλις εκατόν χρόνια. Οι συνεισφορές της αρχαίας Ελλάδας στον παγκόσμιο πολιτισμό είναι τόσες πολλές, τόσες ανάριθμες που μπορούμε να αναφέρουμε μόνο λίγα ονόματα και γεγονότα. Η κατοικία των θεών στον Όλυμπο που χάρισε το όνομά του στους μοντέρνους ολυμπιακούς αγώνες. Οι Δελφοί με το μαντείο τους και φυσικά η Αθήνα με την Ακρόπολη και τον Παρθενώνα. Ο βυζαντινός πολιτισμός είχε εδώ μετά μεγάλη επιρροή και οι σταυροφόροι επίσης άφησαν εδώ τα ίχνη και τις αναμνήσεις τους. Τελειώνουμε την πτήση μας πάνω από την Ευρώπη στην πιο ανατολική άκρη του νησιού της Κρήτης. Ο μοναδικός τόπος στην Ευρώπη όπου φυτρώνουν μηκαλλιεργημένοι φοίνικες και επίσης ο τόπος όπου, κατά το μύθο, βγήκε ο ταύρος από τη θάλασσα και πάτησε τη στεριά. Στη ράχη του καθόταν η Ευρώπη που χάρισε το όνομά της στη νέα ήπειρο.

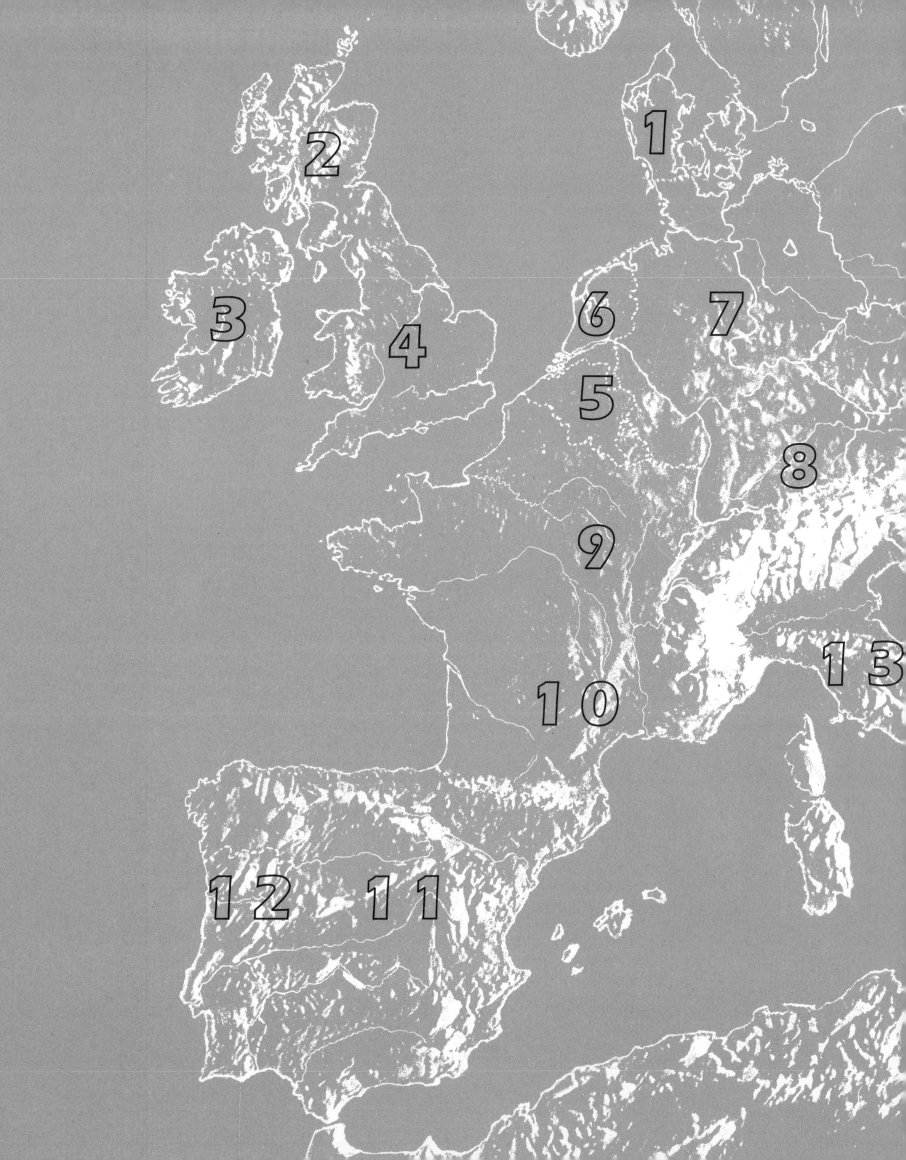

1
DANMARK

36–45

2
United Kingdom
SCOTLAND

46–53

3
IRELAND–EIRE

54–61

4
United Kingdom
ENGLAND & WALES

62–75

5
BELGIE–BELGIQUE
& LUXEMBOURG

76–89

6
NEDERLAND

90–101

7
Bundesrepublik
DEUTSCHLAND I

102–115

8
Bundesrepublik
DEUTSCHLAND II

116–125

9
FRANCE I

126–139

10
FRANCE II

140–149

11
ESPAÑA

150–161

12
PORTUGAL

162–169

13
ITALIA I

170–179

14

15

14
ITALIA II

180–189

15
ΕΛΛΑΣ
(Ellas)

190–196

7
Bundesrepublik
DEUTSCHLAND I
102-115

103: Helgoland, Emden
104: Lübeck, Bremen
105: Hamburg
106: Hannover
107: Münster
108: Duisburg
110: Düsseldorf
111: Leverkusen
112: Bonn, Aachen
113: Köln
114: Eifel
115: Mosel

8
Bundesrepublik
DEUTSCHLAND II
116-125

117: Frankfurt am Main
118: Bamberg, Nürnberg
119: Oberpfalz
120: Garmisch-Partenkirchen
121: München, Ammersee
122: Lindau
124: Stuttgart
125: Hohenzollern

9
FRANCE I
126-139

127: Strasbourg
128: Paris
130: Cassel, Arras
131: Bergues
132: Saint-Malo
133: Mont-Saint-Michel
134: Chartres
135: Orleans, Fontainebleau
136: Chenonceaux
137: Chambord
138: La Rochelle
139: Auvergne

10
FRANCE II
140-149

141: Mont-Blanc, Grenoble
142: Marseille, Saint-Honorat
143: Monaco
144: Camargue
145: La Grande-Motte
146: Narbonne, Nîmes
147: Avignon
148: Toulouse
149: Carcassonne

11
ESPAÑA
150-161

151: Tossa de Mar, Lloret de Mar
152: Calatayud
153: Zaragoza
154: Valencia
155: Alicante, Benidorm
156: Málaga
157: Granada, Córdoba
158: Madrid
160: Toledo
161: El Escorial

12
PORTUGAL
162-169

163: Sintra, Obidos
164: Belém
165: Cascais
166: Lisboa
168: Albufeira

13
ITALIA I
170-179

171: Genova, Sestri Levante
172: Milano
174: Sirmione
175: Verona
176: Venezia
178: Firenze

14
ITALIA II
180-189

181: Elba
182: Roma
184: Vesuvio, Pompeï
185: Napoli
186: Palermo
187: Sicilia
188: Castel del Monte, Capo Rizzuto
189: Apulia

15
ΕΛΛΑΣ
(Ellas)
190-196

191: Κέρκυρα, Πάργα
(Kerkira/Korfu, Parga)
192: Πάτρα, Αθήνα
(Patras, Athinai)
194: Αντίπαρος, Νάξος
(Antiparos, Naxos)
195: Μύκονος
(Mykonos)
196: Σαντορίνη/Θήρα, Βάι
(Santorin/Thira, Vaion)

1
DANMARK

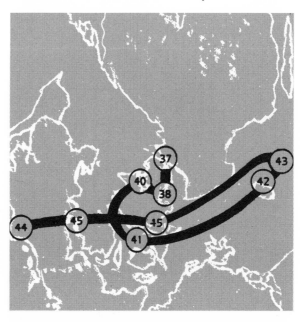

Slottet Kronborg overvåger Sundet, farvandet mellem Danmark og Sverige. Denne del af Sverige (Skåne) var indtil 1660 en del af Danmark. Slottet fra det 17. århundrede er opført i flamsk renæssancestil. Shakespeares skuespil Hamlet finder ifølge legenden sted på dette slot. På fæstningsvoldene kan man fundere over 'to be or not to be'.

Schloß Kronborg in Helsingør hält Wache am Öresund, der Meerenge zwischen Dänemark und Südschweden (Schonen), das bis 1660 zu Dänemark gehörte. Das Schloß wurde im 17. Jahrhundert im flämischen Renaissancestil erbaut. Hier lebte nach einer alten Überlieferung Hamlet, dessen tragisches Schicksal Shakespeare in einem packenden Drama nacherzählt hat. Die Festungsmauern sind der passende Ort, um über Hamlets Frage 'Sein oder Nichtsein' nachzusinnen.

Castle Kronborg at Helsingør (Elsinore) keeps watch over the Sont, the straits between Denmark and Sweden. This part of Sweden (Skane) was Danish territory until 1660. The 17th century castle was built in the Flemish Renaissance style. According to legend this was the castle where the tragedy of Hamlet, made famous by Shakespeare, was played out. The fortress walls provide a suitable setting for anyone to muse upon the question 'To be or not to be".

El castillo Kronborg custodia el Sund, la vía fluvial entre Dinamarca y Suecia. Esta parte de Suecia (Skåne) fue hasta 1660 territorio danés. El castillo (s. XVII) fue construido en el estilo renacentista flamenco. Según cuenta la tradición aquí tuvo lugar la leyenda de Hamlet, tan magníficamente descrita por Shakespeare en la obra del mismo nombre. Desde las murallas uno puede meditar sobre 'ser o no ser'.

Le château fort Kronborg monte la garde sur le Sund, la voie maritime passant entre le Danemark et la Suède. Cette partie de la Suède (Skåne) fut, jusqu'en 1660, territoire danois. Le château du 17e siècle est construit en style renaissance flamand. Selon la tradition, la légende d'Hamlet de Shakespeare s'est jouée ici. Sur les murs fortifiés, on peut rêver à être ou ne pas être.

Il castello di Kronborg controlla il Sund, la via marittima che si trova tra la Danimarca e la Svezia. Questa parte della Svezia (Skåne) fu fino al 1660, territorio danese. Il castello del XVII secolo è costruito in stile rinascimentale fiammingo. Secondo la tradizione è qui che si è svolta la tragedia di Amleto. Sulle mura fortificate si può ancora meditare su 'essere o non essere'.

Het slot Kronborg te Helsingør houdt de wacht aan de Sont, de waterweg tussen Denemarken en Zweden. Dit deel van Zweden (Skåne) was tot 1660 Deens gebied. Het zeventiende-eeuwse kasteel is in Vlaamse renaissancestijl opgetrokken. Volgens de traditie speelt hier de legende van Hamlet, door Shakespeare zo schitterend gevat in zijn gelijknamig drama. Op de vestingmuren kan men mijmeren over 'to be or not to be'.

O castelo Kronborg em Helsingør domina Sundet, o canal entre a Dinamarca e a Suécia. Esta parte da Suécia (Skåne) foi território dinamarquês até 1660. O castelo do s. XVII foi construido no estilo renascença flamengo. Segundo a tradição do drama do mesmo nome de Shakespeare. Nos muros da praça forte pode-se refletir sobre 'to be or not to be', ser ou não ser.

Το κάστρο Κρόνμπορκ στο Χέλσινγκαιρ κρατάει σκοπιά στο Σούνδη, τον πλωτό δρόμο ανάμεσα στη Δανία και τη Σουηδία. Αυτό το κομμάτι γης της Σουηδίας [Σκώνε] ήταν μέχρι το 1660 δανέζικο έδαφος. Το κάστρο του δέκατου έβδομου αιώνα ανορθώθηκε σε ρυθμό φλαμανδικής αναγέννησης. Κατά την παράδοση παίζει εκεί ο θρύλος του Χάμλετ, που τόσο θαυμάσια αποδίδεται από το Σαίξπηρ. Στα τείχη του φρουρίου μπορεί κανείς να ρεμβάσει το 'to be or not te be'.

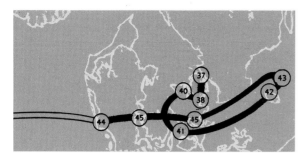

København er én af Europas mest charmerende hovedstæder. Byen, der ligger ved Sundet på øen Sjælland, har brede boulevarder og smukke kanaler og står for en stor del stadig i sin oprindelige skikkelse fra det 18. århundrede. På Rådhuspladsen står det smukke rådhus fra 1905, den danske arkitekt Martin Nyrops mesterværk. Lige overfor

Kopenhagen ist eine der bezauberndsten Haupstädte Europas. Die auf der Insel Seeland am Westufer des Öresunds gelegene Metropole beeindruckt durch breite Boulevards und schmucke Kanäle; in der Altstadt sind noch viele Gebäude aus dem 17. und 18. Jahrhundert erhalten. Das prächtige Rathaus aus der Jahr 1905 ist ein Meisterwerk des dänischen Architekten Martin Nyrops. Gegenüber liegt der einzigartige Vergnügungspark Tivoli, den König Christian VIII. im Jahre 1843 schaffen ließ.

Copenhagen is one of Europe's most charming capitals. Situated on Sjaelland on the Sont, the city has handsome boulevards and beautiful canals. A large part of the original 18th-century buildings still remain. The splendid town hall dating from 1905, a masterpiece by the Danish architect Martin Nyrops, stands on the Rådhuspladsen. In the foreground are the famous Tivoli gardens, founded in 1843 by King Christian VII.

Una de las capitales europeas más atractivas es Copenhague. La ciudad, situada en Sjaelland, al Canal del Sund, tiene amplias avenidas y hermosos canales, y en gran parte todavía se conserva como era en el s. XVIII. En la Rådhuspladsen se halla un hermoso ayuntamiento de 1905, una obra maestra del arquitecto Martin Nyrop. Delante vemos el parque de diversiones Tivoli que fue fundado en 1843 por el rey Christián VIII.

L'une des capitales les plus charmantes d'Europe est Copenhague. La ville, située sur l'île de Sjaelland, au bord du Sund, possède des boulevards royaux et de jolis canaux et une bonne partie de la ville possède toujours ses maisons du 18e siècle. L'hôtel de ville, remarquable, qui date de 1805 se trouve sur la Rådhuspladsen, et est le chef-d'œuvre de l'architecte danois Martin Nyrop. Devant cet hôtel de ville on trouve le parc d'amusement unique du Tivoli, créé en 1843 par le roi Christian VIII.

Copenaghen è senz'altro una delle città più attraenti d'Europa. La città costruita sulla Sjaelland, in riva al Sundet, possiede larghi viali e deliziosi canali e parte della città é nello stile del XVIII secolo. Nella piazza Rådhuspladsen si trova l'elegante municipio, datato 1905, capolavoro dell'architetto danese Martin Nyrop. Davanti al municipio si trova il celebre parco dei divertimenti di Tivoli, creato nel 1843 dal re Christiano VIII.

Eén van Europa's meest charmante hoofdsteden is Kopenhagen. De stad, gelegen op Sjaelland, aan de Sont, heeft royale boulevards en fraaie kanalen, en is voor een goed deel nog origineel achttiendeeeuws. Aan de Rådhuspladsen staat het fraaie stadhuis uit 1905, het meesterwerk van de Deense architect Martin Nyrop. Ervoor zien we het unieke vermaakspark Tivoli, dat in 1843 gesticht werd door Koning Christian VIII.

Uma das cidades europeias com mais encanto é Copenhague. A cidade, situada no Sjaelland, à margem do Sundet, possui avenidas espaçosas e canais graciosos, e nu sua grande parte é ainda original do século XVIII. Na Rådhuspladsen está a bonita câmara municipal que data de 1905, a obra-mestre do arquitecto dinamarquês Martin Nyrop. À frente vê-se o parque de divertimento Tivoli, único no género, que foi fundado em 1843, pelo Rei Christian VIII.

Μια από τις πιο γοητευτικές ευρωπαϊκές πρωτεύουσες είναι η Κοπεγχάγη. Η πόλη, που βρίσκεται στο Ζέλανδ, στο Σούνδη, έχει ευρύχωρες λεωφόρους και υπέροχα κανάλια και για ένα μεγάλο μέρος είναι πρότυπο δέκατου όγδοου αιώνα. Στο Ρωδχουσπλάδσεν βρίσκεται το ωραίο δημαρχείο από το 1905, το αριστούργημα αυτό του Δάνου αρχιτέκτονα Μάρτιν Νύροπ. Μπροστά του βλέπουμε το μοναδικό λούνα παρκ Τίβολι, που ιδρύθηκε το 1843 από το βασιλιά Χρίστιαν Η΄.

ligger den enestående forlystelsespark
Tivoli, der blev stiftet af kong Christian d. VIII
i 1843.

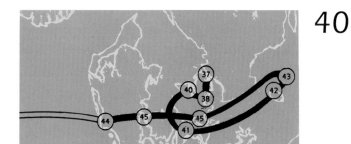

På øen Sjælland ligger slottene som en fyrstekrone omkring Danmarks hovedstad København. Den kongelige residens Fredensborg blev bygget i det 18. århundrede. Slottet Frederiksborg i Hillerød blev opført i det 17. århundrede til Christian d. IV. Slottet er bygget i den såkaldte Vredeman de Vries-renæssancestil.

Til sidst slottet Vallø. Men også på de andre øer blev der bygget slotte. Slottet Tårs på øen Lolland ser endog mere ud af en fæstning. Det er i øvrigt ikke så mærkeligt, da de nordtyske hansepartnerne var nær ved. Blev der således ikke drevet handel, blev der ført krig som f.eks. i 1510, hvor Lübeck afbrændte den nærliggende by Nakskov.

Come una principesca corona intorno alla capitale Copenaghen, si trovano sull'isola Sjaelland magnifici castelli. La residenza reale Fredensborg risale al XVIII secolo. Frederiksborg a Hillerød fu costruito nel XVII secolo per il re Cristiano IV nel cosiddetto stile rinascimentale Vredeman de Vries. E infine il castello di Vallø. Anche sulle altre isole sono stati costruiti dei castelli. Il castello di Tårs sull'isola di Lolland sembra essere in grado di difendersi molto bene. La cosa non sorprende poiché le città anseatiche del Nord della Germania erano vicine e quando non ci si dedicava al commercio, si faceva la guerra, come nel 1510, quando Lubecca mise a fuoco interamente la vicina città di Nakskov.

Als een vorstelijke kroon rond de Deense hoofdstad Kopenhagen liggen prachtige kastelen op het eiland Sjaelland. De koninklijke residentie Fredensborg werd in de 18de eeuw opgetrokken. Frederiksborg te Hillerød in de 17de eeuw gebouwd voor koning Christian IV in de zogenaamde Vredeman de Vries-renaissancestijl. En tenslotte het kasteel Vallø.

Ook op de andere eilanden werden kastelen gebouwd. Tårs op het eiland Lolland ziet er zelfs heel wat weerbaarder uit. Niet zo verwonderlijk overigens, want de Noordduitse Hansepartners waren dichtbij. En als er geen handel gevoerd werd dan was er wel oorlog, zoals in 1510 toen Lübeck de nabijgelegen stad Nakskov geheel platbrandde.

Die Hauptstadt Dänemarks wird auf der Insel Seeland von einem Kranz prächtiger Schlösser eingefaßt. Die königliche Residenz Fredensborg wurde im 17. Jh erbaut. Schloß Frederiksborg in Hillerød wurde im 17. Jahrhundert für König Christian IV. im sogenannten Vredeman-de-Vries-Renaissancestil erstellt. Als drittes ist Schloß Vallø zu nennen. Schlösser errichtete man freilich auch auf anderen dänischen Inseln. Trutzig wirkt Schloß Tårs auf der Insel Lolland – kein Wunder, waren doch die norddeutschen Hansestädte nicht fern, mit denen man nicht nur Handel trieb, sondern auch Kriege führte, so etwa im Jahr 1510, in dem die Lübecker die nahegelegene Stadt Nakskov dem Erdboden gleichmachten.

Magnificent castles are situated on the island of Sjaelland like jewels in a crown, around Copenhagen, the capital of Denmark. The royal residence at Fredensborg was built in the 18th century. Frederiksborg Castle in Hillerod was built in the 17th century for King Christian IV in the so-called Vredeman de Vries Renaissance style. Finally, there is Vallø Castle. Castles were also built on the other islands. Tårs Castle on the island of Lolland looks to have much stronger defences, this is not surprising, because with the North-German Hanse partners nearby, there were always sporadic wars, as in 1510, when the citizens of Lübeck burned down the adjacent city of Nakskov.

En la isla Seeland, rodeando la capital danesa Copenhague, como si fueran su corona real, se encuentran magníficos castillos. La residencia real, Fredensborg, se construyó en el s. XVIII. El castillo Frederiksborg en Hillerød fue construido para el rey Cristián IV en un estilo renacentista denominado 'Vredeman de Vries'. Y por fin el Castillo Vallø. Pero también en otras islas se construyeron castillos. El castillo Taars en la isla Laaland tiene incluso una apariencia más robusta. Cosa en realidad no muy sorprendente ya que las ciudades compañeras del ansa del norte de Alemania estaban muy cerca. Y cuando no tenían algo que comerciar entonces había guerra, como en 1510, año en el que Lübeck incendió la vecina ciudad Nakskov.

Autour de la capitale Copenhague se trouvent de magnifiques châteaux sur l'île Sjaelland. La Résidence Fredensborg date du 18e siècle. Frederiksborg à Hillerod fut construit au 17e siècle pour le roi Christian IV dans le style renaissance Vredeman de Vries. Et enfin le château de Vallø. Mais des châteaux ont également été construits sur les autres îles. Le château de Tårs, sur l'île de Lolland paraît même encore beaucoup plus capable de se défendre. Ce qui n'est d'ailleurs pas surprenant, car les villes hanséatiques du Nord de l'Allemagne étaient proches et lorsque l'on ne faisait pas de commerce, c'était la guerre, comme en 1510, lorsque Lübeck détruisit complètement par le feu la ville proche de Nakskov.

Na ilha Sjaelland encontram-se maravilhosos castelos situados como uma coroa majestosa à volta de cidade de Copenhaga. A residência Fredensborg foi construida no séc. XVIII. O castelo Fredensborg em Hillerød foi construido para o rei Christian IV no estilo renascença Vredeman de Vries, no séc. XVII.
E finalmente o castelo Vallø.

Mas tambem nas outras ilhas se construiram castelos. O castelo Tårs, na ilha Lolland tem até aspecto mais resistente. Não é de admirar, pois os companheiros de Hanse encontravam-se mais próximos. E, quando não havia negócios, havia guerra, como em 1510 quando Lübeck incendiou totalmente a cidade próxima de Nakskov.

Σαν βασιλικό στεφάνι γύρω από τη δανέζικη πρωτεύουσα Κοπεγχάγη βρίσκονται τα θαυμάσια κάστρα στο νησί Ζέλανδ. Η βασιλική κατοικία Φρέντενσμποργκ στο Χίλλεραιδ χτίστηκε το 17ο αιώνα για το βασιλιά Χρίστιαν Δ΄ στο λεγόμενο αναγεννητικό ρυθμό Βρέντεμαν ντε Βρης.
Και τελικά το κάστρο Βάλλο. Αλλά και στα άλλα νησιά

χτίστηκαν κάστρα. Το κάστρο Τωρς στο νησί Λόλλαντ φαντάζει ακόμα πιο αμυντικό. Δεν είναι όμως παράξενο, γιατί οι συνέταιροι της Χανσεατικής Ένωσης της Βόρειας Γερμανίας ήταν κοντά. Αν δεν υπήρχε εμπόριο, υπήρχε όμως μόλεμος όπως το 1510 όταν η Λυβέκκη ισοπέδωσε όλη την κοντινή πόλη Νάξκοβ, καίγοντάς την.

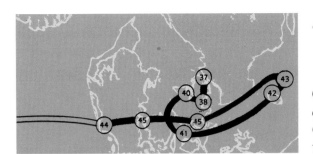

Olskirken ligner et fort. For de mange besøgende nu om dage er man mindre bange! Christiansø, Frederiksø og Ertholmene er fremskudte poster i Østersøen.

Festungsgleich wirkt die Olskirche auf Bornholm, heute ein beliebtes Touristenziel. Dänische Vorposten in der Ostsee sind Christiansø, Frederiksø und Ertholmene.

The Olskirke looks like a fortress, though today there is no longer any fear of invasion. Christiansø, Frederiksø and Ertholmene are all outposts in the Baltic Sea.

La Olskirke parece un fuerte. Pero ahora ya no se teme a los visitantes. Cristianson, Frederikson y Ertholmene, puestos avanzados en el mar Báltico.

L'Olskirke ressemble à un fort. Aujourd'hui, on a beaucoup moins peur des innombrables visiteurs! Christiansø, Frederiksø et Ertholmene sont des avant-postes sur la Baltique.

La Olskirke assomiglia ad una fortezza, ma oggi essa suscita minor timore nei visitatori! Cristiansø, Frederiksø e Ertholmene sono avamposti sul Mar Baltico.

De Olskirke lijkt op een fort. Voor de vele bezoekers nu is men minder bang! Christiansø, Frederiksø en Ertholmene, buitenposten in de Oostzee.

A Olskirke parece um forte. Dos visitantes actuais não se tem tanto medo! Christiansø, Frederiksø e Ertholmene, postos exteriores no Mar do Norte.

Το Ολσκίρκε μοιάζει σαν φρούριο. Αλλά κανείς δεν φοβάται πια τους πολλούς επισκέπτες. Τα Χρίστιανσο και Ερθολμένε είναι προφυλακές στη Βαλτική θάλασσα.

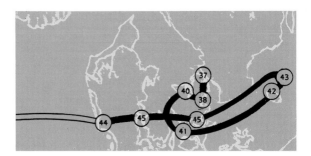

Für die über 100 bewohnten Inseln Dänemarks sind Brücken sehr wichtig. 1937 war die Storstrømsbrücke mit ihren 3211 m sogar die längste Brücke Europas; sie wurde 1985 durch die Farøbrücke ersetzt. Eine West-Ost-Verbindung über den Kleinen Belt zwischen der Halbinsel Jütland und Fünen wurde erst 1935 geschaffen; sie wurde 1970 durch die Lillebaeltsbrücke ergänzt. Der bedeutendste Hafen an der Westküste Jütlands ist Esbjerg. Wichtig ist er nicht nur für Fischerei und Handel, sondern auch als Stützpunkt für die Erdöl- und Erdgasbohrungen in der Nordsee.

Bridges are of the utmost importance to Denmark, which has more than a hundred islands. In 1937, the Storstrømsbrø, which is 3211 metres long, was the longest bridge in Europe. In 1985, a new bridge was put into service on this Southern route, the Farøbroerne. In 1935, a permanent connection was added for traffic going East and West, the Lillebaeltsbroerne. Esbjerg, on the West coast of Jylland, is the most important harbour. In addition to being a fishing port, off-shore industry is also very important here.

Los puentes son vitales para las más de cien islas danesas. El Storstrømsbro era en 1937 el más largo de Europa. En 1985 se construyó otro nuevo puente en esta ruta al sur, el Farøbroerne. La circulación entre este y oeste sobre el Pequeño Belt hacia Jutlandia fue favorecida con un puente en 1935. En 1970 se añadió un segundo puente, el Lillebæltsbroerne. Esbjerg, en la costa occidental de Jutlandia es el puerto más importante. Salvo como puerto de pescadores, su off-shore es muy importante.

Pour les cent et quelques îles du Danemark, les ponts sont très importants. Le pont du Storstrømsbro, long de 3211 m, était même en 1937 le plus long d'Europe. En 1985, un nouveau pont, le Farøbroerne fut mis en service sur cet itinéraire en direction du sud. Le trafic est-ouest par dessus le Petit-Belt (Lille Baelt) en direction du Jylland, a été doté en 1935 d'une liaison terrestre ferme. En 1970, on y a ajouté un nouveau pont, le Lillebæltsbroerne. Esbjerg sur la côte Ouest du Jylland est le port le plus important. Outre le port de pêche, l'off-shore y est très important.

Broer er af meget stor betydning for de mere end hundred danske øer. I 1937 var Storstrømsbroen med sine 3211 m endog Europas længste bro. I 1985 tog man på denne sydgående rute de nye Farøbroer i brug. Øst-vesttrafikken over Lillebælt til Jylland fik i 1935 en fast broforbindelse. I 1970 blev der åbnet endnu en Lillebæltsbro.
Esbjerg på Jyllands vestkyst er den vigtigste havn. Ikke kun fiskerihavnen, men også offshore- og færgehavnen, er af stor betydning.

A causa delle numerosissime isole della Danimarca, i ponti sono molto importanti. Il ponte Strorstrømsbroen, lungo 3211 metri, era già dal 1937 il ponte più lungo d'Europa. Nel 1985 fu costruito sulla stessa strada, in direzione del Sud, il ponte Farøbroerne. Nel 1935 il traffico da est e ovest sul Piccolo Belt fu regolato grazie ad un ponte. Nel 1970 vi è stato aggiunto un nuovo ponte, il Lillebæltsbroerne. Esbjerg, sulla costa occidentale dello Jùlland è il porto più importante, sia per la pesca che come porto per offshore.

Voor de eilanden van Denemarken zijn bruggen erg belangrijk. De 3211 m lange Storstrømsbro was in 1937 de langste van Europa. In 1985 werd op deze route naar het zuiden een nieuwe brug in gebruik genomen, de Farøbroerne. Het oost-westverkeer over de kleine Belt naar Jutland kreeg in 1935 een vaste oeververbinding. In 1970 werd daar een nieuwe brug aan toegevoegd, de Lillebæltsbroerne. Esbjerg aan de westkust is de belangrijkste haven voor de visserij en de off-shore.

Pontes são de grande importância para as mais de cem ilhas da Dinamarca. A ponte de Storstrøm de 3211 m, era em 1937 até a mais comprida da Europa. Em 1985 foi inaugurada uma ponte nova, a Farøbroerne, nesta rota para o sul. O tráfego entre o oriente e o ocidente através do pequeno Belt para Jylland passou a realizar-se, em 1935, por uma ponte. Em 1970 foi adicionada uma ponte nova, a Lillebæltsbroerne. Esbjerg, na costa ocidental de Jylland, é o porto mais importante.

Για τα περισσότερα από τα εκατό νησιά της Δανίας οι γέφυρές τους είναι πολύ σημαντικές. Η γέφυρα Στόρστομσμπρο που είναι 3211μ. ήταν το 1937 μάλιστα η μεγαλύτερη της Ευρώπης. Από το 1985 λειτουργεί σ'αυτή τη διαδρομή προς το Νότο μια καινούρια γέφυρα, η Φαρομπρούρνε. Στο μικρό Μπελτ στη Γιουτλάνδη δημιουργήθηκε το 1935 σταθερός σύνδεσμος των ακτών για την ανατολικοδυτική κίνηση. Το 1970 προστέθηκε καινούρια γέφυρα, η Λιλλεμπαλτσμπρούρνε. Το Έσμπεργκ στη δυτική ακτή της Γιουτλάνδης είναι το πιο σημαντικό λιμάνι. Εκτός από ψαρολίμανο είναι και στα ανοιχτά πολύ απουδαίο επίσης με γραμμές φερυμπώτ με τη Μεγάλη Βρετανία και Ολλανδία.

2
United Kingdom
SCOTLAND

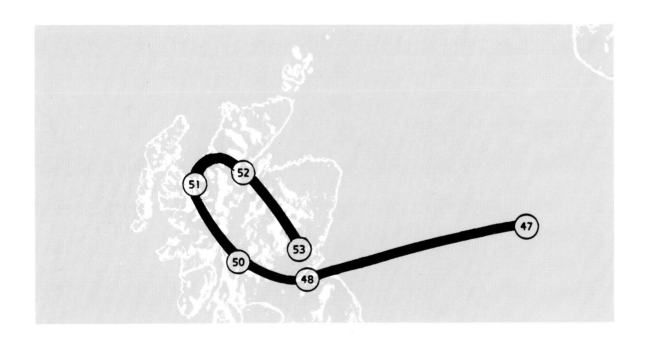

Traditionally, the North Sea has always been of great economic significance to the fishing industry. In an attempt to protect fish stocks the EC have acted in outlining a common policy of restrictive fishing quotas. Since 1960 the North Sea has also become increasingly important in the development of oil and natural gas deposits. Off-shore exploration is carried out on permanent platforms, with agreements having been reached regarding the division of the continental shelf between the different North Sea states.

Fra gammel tid har Nordsøen været af stor betydning for fiskeriet. Det store fiskeri foregår først og fremmest med trawlere. men også det mindre fiskeri, som kutteren på billedet, der fanger frabber ved Helgoland, er meget aktivt. EF har udarbejdet en fælles fiskeripolitik, der gennem fangstkvoter skal beskytte fiskebestanden. Efter 1960 er naturgas- og olieudvinding blevet stærkt udviklet på Nordsøens. Udvindingen til søs foregår fra faste platforme. Nordsøens såkaldte kontinentalsokkel er gennem traktater blevet delt mellem nordsøstaterne.

Desde el punto de vista económico el Mar del Norte tiene un gran significado para la pesca. La Comunidad Europea ha desarrollado una política comunitaria de pesca que por medio de un límite de pesca quiere defender el mundo piscícola. La extracción de gas y petróleo en el Mar del Norte se ha desarrollado mucho después de 1960. La perforación se hace desde plataformas fijas. La así llamada plataforma continental del Mar del Norte ha sido dividida por medio de un acuerdo entre los estados de este mar.

Dal punto di vista economico il Mar del Nord è sempre stato molto importante per la pesca. La Comunità europea ha elaborato un piano comune per proteggere la quantità di pesce esistente imponendo delle quote massime di pesca.
Dopo il 1960 nel Mar del Nord vi è stato un notevole sviluppo dell'industria del petrolio e del gas metano. L'estrazione è effettuata per mezzo di piattaforme fisse. La piattaforma continentale del Mar del Nord è stata suddivisa fra gli Stati costieri di questo mare.

Economicamente é o Mar do Norte desde há muito tempo de grande importância para a pesca. Pela CE foi elaborada uma política de pesca, que exige um límite de apanha, para proteger a criação do peixe. A partir de 1960, a exploração da nafta e do gás natural desenvolveu-se enormemente, no Mar do Norte. A exploração no alto-mar realiza-se com auxílio de plataformas fixas. A chamada 'chapa continental' do Mar do Norte foi dividida, por contracto, entre os estados do Mar do Norte.

Die Fischgründe der Nordsee waren seit alters von großer wirtschaftlicher Bedeutung. Heute betrieben die Länder der EG eine gemeinsame Fischereipolitik; jährlich festgelegte Fangquoten dienen dem Schutz der Fischbestände. Seit 1960 nahm die Erdöl- und Erdgasförderung in der Nordsee einen raschen Aufschwung. Gefördert wird von künstlichen Inseln (Plattformen) aus, die auf dem Festlandsockel errichtet werden. In die Förderzonen teilen sich die Anrainerstaaten der Nordsee.

Du point de vue économique, la mer du Nord a toujours été très importante pour la pêche. La CEE a élaboré une politique de pêche commune qui veut protéger le peuplement en poisson en imposant des quotas de prise. Après 1960, l'extraction du pétrole et du gaz naturel en mer du Nord a connu un développement très marqué. L'extraction off-shore ou en mer est opérée à partir de plates-formes fixes. Le plateau continental de la mer du Nord a été réparti par traité entre les états riverains de la mer du Nord.

Economisch is de Noordzee van oudsher van grote betekenis voor de visserij. Door de EG is een gemeenschappelijk visserijbeleid uitgewerkt dat door het opleggen van vangstquota de visstand wil beschermen. Na 1960 is de aardgas- en oliewinning in de Noordzee sterk ontwikkeld. Buitengaatse winning (goed nederlands voor off-shore) geschiedt vanaf vaste platforms. Het zogenaamde continentale plat van de Noordzee is bij overeenkomst door de Noordzeestaten verdeeld.

Οικονομικά είναι από αμνημόνευτα χρόνια η Βόρειος Θάλασσα πολύ σημαντική για την αλιεία. . Η ΕΟΚ επινόησε κοινή αλιευτική πολιτική για να προστατεύει το απόθεμα ψαριών, επιβάλλοντας αλιευτική ποσόστωση. Μετά το 1960 στη Βόρειο Θάλασσα αναπτύχτηκε σημαντικά η παραγωγή φυσικού αερίου και πετρελαίου. Η παραγωγή στα ανοιχτά γίνεται από σταθερές πλατφόρμες. Η λεγόμενη ηπειρωτική υφαλοκρηπίδα της Βόρειου Θάλασσας μοιράστηκε με σύμβαση από τα κράτη της Βόρειου Θάλασσας.

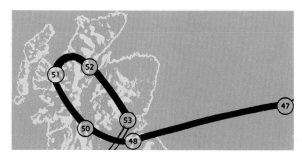

Edinburgh, the Scottish capital, owes its name of the 'Athens of the North' to its architectural and cultural renaissance during the early 19th century. Despite the fact that Scotland has been under British rule since 1707 – its king and nobility had already left for London in 1603 – it has still managed to preserve its own identity.

Den skotske hovedstad Edinburgh kaldes også 'Nordens Athen' på grund af de mange kulturelle og videnskabelige institutioner, der findes her. Selvom Skotland allerede i 1707 blev en del af Storbritannien, har Edinburgh alligevel været i stand til at bevare sin egen identitet. Og omend Glasgow, der har dobbelt så mange indbyggere, næsten 1 millioner, er det kommercielle centrum, er Edinburgh den ubestridte hovedstad. Den international Festival of Music and Drama har siden 1947 givet byen verdensry.

La capital escocesa Edimburgo debe su apodo 'Athenas del Norte' a las muchas culturas e instancias científicas que han estado ahí. Aunque Escocia forma parte desde 1707 del Reino Unido, ha sabido mantener su propia identidad. Edimburgo es la indiscutida capital aunque Glasgow tenga dos veces más habitantes, casi un millón, y sea el centro comercial. El Festival Internacional de Música y Drama le da desde 1947 una fama mundial.

La capitale della Scozia, Edinburgo, deve il suo nome di Atene del Nord, alle numerose istituzioni culturali e scientifiche che vi si trovano. Sebbene la Scozia faccia parte del Regno Unito, già dal 1707, ha saputo conservare intatta la propria identità.
Benchè Glasgow, con il suo milione d'abitanti, sia il centro commerciale, Edinburgo rimane la vera capitale. Il Festival Internazionale di Musica e Dramma che vi si svolge fin dal 1947, gode di fama mondiale.

A capital escocesa, Edinburgh, recebeu o seu cognome 'A Athenas do Norte', graças às muitas instituições culturais e científicas, que possui. Embora a Escócia faça parte do Reino Unido, desde 1707, conseguiu ela manter a sua identidade. E embora Glasgóvia tenha quase o dobro da quantidade de habitantes, à volta de um milhão, e seja o centro do comércio, Edinburgh é a capital incontestável. O Festival Internacional da Música e do Drama concede à cidade desde 1947 uma reputação mundial.

Den Beinamen 'Athen der Nordens' verdankt die schottische Hauptstadt Edinburgh ihren zahlreichen kulturellen und wissenschaftlichen Einrichtungen. Obwohl Schottland seit 1707 zum Vereinigten Königreich gehört, hat es doch bis heute seine Eigenart bewahren können. Mag auch Glasgow mit fast doppelt soviel Einwohnern die schottische Handelsmetropole sein, Edinburgh ist nach wie vor die unbestrittene Hauptstadt Schottlands. Weltruf hat die Stadt auch durch die 1947 gegründete Internationale Festspielwoche (International Festival of Music und Drama) erlangt.

Le ville écossaise d'Edimbourg doit son surnom d'Athènes du Nord aux nombreuses institutions culturelles et scientifiques que l'on y rencontre. Bien que l'Ecosse fasse partie du Royaume-Uni depuis 1707, elle a su garder son identité propre. Et si Glasgow, avec deux fois plus d'habitants c'est-à-dire près d'un million, est le centre commercial de l'Ecosse, Edimbourg en est la capitale incontestée. L'International Festival of Music and Drama confère une réputation mondiale à la ville depuis 1947.

De Schotse hoofdstad Edinburgh dankt zijn bijnaam 'Athene van het Noorden' aan de vele culturele en wetenschappelijke instellingen die hier aanwezig zijn. Hoewel Schotland al sedert 1707 een onderdeel is van het Verenigd Koninkrijk, heeft het zijn eigen identiteit weten te bewaren. Glasgow mag dan met 2 keer zoveel inwoners, bijna een miljoen, het commerciële centrum zijn, Edinburgh is de onbetwiste hoofdstad. Het International Festival of Music and Drama geeft sedert 1947 de stad ook een wereldreputatie.

Το Εδιμβούργο, η πρωτεύουσα της Σκωτίας, οφείλει το παρατσούκλι της 'η Αθήνα του Βορρά' στα πολλά πολιτιστικά και επιστημονικά ιδρύματά της. Μολονότι η Σκωτία από το 1707 ήδη αποτελεί μέρος του Ηνωμένου Βασιλείου, ήξερε να δια φυλάξει τη δική της ταυτότητα. Η Γλασκώβη μπορεί να είναι με δυο φορές περισσότερους κατοίκους, περίπου ένα εκατομμύριο, το οικονομικό κέντρο της Σκωτίας, το Εδιμβούργο παραμένει η αναμφισβήτητη πρωτεύουσα. Το διεθνές Φέστιβαλ Μουσικής και Δράματος χαρίζει από το 1947 στην πόλη αυτή μια παγκόσμια φήμη.

Though Glasgow, with nearly twice the population (almost one million), is the country's main commercial centre, Edinburgh still remains the unchallenged capital. The Edinburgh International Festival of Music and Drama started in 1947, together with the subsequent development of the Fringe, has given this city a world-wide reputation.

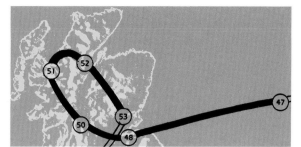

50 Loch Alsh

Skye, an island off the West coast of Scotland and one of the Hebrides group, is known as the 'Misty Isle'. This island, with its volcanic lakes and ruined fortress, can be reached by ferry from Kyle of Lochalsh on the mainland. Situated in the heart of the Scottish Highlands is the extensive Rannoch Moor. Due to its unique marshland flora a large part is now protected as a nature reserve.

Skye, en ø ud for Skotlands vestkyst, der hører til Hebriderne, kaldes også 'Misty Isle', og fra Kyle of Lochalsh er der færgeforbindelse til denne ø med dens vulkansøer og borgruiner.
Midt i det skotske højland ligger Moor of Rannoch, et udstrakt moseområde, hvoraf en stor del er beskyttet naturområde på grund af den enestående moseflora.

Skye, eine Hebrideninsel vor der schottischen Westküste, ist als 'Nebelinsel' bekannt. Von Kyle of Lochalsh aus kann man die Insel mit ihren Kraterseen und malerischen Burgruinen per Fähre erreichen.
Im Herzen der schottischen Highlands liegt das ausgedehnte Rannoch-Moor, das wegen seiner einzigartigen Sumpfflora größtenteils zum Naturschutzgebiet erklärt worden ist.

Skye, una isla frente a la costa occidental de Escocia que pertenece a las Hébridas, es conocida como 'Misty Isle', y desde Kyle of Lochalsh podemos llegar con un transbordador a esta isla con sus lagos volcánicos y sus ruinas. En medio de las Highlands escocesas se encuentra Moor of Rannoch, una extensa zona pantanosa que en gran parte es una reserva natural por su especial flora pantanosa.

Skye, une île qui se trouve devant les côtes occidentales de l'Ecosse et qui fait partie des Hébrides est connue comme la 'Misty Isle' (l'île des Brumes) et de Kyle ou Lochalsh, nous pouvons atteindre cette île, ses lacs volcaniques et ses ruines médiévales au moyen du bac. Au centre des Highlands se trouve le Moor de Rannoch, une zone marécageuse étendue dont une grande partie est zone naturelle protégée en raison de sa flore unique.

Skye, un'isola davanti alla costa occidentale della Scozia e che appartiene al gruppo delle Ebridi, è conosciuta con il nome di Misty Isle (isola delle Brume). La si può raggiungere con un traghetto da Kyle o da Lochalsh. E celebre per i laghi vulcanici e per i ruderi di castelli medievali. Al centro degli altipiani scozzesi si trova Moor of Rannoch, una vasta zona paludosa che è in gran parte zona protetta a causa della sua rara flora.

Skye, een eiland voor de westkust van Schotland dat tot de Hebriden behoort, is bekend als 'Misty Isle' en vanuit Kyle of Lochalsh kunnen we dit eiland met zijn vulkanische meren en burchtruïnes met de veerpont bereiken. Midden in de Schotse Highlands ligt het Moor of Rannoch, een uitgestrekt moerassengebied, waarvan een groot gedeelte beschermd natuurgebied is vanwege de unieke moerasflora.

Skye, uma ilha na costa ocidental da Escócia, que faz parte das Hebridas, é conhecida como a 'Misty Isle' e partindo de Kyle ou Lochalsh pode-se atingir esta ilha, com lagos vulcânicos e ruínas de castelos, por meio de barcos. No centro do Planalto Escocês encontra-se o Moor of Rannoch, um imenso terreno pantanoso, do qual uma grande parte é protegida como Região da Natureza, pela sua flora sem igual.

Το Σκάυ, ένα νησί μπροστά στη δυτική ακτή της Σκωτίας που ανήκει στις Εβρίδες είναι γνωστό σαν 'ομιχλώδες νησί' και από το Κάιλ οφ Λοχ Αλτζ μπορούμε να πάμε με φερυμπώτ σε αυτό το νησί με τις υφαιστειακές λίμνες και τα φρουριακά ερείπια του. Μέσα στην Ορεινή Σκωτία βρίσκεται το Μουρ οφ Ράννοχ, ένας εκτεταμένος βαλτότοπος που ένα μεγάλο μέρος του είναι προστατευόμενος φυσικός χώρος λόγω της μοναδικής χλωρίδας του βάλτου.

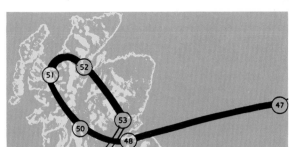

En solopgang ved den legendariske sø Loch Ness, hvor Castle of Urquhart synes at holde vagt. Får vi et glimt af uhyret? Lidt vest for Edinburgh har en karakterikstisk jernbanebro med en længde af 2460 m siden 1890 slået bro over floden Firth of Forth. Foran ser vi trafikbroen fra 1962, der med sine 2751 m er Europas længste hængebro og en af de længste i verden. Ophænget i midten er alene 1100 m langt. Floden Forth, der udspringer på Ben Lomond i det skotske højland, munder her via en fjord ud i Nordsøen.

Sonnenaufgang am sagenumwobenen Loch Ness, über dem Urquhart Castle Wache hält. Wird das Ungeheuer eines Tages zu sehen sein? Westlich von Edinburgh wird der Firth of Forth von einer berühmten, 2460 m langen Eisenbahnbrücke überspannt, die 1890 fertiggestellt wurde. Im Vordergrund sehen wir die 1962 errichtete Straßenbrücke, mit 2571 m die längste Hängebrücke Europas und eine der längsten der Welt; allein das Mittteljoch überbrückt 1100 m. Der am Ben Lomond in den Highlands entspringende Fluß Forth mündet hier in

einen Fjord (Firth), ehe er sich in die Nordsee ergießt.

Un amanecer en el legendario Loch Ness donde el Castillo Urquhart parece vigilar. ¿Se dejará ver el monstruo? Hacia el oeste de Edimburgo se halla desde 1890 sobre el Fiordo de Forth un característico puente de ferrocarril de 2460 m. Delante vemos el puente de circulación de 1962, que con sus 2751 m. es el puente colgante más largo del mundo. Ya sólo la distancia que cuelga en medio es de 1100 m. El Forth, que nace en Ben Lomond en las Highlands desemboca por medio de un fiordo en el Mar del Norte.

Lever de soleil aux abords du légendaire Loch Ness où le Castle of Urquhart semble monter la garde. Le monstre se laissera-t-il encore apercevoir? Quelque peu à l'ouest d'Edimbourg, le Firth of Forth est franchi depuis 1890 par un pont de chemin de fer caractéristique d'une longueur de 2460 m. Devant celui-ci, nous voyons le pont, ouvert à la circulation automobile en 1962, qui, avec ses 2751 m, est le pont suspendu le plus long d'Europe et l'un des plus

longs au monde. Rien que la portée centrale atteint 1100 m. Le Forth qui prend naissance à Ben Lomond dans les Highlands se jette ici dans la mer du Nord par un fjord.

Ed ecco l'alba sul leggendario Loch Ness in cui sembra che il Castle of Urquhart monti la guardia. Potremo scorgere il celebre mostro? Ad ovest di Edinburgo il Firth of Forth è attraversato fin dal 1980 da un ponte ferroviario lungo 2460 metri. In primo piano possiamo vedere il ponte stradale del 1962 che con i suoi 2751 metri è il più lungo ponte europeo ed uno dei più lunghi del mondo. La campata centrale misura ben 1100 metri! Il Forth nasce a Ben Lomond negli altipiani scozzesi e sfocia nel Mar del Nord attraverso un fiordo.

Een zonsopgang bij het legendarische Loch Ness waar het Castle of Urquhart lijkt te waken. Zal het monster zich nog zal laten zien? Even ten westen van Edinburgh wordt Firth of Forth al sedert 1890 overbrugd door een karakteristiek spoorbrug van 2460 m lengte. Ervoor zien we de verkeersbrug van 1962, met zijn 2751 m de langste hangbrug van Europa en een van de langste ter wereld. Alleen de middenoverspanning is al 1100 m. De Forth, die ontspringt op Ben Lomond in de Schotse Highlands, mondt hier via een

fjord (firth) uit in de Noordzee.

Um pôr do sol no Loch Ness legendário, onde o Castelo de Urquhart parece vigiar. O monstro quererá mostrar-se ainda? Firth of Forth, um pouco a ocidente de Edinburgh, é atravessada por uma ponte ferroviária característica, com um comprimento de 2460 m, já desde 1890. Mais próximo vemos a ponte para automóveis de 1962; com os seus 2751 m, a ponte suspensa mais comprida da Europa e uma das mais compridas do mundo. Só o vão central já tem 1100 m. O Forth, com nascente em Ben Lomond, no Planalto Escocês, desagua aqui no Mar do Norte, via um fjord.

Μια ανατολή του ηλίου στο θρυλικό Λοχ Νες που το Κάστρο του Ουρκουάρτ μοιάζει να κρατάει σκοπιά. Το τέρας θα φανερωθεί ακόμα; Λίγο δυτικά από το Εδιμβούργο γεφυρώνεται το Φιρθ οφ Φορθ ήδη από το 1890 από χαρακτηριστική σιδηροδρομική γέφυρα με μήκος 2460μ. Μπροστά της βλέπουμε τη γέφυρα οδικής κυκλοφορίας από το 1962 που με τα 2751μ της είναι η μεγαλύτερη κρεμαστή γέφυρα της Ευρώπης και από τις μεγαλύτερες στον κόσμο. Μόνο το μέσο γεφυρόζευγμα είναι κιόλας 1100μ. Το Φορθ που πηγάζει στο Μπεν Λόμοντ στην Ορεινή Σκωτία, χύνεται εδώ μέσω φιόρδου στη Βόρειο Θάλασσα.

Sunrise over the legendary Loch Ness with Urquhart Castle seemingly standing guard. Just to the West of Edinburgh is the Firth of Forth with its famous iron railway bridge; it

is 2460 metres long, and was completed in 1890. In the foreground is the suspension bridge carrying the motorway built in 1962. With a total length of 2751 metres, it is the longest bridge in Europe and one of the longest in the world. The middle section alone is 1100 metres long. The River Forth, which springs from Ben Lomond in the Scottish Highlands, flows into the firth here before draining into the North Sea.

3
IRELAND–EIRE

Ireland's West coast has been heavily marked by the Atlantic Ocean, the rugged coastline with its harsh cliffs is still of great danger to shipping. The Cliffs of Moher, to the South of Galway Bay, are some of the most famous in Ireland and offer a splendid view over the bay.

Atlanterhavet har skåret sig dybt ind i Irlands vestlige klippekyst. Denne kystlinie er vedvarende en trussel for skibbrudne. På sydsiden af Galwaybugten ligger de imponerende Cliffs of Moher, hvorfra man fra toppen har en pragtfuld udsigt.

Die vom Atlantik zerklüftete, klippenreiche Westküste Irlands ist auch noch heute für die Schiffahrt gefährlich. Eindrucksvoll sind die Moher-Klippen am Südrand der Bucht von Galway. Wenn man auf den Klippen steht, hat man einen wunderschönen Blick über die Bucht.

La costa occidental de Irlanda ha sido profundamente tallada por el Atlántico y está llena de escollos. Esta costa de escollos continua siendo un peligro de naufragios. Los Escollos de Moher al sur de la Bahía de Galway son impresionantes; encima de ellos se puede disfrutar de una espléndida vista.

La côte occidentale de l'Irlande est découpée par l'océan Atlantique et parsemée de récifs. Cette côte de récifs reste un danger permanent pour les bateaux. Les Cliffs of Moher sur la côte Sud de la baie de Galway sont impressionnants et permettent de jouir d'une vue magnifique.

La costa occidentale dell'Irlanda è profondamente intagliata dall'Oceano Atlantico e disseminata di scogliere. Questa costa rocciosa costituisce un pericolo permanente per le barche.
Impressionanti sono le Cliffs of Moher sulla costa meridionale dalla Baia di Galway da cui si gode di una vista magnifica.

De westkust van Ierland is diep uitgesneden door de Atlantische Oceaan en bezaaid met klippen. Deze klippenkust blijft een gevaar voor schipbreukelingen. Imponerend zijn de Cliffs of Moher aan de zuidkant van de Baai van Galway en vanop de klippen heeft men een prachtig uitzicht.

A costa Ocidental da Irlanda é profundamente invadida pelo Oceano Atlântico e está semeada de rochedos. Esta costa rochosa ainda é um perigo de naufrágio. Os Cliffs of Moher, Recifes de Moher, na parte sul da Baía de Galway são impressionantes e a vista dos rochedos íngremes é formidável.

Η δυτική ακτή της Ιρλανδίας είναι βαρειά δαντελωτή και στρωμένη με βράχους. Αυτή η βραχώδης ακτή παραμένει κίνδυνο για τους ναυαγούς. Εντυπωσιακοί είναι οι βράχοι του Μοχέρ της νότιας πλευράς του κόλπου του Γκώλουεϊ, από τους βράχους αυτούς έχει κανείς θαυμάσια θέα.

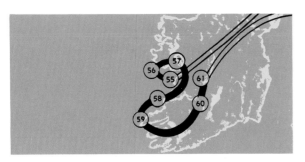

In Galway there are clear signs of the Spanish influence, resulting from centuries of trade with the Iberian Peninsula. According to legend, Columbus passed by this point

Det er tydeligt at se den spanske indflydelse på Galway, der skyldes århundreders handelsforbindelser med den Iberiskehalvø.
Ifølge overleveringen skulle Columbus have været denne vej omkring, før han tog turen over til Amerika. Fra den spanske havn sejler færgen nu til Aranøerne. Tre små øer med utallige forhistoriske levn og tidlige kristne bygningsværker. Det rigtige Irland, hvor man stadig taler irsk.

En Galway se puede notar la influencia española, consecuencia de los lazos comerciales mantenidos con la Península Ibérica durante muchos siglos.
Colón habría pasado por aquí antes de ir a América, cuenta la tradición. De la Puerta Española sale ahora un transbordador hacia las islas Aran: tres islillas con multitud de restos prehistóricos y construcciones del temprano cristianismo. La verdadera Irlanda donde el irlandés sigue siendo el idioma de la calle.

Galway presenta un chiaro influsso spagnolo, conseguenza delle relazioni commerciali che essa ebbe per secoli con la penisola iberica.
La leggenda narra che Cristoforo Colombo venne qui prima di partire per l'America. Dal Porto Spagnolo parte ora il traghetto per le isole Aran, tre isolette con numerosi resti preistorici e costruzioni del primo cristianesimo. La vera Irlanda in cui l'irlandese è ancora la lingua ufficiale.

Galway mostra claramente a influência espanhola, consequência das relações durante séculos com a Península Ibérica.
Cristovão Colombo teria passado por aqui, antes de ir para a América, segundo a tradição. Do Porto Espanhol parte presentemente um barco para as ilhas de Arane. Três ilhas com inúmeros restantes prehistóricos e construções do início da cristandade. A verdadeira Irlânda, onde o irlandês ainda é a língua comum.

Irlands jahrhundertelange Handelsbeziehungen mit der Iberischen Halbinsel haben im Stadtbild von Galway deutliche Spuren hinterlassen. Nach einer alten Überlieferung soll Kolumbus auf seiner Fahrt in die Neue Welt hier Station gemacht haben. Heute legen an der Spanischen Pforte die Fähren an, die Galway mit den Aran-Inseln verbinden, drei kleinen Inseln mit zahlreichen vorgeschichtlichen und frühchristlichen Bauzeugnissen. Sie gehören zum 'richtigen' Irland, in dem noch das keltische Irisch gesprochen wird.

Galway montre une influence espagnole certaine, suite aux relations commerciales séculaires avec la péninsule Ibérique. Colomb serait venu ici avant de se rendre en Amérique, ainsi le veut la tradition! Du port espagnol, un bac vous conduit aux îles d'Aran. Trois petits îlots avec de nombreux vestiges préhistoriques et des constructions datant des premiers âges de la chrétienté. La véritable Irlande où l'irlandais est encore la langue véhiculaire.

Galway vertoont duidelijke Spaanse invloed, als gevolg van eeuwenoude handelsbetrekkingen met het Iberische schiereiland.
Columbus zou hier langs gegaan zijn voordat hij naar Amerika ging, wil de overlevering! Van de Spaanse Poort vertrekt nu de veerboot naar de Araneilanden. Drie eilandjes met talloze prehistorische resten en vroeg-christelijke bouwwerken. Het echte Ierland waar Iers nog voertaal is.

Το Γκώλουεϊ δείχνει ολοφάνερη Ισπανική επίδραση, που είναι συνέπεια των αιωνόβιων εμπορικών σχέσεων με την Ιβηρική χερσόνησο.
Κατά την παράδοση ο Κολόμβος θα προσπερνούσε από εδώ πριν πάει στην Αμερική. Από την Ισπανική πύλη ξεκινάει τώρα το φερυμπώτ για τα νησιά 'Αραν, τρία νησάκια με ανάριθμα προϊστορικά υπολείμματα και χτίσματα από την πρωτη-χριστιανική εποχή. Η γνήσια Ιρλανδία που τα ιρλανδικά είναι ακόμα η επίσημη γλώσσα.

before embarking on his voyage to America. Nowadays, a ferry departs from the Spanish Gateway on its way to the Aran Islands, three small islands with numerous prehistoric remains and early Christian architecture. Irish is still the official language of this part of Ireland.

the best-known of many pop groups to
come from this city.

The city of Caernarvon possesses one of the best preserved mediaeval castles, the construction of which dates from 1283. Traditionally this is where the investiture of England's heir to the throne, the Prince of Wales, is held. The centre of Cardiff, the capital of Wales, was established in Cathay's Park at the beginning of the century. Nearly all the public buildings in the city are built in white Portland stone.

I byen Caernarvon ligger en af de bedst bevarede middelalderborge, hvis opførelse påbegyndtes i 1283. Traditionen tro indsættes den britiske kronprins her som Prins of Wales.
I Wales hovedstad, Cardiff, anlagdes centrum i begyndelsen af dette århundrede i Catheys Park. Næsten alle offentlige bygninger er opført i hvide portlandsten.

In Carnavon (Caernarvon) erhebt sich eine der besterhaltenen mittelalterlichen Burgen Europas, mit deren Bau 1283 begonnen wurde. Hier wird traditionsgemäß dem britischen Thronfolger der Titel des Prinzen von Wales verliehen. Hauptstadt von Wales ist Cardiff (Caerdydd), dessen modernes Zentrum zu Beginn unseres Jahrhunderts im Catheys Park errichtet wurde. Fast alle öffentlichen Gebäude wurden aus weißem Portlandstein erstellt.

La ciudad Caernarvon posee uno de los castillos medievales mejor conservados, cuya construcción comenzó en 1283. Aquí se hace la tradicional investidura del heredero del trono como Príncipe de Gales.

En la capital de Gales, Cardiff, el centro se construyó a principios de siglo en Catheys Park. Casi todos los edificios públicos son de piedra de Portland blanca.

La ville de Caernarvon possède un des châteaux moyennâgeux les mieux fortifiés, dont la construction commença en 1283. C'est ici que le successeur au trône de Grande-Bretagne est fait, comme le veut la tradition, Prince de Galles.

Dans la capitale, Cardiff, le centre a été aménagé au début de ce siècle dans Catheys Park. Preque tous les bâtiments publics sont en pierre blanche de Portland.

A Caernarvon si trova uno dei castelli medievali meglio conservati, la cui costruzione fu iniziata nel 1283. E' qui che per tradizione il successore al trono di Gran Bretagna riceve il titolo di Principe di Galles.

A Cardiff, capitale del Galles, il centro è stato costruito, all'inizio di questo secolo, a Catheys Park. Quasi tutti gli edifici pubblici sono costruiti in pietra bianca di Portland.

De stad Caernarvon bezit een van de best bewaarde middeleeuwse kastelen, waarvan de bouw in 1283 begon. Hier wordt traditioneel de Britse troonopvolger tot Prins van Wales ingehuldigd.

In de hoofdstad van Wales, Cardiff, werd het centrum in het begin van deze eeuw aangelegd in Catheys Park. Vrijwel alle openbare gebouwen zijn van witte Portlandsteen.

A cidade de Caernarvon possui um dos mais bem conservados castelos medievais, cuja construção se iniciou em 1283. Aqui é, tradicionalmente, nomeado o pretendente à coroa britânica, com Príncipe de Wales.

Na capital de Wales, Cardiff, foi o centro instalado, no início deste século, no Catheys Park. Quase todos os edifícios públicos são de pedra branca de Portland.

Η πόλη Καρνέβον κατέχει ένα από τα καλύτερα συντηρημένα μεσαιωνικά κάστρα, που το χτίσιμό του άρχισε το 1283. Εδώ, παραδοσιακά, ο Βρετανός διάδοχος στέφεται πρίγκηπας της Ουαλίας.

Στην πρωτεύουσα της Ουαλίας, Κάρντιφ, χτίστηκε στις αρχές του αιώνα το κέντρο στο Κάθεϋς Παρκ. Περίπου όλα τα δημόσια κτίρια χτίστηκαν με το άσπρο τσιμέντο πόρτλαντ.

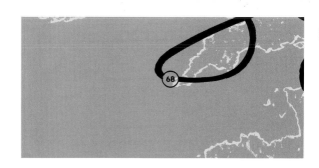

The Cornish peninsula is famous for its 'cores': coves surrounded by high rock faces. In the past these were notorious smugglers' dens. The spectacular cliff at Land's End is the most South-Westerly point of England. A solitary lighthouse in the sea marks the boundary between land and the Atlantic Ocean.

Halvøen Cornwall er berømt for sine 'cores'; bugte omgivet af høje klipper. Tidligere var det berygtede smuglerreder. Den iøjnefaldende klippe Land's End er Englands sydvestligste punkt. Et ensomt fyrtårn ude i havet angiver grænsen mellem Atlanterhavet og fastlandet.

Kennzeichend für die Küsten Cornwalls sind die 'cores', von steilen Felsklippen eingefaßte Buchten, einst berüchtigte Piratennester. Die spektakulären Klippen von Land's End markieren den südwestlichen Punkt Englands. Ihnen ist im Atlantischen Ozean ein einsamer Leuchtturm vorgelagert.

La península Cornwall es famosa por sus 'cores': bahías rodeadas de altos acantilados. En el pasado fueron nidos de contrabandistas. El espectacular acantilado Land's End es el punto más al sudoeste de Inglaterra. Un faro solitario en el mar señala la frontera entre la tierra y el Océano Atlántico.

La presqu'île de Cornouailles est connue pour ses "cores", des baies entourées de hauts rochers. Autrefois, ces cores abritaient de nombreux contrebandiers. Le rocher spectaculaire de Land's End est le point de l'Angleterre le plus au Sud-Ouest. Un phare solitaire, en pleine mer, signale la frontière entre la terre et l'océan Atlantique.

La penisola di Cornovaglia è celebre per i suoi 'cores': baie circondate da alte rocce. In passato essi erano un nascondiglio per i contrabbandieri. La spettacolare roccia di Land's End costituisce l'estrema punta meridionale dell'Inghilterra. Un faro solitario, in mare aperto, indica la divisione tra la terra e l'Oceano Atlantico.

Het schiereiland Cornwall is beroemd om zijn 'cores'; baaien omgeven door hoge rotsen. Vroeger waren het beruchte smokkelaarsnesten. De spectaculaire rots Land's End is de meest zuidwestelijke punt van Engeland. Een eenzame lichttoren in zee geeft de grens aan tussen land en Atlantische Oceaan.

A península Cornwall é famosa pelos seus 'cores': baías cercadas por rochas altas. Em tempos antigos serviam elas de 'ninhos' de contrabandistas. O rochedo Land's End espectacular é o ponto mais ao sudeste da Inglaterra. Um farol solitário no mar indica a fronteira entre a terra e o Oceano Altântico.

Η χερσόνησος Κορνουάλης είναι φημισμένη για τα 'cores' της, κόλπους τριγυρισμένους από ψηλούς βράχους. Παλαιά ήταν φωλιές των περιβόητων λαθρεμπόρων. Ο θεαματικός βράχος Λαντς Εντ είναι η πιο νοτοδυτική άκρη της Αγγλίας. Ένας απομονωμένος φάρος στη θάλασσα δείχνει το σύνορο ανάμεσα ξηρά και Ατλαντικό Ωκεανό.

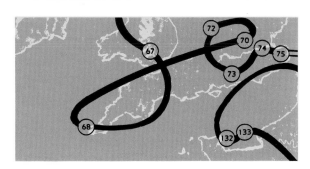

The place where the Romans once founded a trading post is now the City of London, the centre of national and international trade in insurance, stocks and shares and raw materials. Once it was also the focal point of the British Commonwealth and of the power of the Pound. St. Paul's Cathedral, designed by the famous architect Sir Christopher Wren, was built between 1673-1711.

West of the City of London lies the seat of British democracy, the Palace of Westminster (Houses of Parliament), rebuilt between 1840 and 1860, in neo-Gothic style, so that it would not clash too much with the Gothic style of near by Westminster Abbey. The Abbey is renowned for its numerous chapels and tombs of celebrated figures in politics and the arts. British monarchs have been crowned in Westminster Abbey since the beginning of the 14th century.

En el mismo lugar en que en tiempos pasados fundaran los romanos un centro comercial, se encuentra actualmente la City de Londres, el centro nacional e internacional del comercio, de la industria, de los seguros, de la bolsa de valores y materias primas. En un tiempo fue también el centro de la Mancomunidad Británica y del poder de la libra británica. La Catedral de San Pablo, construida entre 1673 y 1711, es una obra de Christopher Wren.
Al sur de la ciudad comercial se halla el corazón de la democracia británica, el edificio del Parlamento, construido en 1834 en estilo neo-gótico para que no desfigurara junto a la Westminster Abbey, que tiene ese mismo estilo. La Westminster Abbey, famosa por sus muchas capillas y las tumbas de prominentes políticos y artistas, es, además, desde los comienzos del siglo XVI, la iglesia donde tiene lugar la coronación.

A l'endroit où les Romains avaient fondé une cité commerciale, se trouve maintenant la Cité de Londres, le centre du commerce national et international, des assu-rances, de la finance et des matières premières. La Cité fut aussi le pivot du Common-wealth et de la puissance de la livre anglaise. La cathédrale St. Paul, construite entre 1673 et 1711, est l'œuvre de l'archi-tecte Christopher Wren.
Au sud de la cité commerciale se trouve le cœur de la démo-cratie britannique, le Parle-ment (Houses of Parliament), construit, en 1834 en style néogothique pour ne pas paraître déplacé à côté de l'Abbaye gothique de West-minster. L'Abbaye est connue pour ses multiples chapelles et pour les tombeaux de per-sonnalités politiques et artis-tiques. Depuis le début du 14e siècle, l'église est également le théâtre du couronnement des souverains anglais.

Nel luogo in cui i Romani ave-vano fondato una località commerciale, si trova oggi la City di Londra, centro del com-mercio nazionale ed interna-zionale, delle assicurazioni, della finanza e delle materie prime. La City fu in passato il cuore del Commonwealth e della potenza della sterlina inglese. La cattedrale di St. Paul, costruita fra il 1673 e il 1711 è opera dell'architetto Christopher Wren. A sud della City si trova il centro della de-mocrazia britannica, il Parla-mento (Houses of Parliament) costruito nel 1834 in stile neo-gotico, per non sfigurare ac-canto all'abbazia gotica di Westminster. L'abbazia è co-nosciuta per le numerose cap-pelle e per le tombe di perso-nalità politiche ed artistiche. Dall'inizio del XIV secolo l'Ab-bazia di Westminster è sede dell'incoronazione dei sovrani inglesi.

Waar eens de Romeinen een handelsplaats stichtten, be-vindt zich thans de City van Londen, het centrum van na-tionale en internationale han-del, verzekeringen, effecten-en grondstoffenbeurs. Eens ook de spil van het Gemene-best en van de macht van het Britse pond. De Saint Paul's Cathedral, een bouwwerk van de architect Christopher Wren, is gebouwd van 1673-1711. Zuidelijk van de commerciële City ligt het hart van de Britse democratie, the Houses of Parliament, de parlementsge-bouwen, in 1834 in neogoti-sche stijl gebouwd om niet te misstaan naast de gotische Westminster Abbey. Bekend om haar talrijke kapellen en statiegraven van politieke en artistieke prominenten, is Westminster Abbey sedert het begin van de veertiende eeuw tevens de kroningskerk van de Engelse monarchen.

Onde uma vez os romanos fundaram um espólio comer-cial, encontra-se hoje a Cidade de Londres, o centro de co-mércio nacional e internacio-nal, de seguros, de bolsas de valores e de matérias primas. Também foi uma vez o eixo do Commonwealth (União das Nações Britânicas) e da Libra esterlina. A catedral de S. Paulo é uma construção do arqui-tecto Christopher Wren de 1673-1711.
A sul da Cidade comercial está situado o coração da demo-cracia britânica, as Casas do Parlamento, costruidas em 1834, no estilo neo-gótico para não destoar com a West-minster Abbey vizinha. Conhe-cida pelas numerosas capelas e pelos túmulos de figuras prominentes no mundo da política e da arte, a Westmin-ster Abbey é a igreja de co-roação dos monarcas ingleses desde o começo do séc. XIV.

Der, hvor romerne engang oprettede en handelspost, ligger nu The City of London, centrum for den nationale og internationale handel, forsi-kringer, fonds- og råstofbør-sen. Engang var det også centrum for the Commen-wealth og det britiske punds magt. Saint Paul's Cathedral er bygget af arkitekten Christo-pher Wren fra 1673-1711.
Syd for det kommercielle City ligger hjertet i det britiske de-mokrati, The Houses of Parlia-ment, bygget i 1834 i nygotisk stil for ikke at være en for stor kontrast til den gotiske West-minster Abbey. Westminster Abbey er kendt for sine talrige kapeller og statelige gravste-der for fremtrædende politike-re og kunstnere. Fra det 14. århundrede har kirken endvi-dere været kroningskirke for de engelske monarker.

Wo einst die Römer eine Han-delsniederlassung gründeten, erhebt sich heute die Londo-ner City, nationales und inter-nationales Zentrum von Han-del, Versicherungswesen, Banken und Börsen und vor-dem auch der Angelpunkt des Commonwealth und des frü-her als Weltleitwährung star-ken Pfundes Sterling. Die herr-liche St.-Pauls-Kathedrale wur-de von dem großen Architek-ten Sir Christopher Wren 1673-1711 erbaut.
Südlich der City, des Geschäfts-und Bankenzentrums, liegt im Stadtbezirk Westminster das Parlamentsgebäude, das 'Herz' der englischen Demo-kratie. Es wurde 1834 im neu-gotischen Stil errichtet, pas-send zur gotischen Westmin-ster-Abtei. Das im wesentli-chen auf das 13. Jahrhundert zurückgehende Gotteshaus ist durch seine herrlichen Kapel-len und Grabmäler berühmter Persönlichkeiten aus Politik und Kultur bedeutend. Seit dem frühen 14. Jahrhundert ist es englische Krönungskir-che.

Εκεί που κάποτε οι Ρωμαίοι ίδρυσαν εμπορικό σταθμό, βρίσκεται τώρα το Σίτυ του Λονδίνου, το κέντρο του εθνικού και διεθνούς εμπορίου, ασφαλίσεων, και το χρηματιστήριο αξιών και πρώτων υλών. Κάποτε ο αξόνας της κοινοπολιτείας και της εξουσίας της βρεταννικής λίρας. Ο Καθεδρικός ναός του Αγίου Παύλου, ένα οικοδόμημα του αρχιτέκτονα Χρίστοφερ Ουρέν, κτίστηκε από το 1673-1711. Νότια από το εμπορικό Σίτυ βρίσκεται η καρδιά της βρεταννικής δημοκρατίας, τα Χάουσες οφ Πάρλαμεντ, τα κτίρια του αγγλικού κοινοβουλίου, που χτίστηκαν το 1834 σε νεογοτθικό ρυθμό για να είναι ταιριαστά στο γοτθικό αββαείο Ουεστμίνστερ. Γνωστό όχι μόνο για τα ανάριθμα παρεκκλήσιά του και τα

εθιμοτυπικά ταφεία πολιτικών και καλλιτεχνικών διαπρεπόμενων ανθρώπων, αλλά και επειδή το αββαείο Ουεστμίνστερ είναι από τις αρχές του δέκατου τέταρτου αιώνα η εκκλησία που στέφονται οι Άγγλοι μονάρχες.

Oxford, England's oldest university, dates from the beginning of the 12th century, though its precise date of origin is not known. Oxford's assembly of colleges with their characteristic 'quads' makes it one of the most attractive cities in Europe.

The little township of Arundel in West Sussex is dominated by the impressive castle, seat of the Dukes of Norfolk, which dates from Norman times.

Brighton, a town on the Sussex coast, is a popular and typically English seaside resort. The exotic Royal Pavilion with its domes, pagoda roofs and minarets was built by George, Prince of Wales (later Prince Regent and finally George IV).

Oxford, Englands ældste universitet fra begyndelsen af det 12. århundrede, den nøjagtige dato kendes ikke, har ca. fyrre kollegier, der genkendes på deres firkantede gårde, kaldet 'quads'.
Den lille by Arundal i West-Sussex domineres af Nordfolk hertugernes imponerende borg. Den stammer fra normannertiden.
Brighton på Sussexkysten er en meget besøgt og typisk engelsk badeby. Den eksotiske Royal Pavillion er enestående med sine kupler, pagodetage og minareter.

Die älteste Universität Englands wurde 1163 in Oxford gegründet. Heute umfaßt das Universitätszentrum etwa 40 Colleges, die um quadratische Innenhöfe (quads) gelagert sind.
Arundel im westlichen Sussex wird von der eindrucksvollen Burg der Herzöge von Norfolk überragt, die auf die Normannenzeit zurückgeht.
An der Küste von Sussex liegt Brighton, ein ungemein beliebtes und typisch englisches Seebad. Einmalig ist der um 1812 erbaute Royal Pavillon, ein Palast im orientalischen Stil mit Kuppeln, Minaretten und Pagodendächern.

Oxford, la universidad más antigua de Inglaterra, sin fecha conocida pero sí de principios del s. XII, cuenta con unos cuarenta colegios que se reconocen por sus patios cuadrados llamados 'quads'.
El lugar Arundal, en West-Sussex, está dominado por el impresionante castillo de los duques de Norfolk. Data de la época normanda.
Brighton, en la costa Sussex, es un lugar muy visitado, un típico balneario inglés. Especial es el exótico Royal Pavillion con sus cúpulas, techos de pagoda y minaretes.

Oxford, l'université la plus ancienne de l'Angleterre, qui remonte au début du 12e siècle (la date exacte de son origine n'est pas connue), compte environ 40 collèges qui sont reconnaissables aux places intérieures carrées, dénommées "quads".
Arundal, une petite localité du West-Sussex, est dominée par l'imposant château des comtes de Norfolk. Il date de l'époque normande.
Brighton sur la côte du Sussex, est une ville balnéaire très fréquentée, typiquement anglaise. Une attraction unique est constituée ici par le Royal Pavillon avec ses coupoles, ses toits de pagode et ses minarets.

Oxford, a universidade mais antiga da Ingalterra, data do início do século XII, mas uma data exacta não se conhece, possui à volta de quarenta colégios, que se reconhecem pelos seus páteos quadrados, aos quais se dá o nome de 'quads'.
A vila de Arundal, em West-Sussex, é dominada por um castelo impassante do duque de Norfolk. Ele data do período dos Normandos.
Brighton, na costa de Sussex, é uma praia balneária típica inglesa e muito procurada. Exclusivo é o exótico Royal Pavillion com as suas cúpulas, telhados de pagodes e minaretes.

Το πιο παλαιό πανεπιστήμιο της Αγγλίας από τις αρχές του δωδέκατου αιώνα, η ακριβής ημερομηνιά δεν είναι γνωστή, μετράει περίπου σαράντα κολέγια που αναγνωρίζονται από τις τετραγωνικές αυλές που ονομάζονται 'quads'.
Το χωριό Άρενταλ στο δυτικό Σάσεξ κυριαρχείται από το εντυπωσιακό κάστρο των δούκων του Νόρφολκ που χρονολογείται από τη Νορμανδική εποχή.
Μπράιτον στην ακτή του Σάσεξ είναι τυπική αγγλική παραθαλάσσια πόλη που την επισκέπτονται ευχάριστα. Μοναδικό είναι το εξωτικό Ρόυαλ Παβίλιον με τους θόλους, τις στέγες παγόδας και μιναρέδες.

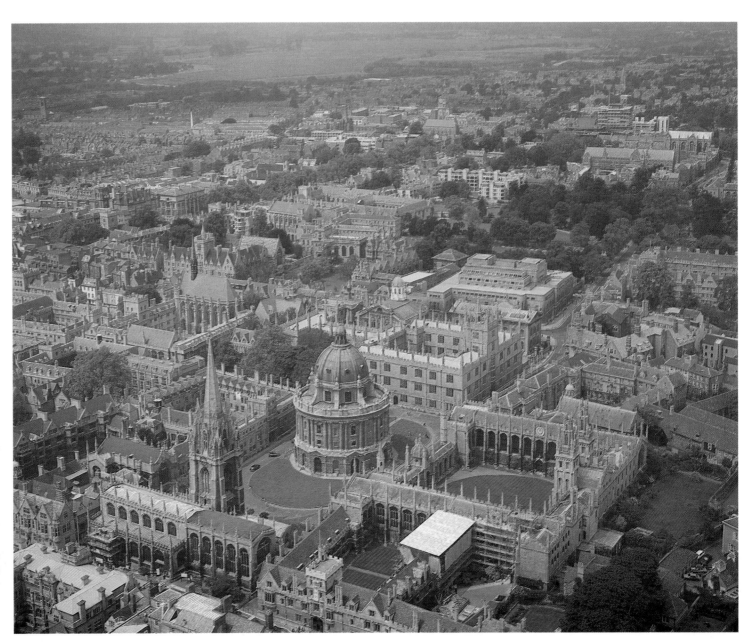

Oxford, la più antica università inglese che risale all'inizio del XII secolo (non se ne conosce la data esatta) comprende circa 40 'colleges', riconoscibili dai cortili interni quadrati, chiamata 'quads'.
Arundal, una piccola località del West Sussex, è dominata dal maestoso castello dei conti di Norfolk di epoca normanna.
Brighton, sulla costa del Sussex è una città balneare tipicamente inglese, in cui il Royal Pavillion, con cupole, tetti a pagoda e minareti, costituisce un'attrattiva del tutto particolare.

Oxford, Engelands oudste universiteit, uit het begin van de twaalfde eeuw een exacte datum is niet bekend, telt ongeveer veertig colleges die herkenbaar zijn aan de vierkante binnenplaatsen 'quads' genoemd.
Het plaatsje Arundal, in West-Sussex, wordt gedomineerd door het imposante kasteel van de hertogen van Norfolk. Het dateert uit de Normandische tijd.
Brighton aan de kust van Sussex is een graag bezochte en typisch Engelse badplaats. Uniek is het exotische Royal Pavillion met zijn koepels, pagodedaken en minaretten.

The romantic 13th century Leeds Castle is situated near the town of Maidstone in the hilly countryside of Kent – the 'Garden of England'.

Canterbury, with its cathedral and Anglican archbishop, has been the ecclesiastical centre of England since the 6th century.

Nær Maidstone, i Kents bølgende landskab, Englands have, ligger det romantiske Leeds Castle fra det 13. århundrede.
Canterbury har sin katedral og sin ærkebiskop og har lige siden det 6. århundrede været Englands åndelige centrum.
Lige siden romerne har Dover været porten til England. I det 12. århundrede blev byen forstærket med en borg på toppen af de hvide kridtklipper.

In der hügeligen Grafschaft Kent, dem 'Garten Englands', liegt unweit von Maidstone das romantische Leeds Castle aus dem 13. Jahrhundert.
Canterbury ist mit Kathedrale und anglikanischem Erzbischof seit dem 6. Jahrhundert der geistliche Mittelpunkt Englands.
Seit der Römerzeit ist Dover das Einfallstor Englands. Im 12. Jahrhundert wurde die Stadt durch eine über den weißen Kreideklippen errichtete wehrhafte Burganlage gesichert.

En el paisaje ondeante de Kent, el jardín de Inglaterra, se encuentra el romántico castillo Leeds del S. XIII, cerca de Maidstone.
Canterbury tiene su catedral y su arzobispo anglicano; ya desde el s. VI es el centro espiritual de Inglaterra.
Ya desde la época romana Dover es la puerta de entrada a Inglaterra. En el s. XII se fortalecieron con una fortaleza sobre los blancos cantiles de creta.

Dans le paysage ondulé du Kent, le jardin de l'Angleterre, le château romantique du 13e siècle, le Leeds Castle orne les environs de Maidstone.
Canterbury a sa cathédrale et son archevêque anglican et est, depuis le 6e siècle, le centre spirituel de l'Angleterre. Depuis l'époque romaine déjà. Douvres est la porte d'accès de l'Angleterre. Au 12e siècle, la défence de la ville fut renforcée par une forteresse bâtie sur les rochers calcaires blanchâtres.

Nell'ondulato paesaggio del Kent, il giardino d'Inghilterra, vicino a Maidstone, si trova Leeds Castle, il romantico castello del tredicesimo secolo.
Canterbury, centro sprituale dell'Inghilterra fin dal VI secolo, può vantare la stupenda cattedrale e il vescovo anglicano.
Dover, già dal tempo dei Romani, costituisce la porta d'entrata dell'Inghilterra. Nel XII secolo, per difendere la città, fu costruita una fortezza sulle sue bianche rocce calcaree.

In het golvende landschap van Kent, de tuin van Engeland, staat het romantische dertiende-eeuwse Leeds Castle, vlakbij Maidstone.
Canterbury heeft zijn kathedraal en zijn Anglicaanse aartsbisschop en is al sedert de zesde eeuw het geestelijk centrum van Engeland.
Reeds sedert de Romeinse tijd is Dover de invalspoort voor Engeland. In de twaalfde eeuw werd het versterkt met een vesting op de witte krijtrotsen.

Na païsagem ondulada de Kent, o jardim da Inglaterra, está o romântico Leeds Castle do século XIII, na proximidade de Maidstone.
Canterbury tem a sua catedral e o seu arcebispo anglicano e é já desde o século VI o centro eclesiástico da Inglaterra.
Desde já do tempo romano é Dover a porta de ataques à Inglaterra. No século XII foi ele reforçado com um forte em pedra-gêsso branca.

Στο κυματιστό τοπίο του Κέντ, του κήπου της Αγγλίας, βρίσκεται κοντά στο Μαίντστον το ρομαντικό κάστρο του Λητνς από το δέκατο τρίτο αιώνα.
Το Κάντερμπουρυ κατέχει το Καθεδρικό ναό του και τον Αγγλικανό αρχιεπίσκοπο και αποτελεί ήδη από τον έκτο αιώνα το πνευματικό κέντρο της Αγγλίας.
Από τη ρωμαϊκή εποχή ήδη είναι το Ντόβερ η είσοδος για την Αγγλία. Το δωδέκατο αιώνα οχυρώθηκε με φρούριο στους άσπρους κιμωλόβραχους.

Dover has been the gateway to England since Roman times. In the 12th century a fortress was built on the white chalk cliffs.

5
BELGIE–BELGIQUE & LUXEMBOURG

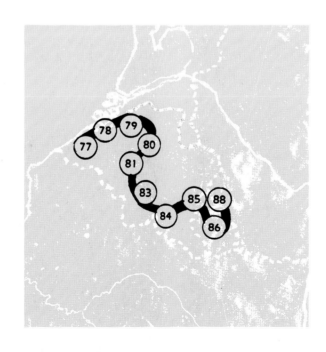

Wereldbekend is het Westvlaamse Brugge, het Venetië van het Noorden, een cultuur-historisch juweel en in de dertiende eeuw het centrum van de Westeuropese handel.

Symbolen van de rijkdom en de autonomie van de stad zijn nog het stoere Belfort en de Lakenhalle.

Ook in Ieper is dat zo of is dat eigenlijk weer zo. Want het is de stad gelukkig niet meer aan te zien dat dit in de Eerste Wereldoorlog vier jaar lang een stad in de frontlijn was.

La ville flamande de Bruges, appelée aussi la Venise du Nord, est connue dans le monde entier. C'est un joyau historique et culturel qui, au 13e siècle, était le centre du commerce en Europe occidentale. Les symboles de la richesse et de l'autonomie de la ville sont aujourd'hui encore le fier beffroi Befroid et la Halle aux Draps.
A Ypres, on dirait que tout revit comme autrefois, car heureusement ce n'est plus la ville qui fut, pendant quatre ans, au centre de combats meurtriers, durant la Première Guerre mondiale.

Brugge, nordens Venedig, beliggende i Vestflanderen er en kulturhistorisk juvel, og byen var i det 13. århundrede centrum for den vesteuropæiske handel. Det tapre Belfort og Lagenhallerne står der endnu som symboler på byens rigdom og autonomi.
Sådan er det også i Ieper eller bedre sådan er nu igen i Ieper. For heldigvis kan man ikke se på byen, at den under den første verdenskrig i fire år var frontlinieby.

Brügge, das 'Venedig des Nordens', ab dem 13. Jahrhundert Zentrum des westeuropäischen Handels, ist mit seinen zahlreichen alten Bauten ein kulturhistorisches Kleinod. Der mächtige Belfried und die Tuchhalle zeugen vom einstigen Reichtum und stolzen Freiheitswillen der westflämischen Stadt.
Auch Ypern war einst ein selbstbewußtes Handelszentrum, das freilich im Ersten Weltkrieg fast völlig zerstört, aber bald nach alten Plänen wiederaufgebaut wurde.

The West Flemish city of Bruges, the 'Venice of the North', is famous all over the world as a jewel of cultural history and the commercial centre of 13th century Western Europe. Symbols of its wealth and autonomy are still to be seen in the carillon and drapers hall.
This is also true of Ypres. For four years this town was in the front-line of the First World War, though today few signs of conflict are left.

Brujas, la famosísima ciudad de Flandes Occidental, la Venecia del Norte, une joya histórico-cultural y el centro en el s. XIII del comercio de la Europa Occidental. Belfort y la Lakenhalle son los símbolos de la riqueza y de la autonomía de la ciudad.
También en Ieper pasa lo mismo o, en realidad, vuelve a pasar lo mismo, pues felizmente ya no se nota que esta ciudad estuvo cuatro años seguidos en el frente en la Primera Guerra Mundial.

Bruges, nella Fiandra occidentale, chiamata anche la Venezia del Nord, è nota in tutto il mondo. Essa è un gioiello storico e culturale, e nel XIII secolo, fu il centro del commercio europeo occidentale.
Simboli della ricchezza e dell'autonomia della città sono ancora oggi Belfort e la Lakenhalle.
A Ieper, tutto vive come un tempo e non si direbbe che la città è stata, per 4 anni, teatro di combattimenti violenti, durante la I guerra mondiale.

De fama mundial é Brugge, na Flândria ocidental, a Veneza do Norte, uma joia de cultura histórica e foi no século XIII o centro do comércio da Europa Ocidental. Símbolos de riqueza e de autonomia da cidade são ainda o potente Belfort e o Lakenhalle.
Em Ieper dá-se o mesmo ou dá-se tambem o mesmo, novamente. Porque felizmente já não se nota na cidade que ela esteve durante quatro anos na inha da frente, da Primeira Guerra Mundial.

Κοσμοξάκουστη είναι η Μπρυζ στη Δυτική Φλάντρα, η Βενετιά του Βορρά, ένα πολιτιστικό-ιστορικό κόσμημα που το δέκατο τρίτο αιώνα ήταν το κέντρο εμπορίου της Δυτικής Ευρώπης. Σύμβολα του πλούτου και της αυτονομίας της πόλης είναι ακόμα το ισχυρό Μπελφόρ και το Λάκενχαλλε. Επίσης στο Ήπερ είναι έτσι, ή καλύτερα πάλι έτσι, γιατί ευτυχώς δεν μπορείτε να δείτε πια ότι το Ήπερ κατά τον πρώτο παγκόσμιο πόλεμο ήταν για τέσσερα χρόνια μια πόλη μετώπου.

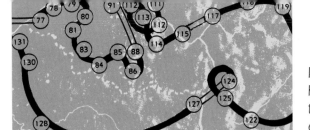

In Gent wordt de toren van het Belfort als het ware ingesloten door twee monumentale kerktorens, die van de Sint-Niklaaskerk en de Sint-Baafskathedraal. Samen vormen ze de fameuze kuip van Gent.

Ook Antwerpen heeft zijn historisch centrum maar voor de verandering laten we nu eens zien dat de Rubensstad aan de Schelde, ook nog steeds een belangrijke, moderne en grote wereldhaven rijk is.

A Gand, la tour du beffroi est, comme enfermée par deux tours d'église monumentales, celle de l'église Saint-Nicolas et celle de la cathédrale Saint-Bavon. Ensemble, elles forment la célèbre 'kuip (cuve) de Gand'.

Anvers possède également son centre historique, mais pour changer un peu disons également que la ville de Rubens, sur l'Escaut, est toujours riche d'un port mondial, important, moderne et de grandes dimensions.

I Gent omfavnes sandt at sige Belforts tårn af Sint-Niklaaskirkens og Sint-Baafskatedralens to monumentale kirketårne. Sammen udgør de Gents berømte bassin.

Antwerpen har også sit historiske centrum, men for forandringens skyld viser vi her, at Rubenbyen ved floden Schelde stadig har en vigtig, stor og moderne verdenshavn.

In Gent wird der Belfried von zwei mächtigen Kirchtürmen (St. Nikolaus und St. Bavo) flankiert. Zusammen bilden sie das Stadtzentrum, den berühmten 'Kessel' von Gent am Zusammenfluß von Leie und Schelde. Auch Antwerpen hat seine historische Altstadt, doch zeigen wir hier zur Abwechslung von der Rubensstadt an der Schelde den bedeutenden modernen Hafen, der die Stadt zu Belgiens 'Tor zum Meer' gemacht hat.

In Ghent, the tower of the carillon is virtually enclosed between the two monumental church towers of the St. Nicholas Church and the St. Bavel's Cathedral. Together they form the celebrated 'Kuip van Gent'.
Antwerp also has its historical centre, but by way of contrast, the photograph shows that Rubens's city on the River Scheldt also boasts a large, important and modern international port.

En Gante la torre del Belfort está, digamos, encerrada entre dos torres monumentales, la de iglesia de San Nicolás y la de la Catedral de San Bavo. Juntas forman el famoso tonel ('Kuip') de Gante.
También Amberes tiene un centro histórico pero para variar un poco mostramos aquí la ciudad de Rubens al Escalda que aún sigue siendo un gran puerto mundial importante y moderno.

A Gand, la torre del 'Beffroi', è come racchiusa fra due torri monumentali, quella di San Nicola e quello di San Bavo. Insieme esse formano la celebre 'Kuip van Gent'. Anche Anversa possiede un centro storico, ma tanto per cambiare, diciamo che la città di Rubens, sulla Schelda, è anche un porto mondiale, importante e moderno.

Em Gent, a torre do Belfort está como encerrada por duas torres de igreja monumentais, a da Igreja S. Nicolau e a catedral de S. Baaf. Em conjunto formam elas a famosa bacia de Gent.
Tambem Antuérpia tem o seu centro histórico, mas para variação mostramos que a cidade de Rubens, situada ao Escalda, possui ainda um porto mundial moderno, grande e de importância.

Στη Γάνδη εσωκλείεται σα να λέμε ο πύργος του Μπελφόρ από δύο μνημειώδη καμπαναριά, αυτό του ναού του Αγίου Νικολάου και αυτό του Καθεδρικού ναού Αγίου Μπάβο. Μαζί αποτελούν το λεκανοπέδιο της Γάνδης.
Η Αμβέρσα επίσης έχει το ιστορικό της κέντρο, αλλά για αλλαγή σας δείχνουμε τώρα ότι η πόλη του Ρούμπενς στο Σκάλδη κατέχει ακόμα μεγάλο διεθνές λιμάνι, μοντέρνο και σπουδαίο.

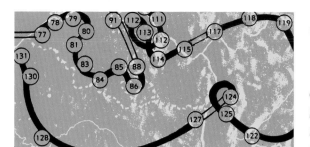

Getuigen van de bouwwoede van de Brabantse steden in de middeleeuwen zijn er nog in overvloed. De Sint-Romboutskathedraal in Mechelen en het Stadhuis van de universiteitsstad Leuven zijn maar enkele spectaculaire voorbeelden. Het Stadhuis aan de Grote Markt te Brussel is het symbool van de gemeentelijke vrijheid en de rijkdom

Il existe de très nombreux témoins, aujourd'hui encore, de la vague de constructions qui a déferlé sur les villes brabançonnes au Moyen Age. La cathédrale Saint-Rombout, à Malines, et l'Hôtel de Ville de la ville universitaire de Louvain n'en sont que quelques exemples spectaculaires.

L'Hôtel de Ville sur la Grand-Place de Bruxelles est le symbole de la liberté et de la richesse des villes dans les Flandres et le Brabant. Il date du 15e siècle et resta miraculeusement épargné par le bombardement français de Bruxelles en 1697.

Zeugnisse der Baurage, die im Mittelalter in den Stadtern Brabants herrschte, sind noch im Überfluß vorhanden. Die kathedrale St. Romuald in Mecheln und das Rathaus der Universitätsstadt Löwen sind nur 2 spektakuläre Beispiele. Das Rathaus am Marktplatz zum Brüssel ist das Symbol der städtischen Freiheit und des Reichtums der spätmittelalterlichen Städte in Flandern und Brabant. Es stammt aus dem 15. Jh. Wunderbarerweise wurde es 1697, während der französischen Beschießung von Brüssel, nicht zerstört.

Hay multitud de téstigos del entusiasmo por la arquitectura en las ciudades de Brabante durante la Edad Media. La Catedral de San Rombout en Malinas y el Ayuntamiento de la ciudad universitaria de Lovaina son unos pocos y espectaculares ejemplos. El ayuntamiento situado en la Plaza grande en Bruselas es el símbolo de la libertad municipal y de la riqueza de las ciudades de la alta Edad Media de Flandres y Brabante. Data del siglo XV y milagrosamente fue perdonado en el bombardeo francés de Bruselas en 1697.

A Câmara Municipal no Praça Grande em Bruxelas é o símbolo da liberdade municipal e da riqueza das cidades medievais mais recentes na Flandres e em Brabante. Data do séc. XV e foi miraculosamente poupada durante o ataque francês a Bruxelas em 1697. Testemunhas do furor para a construção nas cidades de Brabante, na idade média, há ainda em abundância. A catedral de S. Rombout, em Mechelen e a Câmara Municipal da cidade universitária de Leuven são os exemplos mais espectaculares.

Der findes stadig vidnesbyrd i overflod om den brabantse byggegalskab i middelalderen. Sint-Romboudtkatedralen i Mechelen og universitetsbyen Leuvens rådhus er kun enkelte iøjnefaldende eksempler.
Rådhuset på Grote Markt i Bruxelles er et symbol på byens frihed og rigdom i senmiddelalderens Flanderen og Brabant. Det stammer fra det 15. århundrede og blev ved et under sparet ved det franske bombardement af Bruxelles i 1697.

There are many surviving examples of the early building of the cities of Brabant which took place in the Middle Ages. The St. Rombout's Cathedral in Mechelen and the Town Hall of the university city of Louvain are two spectacular examples. The Town Hall on the Grote Markt ('large market') in Brussels is a symbol of the municipal freedom and wealth of the cities of Brabant and Flanders during the late mediaeval era. It dates back to the 15th century and was miraculously spared during the French siege of Brussels in 1697.

Esistono ancora numerosi esempi dell'esplosione edilizia, durante il Medioevo, nelle città del Brabante. Le cattedrale di Saint-Rombout a Mechelen e il municipio della città universitaria di Louvain ne costituiscono degli esempi spettacolari.
Il municipio nella grande Piazza di Bruxelles è il simbolo della libertà e della ricchezza delle città nelle Fiandre e nel Brabante.
Esso risale al XV secolo e rimase miracolosamente indenne durante i bombardamenti francesi del 1697.

Μάρτυρες της οικοδομικής μανίας των πόλεων της Βραβάντης κατά το μεσαίωνα υπάρχουν ακόμα άφθονες. Ο Καθεδρικός ναός του Αγίου Ρόμπαουτ στη Μαλίν και το Δημαρχείο στη πανεπιστημιακή πόλη Λουβαίν είναι μόνο λίγα θεαματικά δείγματα. Το Δημαρχείο στη Μεγάλη Πλατεία στις Βρυξέλλες είναι το σύμβολο της δημόσιας ελευθερίας και των πόλεων στα τέλη του Μεσαίωνα στη Φλάντρα και Βραβάντη. Το Δημαρχείο χρονολογείται από το δέκατο πέμπτο αιώνα που ως εκ θαύματος σώθηκε από το γαλλικό βομβαρδισμό το 1697.

van de steden in Vlaanderen en Brabant.
Het dateert uit de vijftiende eeuw en bleef
als bij wonder gespaard tijdens het Franse
bombardement van Brussel in 1697.

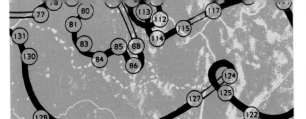

La cathédrale Saint Michel à Bruxelles est un bâtiment gothique qui, avec ses deux tours, trahit une influence française. L'intérieur est de style gothique brabançon. Les vitraux du 16e siècle sont particulièrement remarquables.
Bruxelles est également le siège de la CEE pour lequel le bâtiment du Berlaymont fut

De Sint Michielskathedraal te Brussel is een gotisch bouwwerk dat met zijn twee torens Franse invloed verraadt. Het interieur is in Brabantse gothiek. Bijzonder fraai zijn de zestiende-eeuwse glasramen. Brussel is ook de zetel van de EG waarvoor in de regeringswijk in 1969 het Berlaymont gebouw werd opgericht.
De Condroz, een hooggelegen plateau op de grens van Namen en Henegouwen, is weer een ander gezicht van België.

St. Michelkatedralen i Bruxelles er et gotisk bygningsværk, der med sine to tårne giver udtryk for fransk påvirkning. Interiøret står i brabants gotik. Særligt smukt er glasvinduerne fra det 16. århundrede.
EF-hovedkvarteret ligger også i Bruxelles i Berlaymontbygningen, der blev rejst i regeringsbydelen i 1969.
Condroz, et højtliggende plateau på grænsen mellem Namen og Henegouwen, giver et helt andet billede af Belgien.

Die Brüsseler Stiftskirche St. Michael und St. Gundula ist ein gotischer Bau, dessen Doppeltürme französischen Einfluß verraten. Das Innere im Stil der Brabanter Gotik weist prächtige Glasfenster aus dem 16. Jahrhundert auf. Für die Behörden der EG, die ihren Sitz in Brüssel hat wurde 1969 im Regierungsviertel das Berlaymont-Gebäude errichtet.
Ein anderes Bild von Belgien zeigt uns das Condroz, eine Hochebene an der Grenze zwischen den Provinzen Hennegau und Namur.

St. Michael's Cathedral in Brussels was built in the Gothic style, the two towers show the French influence, whilst the interior is Brabant Gothic. The 16th-century stained glass windows are particularly noteworthy.
Brussels is the official seat of the EC; the Berlaymont Building was built for the EC in 1969 in the city's government district. Another very different area in Belgium is Le Condroz, a high plateau situated on the border between Namur and Hainault.

La Catedral de San Miguel en Bruselas es una obra gótica en la que no se nota la influencia francesa. El interior es del estilo gótico de Brabante. Las vidrieras del siglo XVI son de una gran belleza.
Bruselas es también la sede de la CEE por lo que en 1969 se contruyó el barrio gubernativo Berlaymont.
El Condroz una alta meseta en la frontera entre Namur y Henegouwen, muestra otra cara de Bélgica.

La cattedrale di San Michele a Bruxelles è una costruzione gotica che, con le sue due torri, rivela un influsso francese. L'interno è in stile gotico brabantino. Le vetrate del XVI secolo sono particolarmente preziose.
Bruxelles è anche la sede della Comunità Europea, per cui fu costruito l'edificio di Berlaymont nel 1969. Il Condroz, un altipiano sul confine tra le province di Namur e dell'Hainaut, costituisce un altro aspetto del Belgio.

A catedral de St. Michel em Bruxelas é de arquitectura gótica que denuncia a influência francesa, com as suas duas torres. O interior é gótico brabantino. As janelas do séc. XVI são de especial beleza.
Bruxelas é tambem a sede da CEE, para a qual o edifício Berlaymont foi instalado em 1969, no quarteirão do governo.
O Condroz, um planalto na fronteira entre Namen e Henegouwen, é um outro aspecto da Bélgica muito diferente.

Ο Καθεδρικός ναός του Αγίου Μιχαήλ στις Βρυξέλλες είναι γοτθικό οικοδόμημα που προδίνει τη γαλλική επίδραση με τα δύο καμπαναριά του. Η εσωτερική διακόσμηση του Καθεδρικού ναού είναι βραβαντογοτθική. Εξαιρετικά όμορφα είναι τα παράθυρα με υαλογραφήματα του δέκατου έκτου αιώνα. Οι Βρυξέλλες είναι επίσης η έδρα της ΕΟΚ για την οποία υψώθηκε το 1969 στην κυβερνητική συνοικία το κτίριο Μπερλεϋμόν. Το Κονδρόζ, ένα υψίπεδο στα σύνορα του Ναμύρ και Αινώ, είναι μια άλλη μορφή του Βελγίου.

érigé en 1969 dans le quartier administratif.
Le Condroz, un haut plateau à la frontière
des provinces de Namur et du Hainaut
constitue un autre aspect de la Belgique.

A la lisière des Ardennes et du val de Meuse, il existe de très nombreux châteaux, dont celui, romantique, de Vêves et l'impressionnante forteresse de Laveaux-Ste-Anne. Un peu à l'extérieur de Bastogne, le Mémorial du Mardasson commémore l'offensive des Ardennes à la fin de 1944, la dernière grande offensive allemande de la Deuxième Guerre mondiale.

Aan de rand van de Ardennen en het dal van de Maas zijn er kastelen te kust en te keur, waarvan hier het romantische Vêves en de stoere burcht van Laveaux Ste-Anne. Even buiten Bastogne herinnert het Mémorial du Mardasson aan het Ardennenoffensief van eind 1944, het laatste grote Duitse offensief in de Tweede Wereldoorlog.

There are many castles on the edge of the Ardennes and the valley of the River Meuse. Depicted here are the romantic chateau of Vêves and the powerful fortress of Laveaux Ste.-Anne. The Memorial du Mardasson standing just outside Bastogne commemorates the Ardennes Offensive which took place at the end of 1944, the last major offensive.

På randen af Ardennerne og Maasdalen ligger den ene borg efter den anden, hvoraf vi her viser det romantiske Vêves og Laveaux Ste-Annes stærke borg. Lige uden for Bastogne minder Mémorial du Mardasson os om Ardenneroffensiven i slutningen af 1944, den sidste store tyske offensiv under den anden verdenskrig.

A los pies de las Ardenas y en el valle del Mosa hay castillos de todo tipo, entre ellos el romántico Vêves y el castillo de Laveaux Ste-Anne. A las afueras de Bastogne, el Mémorial du Mardasson recuerda la ofensiva de las Ardenas de finales de 1944, la última gran ofensiva alemana en la Segunda Guerra Mundial.

Zahlreiche Burgen und Schlösser säumen den Rand der Ardennen und das Maastal. Als Beispiele zeigen wir die Burg von Vêves und die trutzige Burganlage von Laveaux Ste-Anne. Unweit von Bastogne erinnert die Mardasson-Gedenkstätte an die Ardennenoffensive des Winters 1944/45, den letzten deutschen Großangriff im Zweiten Weltkrieg.

Al confine delle Ardenne e della valle della Mosa, esistono numerosi castelli, fra cui quello romantico di Vêves e l'imponente fortezza di Laveaux Ste-Anne. Appena fuori Bastogne, troviamo il monumento commemorativo del Mardasson che ricorda l'offensiva delle Ardenne alla fine del 1944, vale a dire l'ultima grande offensiva tedesca.

Na orla das Ardenas e do vale do Mosa há castelos para todos os gostos, dos quais aqui o romântico de Vêves e o vigoroso de Laveaux Ste-Anne. Um pouco fora de Bastogne o Mémorial du Mardasson recorda-nos a ofensiva das Ardenas, no fim de 1944, a última grande ofensiva alemã na Segunda Guerra Mundial.

Στην άκρη των Αρδέννων και στην κοιλάδα του Μόζα βρίσκονται άφθονοι πύργοι, όπως εδώ ο ρομαντικός Βεβ και το ισχυρό όχυρο Λαβώ σαίντε Αν. Λίγο έξω από τη Μπαστώνια το Μνημείο του Μαρντασσόν μας θυμίζει τη μάχη των Αρδέννων στα τέλη του 1944. Ήταν η τελευταία μεγάλη μάχη των Γερμανών κατά το δεύτερο παγκόσμιο πόλεμο.

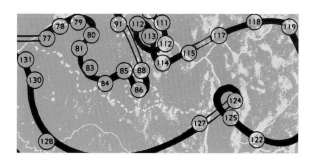

Le Quartier de l'Europe dans la capitale du Grand-Duché de Luxembourg est situé sur la Kirchberg, une colline au nord-est de l'ancienne ville fortifiée, qui fut occupée et défendue pendant des siècles par les troupes espagnoles, françaises, autrichiennes et prussiennes. Le Quartier de l'Europe se compose, entre autres, du Théâtre Municipal, du Centre européen, de la Cour de Justice et du bâtiment Jean Monnet.

I Storhertugdømmet Luxemburgs hovedstad ligger 'quartier de l'Europe' på Kirchberg, en høj nordøst for den gamle fæstningsby, der gennem århundreder blev belejret og forsvaret af spanske, franske, østrigske og preussiske tropper. 'Quartier de l'Europe' består bl.a. af Théâtre Municipal, Det Europæiske Centrum Den Europæiske Domstol og Jean-Monnet-bygningen.

Das 'Europaviertel' in der Hauptstadt des Großherzogtums Luxemburg liegt auf dem Kirchberg, einer Anhöhe im Nordosten der alten Festungsstadt, die im Laufe von Jahrhunderten spanischen, französischen, österreichischen und deutschen Truppen getrotzt hat. Zum Europaviertel gehören unter anderem das Stadttheater, das Europazentrum, der Justizpalast und das Jean-Monnet-Gebäude.

The so-called 'Quartier de l'Europe' in the capital of the Grand Duchy of Luxembourg lies on Mount Kirchberg, a hill to the North-east of the old fortress. Throughout history it has been besieged and defended in turn by Spanish, French, Austrian and Russian troops. The Municipal Theatre, the European Centre, the Court of Justice, and the Jean Monnet building are just a few of the many buildings of interest situated in the 'Quartier de l'Europe'.

El 'barrio de Europa' en la capital del gran ducado de Luxemburgo se encuentra en el Kirchberg, una colina al noreste de la antigua fortaleza, que durante muchos siglos fue atacada y defendida por los ejércitos de España, Francia, Austria y Prusia. El 'cuartel de Europa' contiene entre otros el Teatro Municipal, el Centro Europeo, la Corte de Justicia y el edificio de Jean-Monnet.

Il Quartiere dell'Europa nella capitale del Granducato del Lussemburgo si trova sulla Kirchberg, una collina a nord-est dell'antica città fortificata che fu occupata e difesa per secoli dalle truppe spagnole, francesi, austriache e prussiane. Il Quartiere dell'Europa comprende, fra l'altro, il teatro municipale, il Centro Europeo, la Corte di Giustizia e l'edificio Jean Monnet.

Het 'quartier de l'Europe' in de hoofdstad van het Groothertogdom Luxemburg ligt op de noordoosten van de oude vestingstad, die gedurende eeuwen door Spaanse, Franse, Oostenrijkse en Pruisische troepen werd belegerd en verdedigd. Het 'quartier de l'Europe' bestaat uit ondermeer het Théâtre Municipal, het Europese Centrum, het Hof van Justitie en het Jean-Monnet gebouw.

O 'bairro da Europa' na capital do Grão-Ducado de Luxemburgo encontra-se no Kirchberg, uma colina a nordeste da velha cidade forte; esta foi durante séculos ocupada e defendida por Espanhóis, Franceses, Austríacos e Prussianos. O 'bairro da Europa' é constituido entre outros pelo Teatro Municipal, o Centro Europeu, o Tribunal de Justiça e o Edifício Jean-Monnet.

Το 'καρτιέ της Ευρώπης' της πρωτεύουσας του Δουκάτου Λουξεμβούργου βρίσκεται στο Κίρχμπεργκ, ένας λόφος βορειανατολικά από την παλαιά οχυρωμένη πόλη που επί αιώνες πολιορκήθηκε και υπερασπίστηκε από ισπανικούς, γαλλικούς, αυστριακούς και πρωσσικούς στρατούς. Το 'καρτιέ της Ευρώπης' αποτελείται μεταξύ άλλων από το Θέατρο Μουνισιπάλ, το Ευρωπαϊκό Κέντρο, το Δικαστήριο και το κτίριο Σαν-Μοννέ.

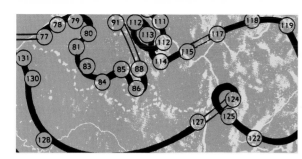

Petite localité, étroitement enserrée par la Sûre. Les ruines du château fort, dont les vestiges les plus anciens datent de 927 environ, sont parmi les plus anciennes du pays. Elles se trouvent encore à une hauteur respectable par rapport au village et nous procurent des vues magnifiques. Comme sur la Lugturm ronde, par exemple, l'avant-poste qui nous paraît si proche, mais qui se trouve de l'autre côté d'une faille profonde.

En lille by i floden Sûres knusende favntag. Borgruinen, hvis ældste rester stammer fra ca. 927, er en af landets ældste. Den ligger højt over landsbyen, og herfra har man en pragtfuld udsigt til f.eks. det runde Lugturm forposten, der synes så tæt ved, men som ligger på den anden side af en dyb kløft.

Piccolo villaggio, strettamente racchiuso dalla Sûre. I ruderi della roccaforte, le cui più antiche vestigia risalgono al 927 circa, sono fra i più antichi del paese. Essi si trovano ad una notevole altezza rispetto al villaggio e consentono di ammirare magnifici panorami. Sulla Lugturm rotonda ad esempio, un avamposto che ci sembra così vicino, ma che si trova dall'altro lato di una faglia profonda.

Von der Sûre umschlungen ist Esch, eine kleine Ortschaft mit einer mächtigen Burg, die in ihren ältesten Teilen auf die Zeit um 927 zurückgeht. Sie liegt hoch über dem Ort. Einen prächtigen Ausblick hat man vom runden Lugturm aus, einem Wachturm außerhalb der Burganlage, der durch eine tiefe Schlucht von ihr getrennt ist.

Een klein dorpje in een knellende omhelzing van de Sûre. De burchtruïne, waarvan de vroegste resten dateren van rond 927, is één van de oudste van het land. Het ligt nog een flink eind boven het dorp en het verschaft ons prachtige uitzichten. Op de ronde Lugturm bijvoorbeeld, de voorpost die zo dichtbij lijkt, maar die aan de andere kant van een diepe kloof ligt.

A small village, almost completely embraced by the River Sûre. The ruined fortress, situated well above the village, is one of the oldest in the country with the earliest parts dating from about the year 927. From the top there is a magnificent view over the round Lugturm, which although it looks near is in fact right at the other end of a steep gorge.

Uma pequena aldeia apertada num abraço do Sûre. As ruínas dum castelo, cujos restos datam de à volta de 927, são as mais velhas do país. Lá se encontram ainda bastante por cima da aldeia, donde se gosa um panorama magnífico. No Lugturm redondo, por exemplo, um posto avançado, que parece estar tão próximo, mas que se encontra no outro lado de um vale profundo.

Un pequeño pueblo abrazado por el Sûre. Las ruinas del castillo, de hacia 927, son de las más antiguas del país. Se encuentra a una buena altura sobre el pueblo y nos ofrece unas hermosas vistas. En el circular Lugturm por ejemplo, un puesto avanzado que parece estar muy cerca pero que se halla al otro lado de la profunda quebrada.

Ένα μικρό χωριό στη σφιχτή αγκαλιά του Συρ. Το φρουριακό ερείπιο, που τα πρώτα υπολείμματά του χρονολογούνται περίπου από το 927, είναι ένα από τα παλαιότερα της χώρας. Βρίσκεται αρκετά ψηλά πάνω από το χωριό και μας χαρίζει πανοραμικές θέες, λόγου χάριν στο στρογγυλό λούγτουρμ. Το εμπροσθοφυλάκιο φαίνεται τόσο κοντά, αλλά βρίσκεται στην άλλη πλευρά της βαθειάς χαράδρας.

6
NEDERLAND

Limburg en Brabant vormen een gezicht van Nederland, dat vaak minder bekend is. Temidden van glooiende Limburgse heuvels vinden we, pal aan de Belgische grens,

Maastricht één van de oudste Nederlandse steden, met monumenten vanaf de Romeinse tijd.

De moderne industriestad Eindhoven, in Noord-Brabant, wordt wegens de aanwezigheid van de reus Philips ook wel 'de lichtstad' genoemd.

Limburg og Brabant danner et billede af Holland, der ikke er så kendt i udlandet. Midt mellem bølgende limburgske bakker finder vi, umiddelbart ved den belgiske grænse Maastricht, én af Hollands ældste byer med monumenter fra romertiden.

Den moderne industriby Eindhoven i Noord-Brabant kaldes også ofte for 'lysbyen', fordi glødelampefabrikanten Philips har hjemme her.

Ein weniger bekanntes Gesicht der Niederlande zeigen uns Limburg und Brabant. Im sanft ansteigenden Limburger Hügelland liegt unweit der belgischen Grenze Maastricht, eine der traditionsreichsten Städte des Landes, deren älteste Bauzeugnisse aus der Römerzeit stammen.

Eindhoven in Nordbrabant ist eine moderne Industriestadt, die ihren Beinamen 'Lichterstadt' dem hier ansässigen Industriegiganten Philips verdankt.

The provinces of Limburg and Brabant form an aspect of the Netherlands which is familiar and appreciated in other countries. Amidst the undulating hills of Limburg, right on the Belgian border, we find the city of Maastricht, one of the oldest cities in the Netherlands. It has monuments dating back to Roman times. Eindhoven, the modern industrial city in North Brabant, is also called 'the city of light' because the gigantic Philips concern has its headquarters there.

Limburgo y Brabante ofrecen una imagen de los Países Bajos que en el extranjero no es muy conocida. En medio de las colinas de Limburgo encontramos, frente a la frontera belga, Maastricht, una de las ciudades más antiguas de los Países Bajos, con monumentos ya de la época romana.

La moderna ciudad industrial Eindhoven, en Brabante Septentrional, debido a la presencia del gigante Philips es conocida también como la 'ciudad de la luz'.

Le Limbourg et le Brabant constituent un aspect des Pays-Bas qui est souvent moins bien connu à l'étranger. Au milieu des collines en pente douce du Limbourg, nous trouvons tout contre la frontière belge, Maastricht, une des villes les plus anciennes des Pays-Bas, avec des monuments qui datent notamment de l'époque romaine.

La ville industrielle d'Eindhoven, dans la province du Nord-Brabant, est appelée parfois également la 'ville-lumière' en raison de la présence de l'entreprise géante Philips.

Il Limburgo e il Brabante costituiscono un aspetto dei Paesi Bassi poco conosciuto all'estero. Il mezzo al paesaggio ondulato del Limburgo, vicino al confine con il Belgio, troviamo Maastricht, una della città più antiche dei Paesi Bassi, con monumenti che risalgono al periodo romano.

La città indistriale di Eindhoven, nel Brabante del Nord è chiamata anche 'ville lumière' (città-luce) a causa della presenza della colossale Philips.

Limburgo e Brabante formam uma fisionomia da Holanda, que no estrangeiro muitas vezes é menos conhecida. Rodeada pelas colinas de Limburgo encontramos, junto à fronteira da Bélgica, a cidade de Maastricht, uma das mais antigas da Holanda, com monumentos desde o tempo romano.

A moderna cidade industrial Eindhoven, na Brabante do Norte, é, às vezes, nomeada 'a cidade da luz', graças à presença da gigante Philips.

Το Λιμβούργο και η Βραβάντη αποτελούν μαζί μια μορφή της Ολλανδίας που στο εξωτερικό συχνά δεν είναι τόσο γνωστή. Μέσα στους κυματιστούς λόφους του Λιμβούργου κόντα στα Βελγικά σύνορα βρίσκουμε το Μάαστριχτ, μια από τις παλαιότερες ολλανδικές πόλεις με μνημεία από τη Ρωμαϊκή εποχή.

Η μοντέρνα βιομηχανική πόλη Άίντχοβεν, στο νομό Βόρεια Βραβάντη, ονομάζεται εξαιτίας της παρουσίας της γιγαντιας Φίλιπς και η πόλη του φωτός.

Biesbosch, en lunefuld labyrint af vand og land, opstod efter St. Elizabethstormfloden i 1421. I horisonten ses broerne ved Moerdijk, forbindelsen mellem provinserne Holland og Brabant. I 1986 fuldførtes Oosterscheldedæmningen, det længste led i Deltakæden, der skal beskytte landet mod stormfloder.

Der Biesbosch ist ein bizarres Labyrinth von Wasser und Land, das seine Entstehung der Elisabethflut des Jahres 1421 verdankt. Am Horizont erkennt man die Brücken von Moerdijk, die Nordbrabant mit Südholland verbinden. 1986 wurde als letztes Glied des Deltaplans der Oosterschelde-Damm fertiggestellt, der das Land vor den Fluten des Meeres schützt.

The 'Biesbosch' is a strange maze of land and water which was formed in the St. Elizabeth Flood of 1421. On the horizon are the bridges of Moerdijk which connect the provinces of Holland and Brabant. In 1986, the 'Oosterschelde Dam' was completed. Built to protect the land against storm floods it was the last link in the Delta Works.

El Biesbosch, un caprichoso laberinto de agua y tierra, que surgió tras la marea de Santa Isabel en 1421. En el horizonte se divisan los puentes sobre el Moerdijk, la conexión entre Holanda y Brabante. En 1986 se finalizó la construcción del dique del Escalda Oriental, el último gran obstáculo en las obras del Delta que debían proteger estas tierras contra mareas vivas.

Le Biesbosch, un labyrinthe capricieux d'eau et de terre ferme, prit naissance après l'inondation de la Sainte Elisabeth, en 1421. A l'horizon, les ponts sur la Moerdijk, liaison entre les provinces de Hollande et de Brabant. C'est en 1986, que la digue de l'Oosterschelde ou digue de l'Escaut oriental fut terminée, en tant que dernier grand maillon des travaux du delta qui ont pour but de protéger les Pays-Bas contre les tempêtes.

Il Biesbosch, un tortuoso labirinto di acqua e terra, formatosi dopo l'inondazione di Santa Elisabetta nel 1421. All'orizzonte, i ponti sulla Moerdijk, collegamento fra il Brabante e l'Olanda. Nel 1986 è stata portata a termine la diga dello Oosterschelde, ultimo anello dei lavori del Delta che hanno come scopo di difendere i Paesi Bassi dalle tempeste.

O Biesbosch, um labirinto caprichoso de água e terra, que teve a sua origem na inundação de Santa Elizabeth, em 1421. No horizonte as pontes de Moerdijk, a ligação entre as províncias Holanda e Brabante. Em 1986 foi terminado o dique no Oosterschelde, o último elo nas Obras do Delta, que têm como finalidade proteger este país contra tempestades.

Το Μπήσμπος, παράξενος λαβύρινθος από νερό και ξηρά, δημιουργήθηκε μετά τη φουσκονεριά του 1421 που πήρε το όνομα Αγία Ελίσαμπετ. Στον ορίζοντα οι γέφυρες του Μούρντεϊκ, οι σύνδεσμοι μεταξύ Ολλανδίας και Βραβάντης. Το 1986 ολοκληρώθηκε το φράγμα στον Ανατολικό Σκάλδη, ο τελευταίος μεγάλος κρίκος στα έργα του Δέλτα, που πρέπει να προστατεύει τη χώρα αυτή από τις φουσκονεριές, όπως το 1421 και πρόσφατα ακόμα το 1953.

De Biesbosch, een grillig labyrinth van water en land, ontstond na de St. Elizabethsvloed van 1421. Aan de horizon de bruggen bij Moerdijk, de verbinding tussen

Holland en Brabant. In 1986 werd de Oosterscheldedam voltooid, de laatste grote schakel in de Deltawerken, die dit land moet beschermen tegen stormvloeden.

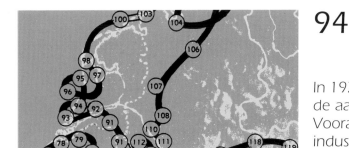

In 1929 werd onder Pernis begonnen met de aanleg van de Eerste Petroleumhaven. Vooral na 1945 heeft de petrochemische industrie hier een grote vlucht genomen. Mede daardoor kon Rotterdam uitgroeien tot de grootste haven ter wereld.
Aan de andere kant van de Nieuwe Waterweg ligt het Westland, een tuinbouwgebied bij uitstek.
Nog weer iets noordelijker: de bloembollenstreek, die vooral in het voorjaar veel toeristen trekt.

I 1929 begyndte man nedenfor Pernis at anlægge den Første Bensinhavn. Særligt efter 1945 har den petrokemiske industri i dette område fået et stort opsving. Bl.a. af den grund er Rotterdam vokset til at blive verdens største havn.
På den anden side af Den Nye Vandvej ligger Westland, et fremtrædende gartneriområde.
Endnu lidt mere mod nord ligger blomsterløgsområdet, der særligt om foråret trækker mange turister.

1929 wurde unterhalb von Pernis mit dem Bau des ersten Erdölumschlaghafens begonnen, und nach dem Zweiten Weltkrieg nahm die petrochemische Industrie Rotterdams einen ungeahnten Aufschwung. Heute ist der Rotterdamer Hafen der größte der Welt.
Jenseits des Nieuwe Waterweg liegt Westland, ein Gartenbaugebiet ganz besonderer Art.
Weiter nördlich erstreckt sich der 'Bloembollenstreek', das Tulpenanbaugebiet, das besonders im Frühjahr viele Touristen anlockt.

In 1929, work commenced near the town of Pernis on the construction of the world's first oil port. The petrochemical industry has assumed enormous proportions, particularly since 1945, and this has contributed to the development of Rotterdam as the world's largest seaport.

On the other side of the 'Nieuwe Waterweg' is Westland, predominantly a horticultural area.

Further to the north is the area where bulbs are cultivated. It attracts a great many visitors, especially in the springtime.

En 1929 se comenzó al sur de Pernis la construcción del primer Puerto Petrolero. Sobre todo tras 1945 la industria petroquímica ha crecido enormemente. En parte gracias a ello Rotterdam se ha convertido en el mayor puerto del mundo.

Al otro lado del Nieuwe Waterweg se halla Westland, el terreno jardinero por excelencia. Un poco más al norte: la zona de los bulbos que, especialmente en la primavera atrae a muchos turistas.

C'est en 1929, près de Pernis, que commença l'aménagement du premier port pétrolier. Mais c'est surtout après 1945 que l'industrie pétrochimique a pris son essor ici. Cette activité a notamment permis à Rotterdam de devenir le plus grand port au monde. Sur l'autre rive du nouveau canal, on trouve le Westland, une terre horticole par excellence.

Puis un peu plus au Nord, la région des oignons à fleurs que attirent de nombreux touristes, au printemps tout spécialement.

Nel 1929, sotto Pernis, fu iniziata la costruzione del primo porto petrolifero, ma è soprattutto dopo il 1945 che l'industria petrolchimica si è sviluppata. Questa attività ha fatto sì che Rotterdam diventasse il più grande porto del mondo. Sull'altra sponda del nuovo canale, si trova il Westland, un'eccellente terra orticola.

Un po' più a nord si trova la regione dei bulbi da fiore, che attira numerosi turisti, soprattutto in primavera.

Em 1929 iniciou-se, junto a Pernis, a construção do Primeiro Porto do Petróleo. Em especial depois de 1945, a indústria petroquímica gosou um enorme desenvolvimento. Graças tambem a isso, poude Roterdão desenvolver-se até ao maior porto do mundo.

No outro lado do Novo Canal, encontra-se a região Westland, especializada em horticultura.

Mais para o norte a região dos campos dos bolbos de flores, a qual especialmente na primavera atrai muitos turistas.

Το 1929, κάτω από το Περνίς, άρχισαν τα έργα για το πρώτο λιμάνι Πετρελαίου. Ιδίως μετά το 1945 η πετροχημική βιομηχανία έχει επεκταθεί τρομερά και γι' αυτό μπόρεσε το Ρότερνταμ να ακμάσει και να γίνει το μεγαλύτερο διεθνές λιμάνι του κόσμου.

Στην άλλη πλευρά του νέου Βάτερβεχ βρίσκεται το Βέστλαντ, μια κατ' εξοχή κηπευτική περιοχή.

Και πάλι λίγο βόρεια η χώρα των βολβών που ελκύει κάθε άνοιξη πολλούς τουρίστες.

De officiële naam van Den Haag is 's-Gravenhage. Het is niet de hoofdstad, die eer is voorbehouden aan Amsterdam, maar wel de residentie van de regering en de Koningin. Vanaf het Binnenhof wordt het land bestuurd en hier klopt het hart van de Nederlandse democratie.

De glorie van het oude Amsterdam, zeventiende-eeuwse grachten met aan weerszijden woon- en pakhuizen. De toren van de Westerkerk draagt een gouden keizerskroon.

Haags officielle navn er 's-Gravenhage (grevernes have). Det er ikke hovedstaden, den ære er forbeholdt Amsterdam, men byen er sæde for regeringen og dronningen. Fra Binnenhof regeres landet, og her banker det hollandske demokratis hjerte.

Det gamle Amsterdams stolthed, kanalerne fra det 17. århundrede med beboelseshuse og pakhuse på begge sider. Tårnet på Westerkerk bærer en gylden kejserskrone.

Der offizielle Name von Den Haag ist 's-Gravenhage. Es ist nicht die Hauptstadt – diese Ehre wurde Amsterdam vorbehalten –, sondern Regierungssitz und königliche Residenz. Vom Binnenhof aus, dem Herz der niederländischen Demokratie, wird das Land regiert. Der Stadtkern Amsterdams stammt im wesentlichen aus dem 17. Jahrhundert. Er ist von Kanälen (Grachten) durchzogen, an denen sich Wohn- und Handelshäuser erheben. Den Turm der Westerkerk ziert eine goldene Kaiserkrone.

The official name of The Hague is 's-Gravenhage'. Though it is not the capital of the Netherlands – that honour belongs to the city of Amsterdam – it is the official seat of both the government and the Queen of the Netherlands. The 'Binnenhof' is the place from which the country is governed, thus forming the heart of Dutch democracy. The glory of Old Amsterdam is shown here; a city of canals built in the 17th century, with a mix of both residential houses and warehouses. The tower of the Westerkerk is capped with an emperor's golden crown.

El nombre oficial de La Haya es 's-Gravenhage. No es la capital, ese honor se lo reserva Amsterdam, pero sí es la residencia del Gobierno y de la Reina. Desde el Binnenhof se dirige el país y aquí late el corazón de la democracia holandesa.
La gloria de la antigua Amsterdam los canales del s. XVII y a ambas orillas las viviendas y almacenes. La torre de la Westerkerk tiene una corona imperial de oro.

Le nom officiel de La Haye est 's-Gravenhage. Ce n'est pas la capitale, cet honneur étant réservé à Amsterdam, mais la résidence du Gouvernement et de la Reine. C'est à partir du Binnenhof qu'est dirigé le pays et c'est ici que bat le cœur de la démocratie néerlandaise.
La gloire de la vieille Amsterdam, avec ses canaux du 17e siècle, bordés de part et d'autre de maisons d'habitation et d'entrepôts. La tour de la Westerkerke porte une couronne impérale en or.

Il nome ufficiale dell'Aia è 's-Gravenhage. Essa non è la capitale, onore riservato ad Amsterdam, ma è la residenza del Governo e della Regina. Il Paese è governato dal Binnenhof ed è qui che batte il cuore della democrazia olandese.
La gloria della vecchia Amsterdam con i canali del XII secolo, fiancheggiati da case private e da magazzini. La torre della Westerkerk reca una corona imperiale d'oro.

O nome oficial de Haia é 's-Gravenhage. Ela não é a capital; essa honra cabe a Amesterdão, mas é sim a residência do governo e da Raínha. No complexo Binnenhof é o país governado e aqui bate o coração da democracia holandesa.
A glória da Amesterdão antiga, canais do século XVII, com a ambos os lados as moradias e os armazens. A torre de igreja 'Westerkerk' está encimada por uma coroa imperial de ouro.

Το επίσημο όνομα της Χάγης είναι 's-Gravenhage. Αυτή δεν είναι η πρωτεύουσα της Ολλανδίας, το 'Αμστερνταμ έχει την τιμή αυτή, αλλά είναι μάλιστα η έδρα της κυβέρνησης και της Βασίλισσας. Από το Μπίννενχοφ κυβερνείται η χώρα και εδώ χτυπάει η καρδιά της ολλανδικής δημοκρατίας. Η δόξα του παλαιού 'Αμστερνταμ φαίνεται από τα κανάλια του δέκατου έβδομου αιώνα με σπίτια και αποθήκες και από τα δυό μέρη. Το καμπαναριό της Βέστερκερκ φοράει χρυσή αυτοκρατορική κορόνα.

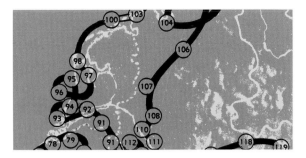

På Zaanse Schans i Zaandam, nordvest for Amsterdam, er der samlet en række karakteristiske zaanse boliger og møller fra de 17. og 18. århundrede. Der er tale om et frilandsmuseum for arkitektur og håndværk fra forgangne tider. Der unge Peter, den senere zar Peter den store af Rusland, lærte her, hvorledes hollænderne byggede skibe, der kunne klare sig på alle have.

Alkmaar er verdensberømt for sine ostekugler og hvidklædte ostebærer. Byen har naturligvis et traditionelt ostemarked. Vægten fra 1582, tæt ved markedet, har et tårn med klokkespil og rytterspil. Mellem Kamperduin og Petten i Nordholland ligger den Hondsbosse Zeewering, et ca. 5 km langt digekompleks. Det blev anlagt efter den ødelæggende St.-Elizabethsstormflod i 1421 og fornyet fra 1870.

Typische Wohnhäuser und Windmühlen erheben sich auf der Zaanse Schans in Zaandam nordwestlich von Amsterdam – ein wahres Freilichtmuseum vergangener Wohn- und Gewerbekultur. Hier konnte vor seiner Thronbesteigung der spätere Zar Peter der Große von den Holländern lernen, wie man Schiffe baut, die allen Stürmen zu trotzen vermochten.

Die von weißgekleideten Trägern beförderten mächtigen Käselaibe von Alkmaar sind weltbekannt. Unweit des historischen Käsemarktes befindet sich die Stadtwaage aus dem Jahr 1582, deren Türmchen ein Glocken- und Reiterspiel ziert.

In den Provinz Nordholland erstreckt sich zwischen Kamperduin und Petten die Hondsbossche Zeewering, ein etwa 5 km langer Deich. Er wurde nach der verhängnisvollen Elisabethsflut 1421 erbaut und nach 1870 erneuert.

At Zaanse Schans in Zaandam, a town to the Northwest of Amsterdam, there are a collection of houses and mills dating from the 17th and 18th century which are characteristic of the Zaan region. This collection of houses and mills forms an open air museum of architecture and the crafts of bygone days. Peter the Great, Tzar of Russia, came here as an apprentice to learn how the Dutch constructed their great sea-going vessels. Alkmaar is famous through the world for its own cheese market and its ball-shaped cheeses and cheese carriers in their traditional white outfits. The Weighing House, built in 1582 near the marketplace, has a turret with a carillon and figures of knights.

A 5 km long wall for protection from the sea was built between Kamperduin and Petten after the disastrous St. Elizabeth's Flood in 1421, and was renewed in 1870.

En el Zaanse Schans en Zaandam, al Noroeste de Amsterdam, se han reunido casas y molinos de la zona de los siglos XVII y XVIII. El conjunto es un museo al aire libre para arquitectura y profesiones artesanales de tiempos pasados. El joven Pedro, que después sería Pedro el Grande de Rusia, aprendió de los holandeses a construir barcos que podían arrostrar todos los mares.

La ciudad de Alkmaar es famosa por sus quesos en forma de bola y sus portadores vestidos de blanco. La ciudad tiene, naturalmente, su mercado folclórico de quesos. El Waag de 1582, cerca del mercado, tiene una torrecita con un carillón y un duelo del caballeros. Entre Kamperduin y Petten, en Holanda Septentrional, se haya el Hondsbosse Zeewering, un complejo de diques de unos cinco kilómetros. Se construyó tras la desastrosa inundación de Santa Isabel de 1421 y se renovó en 1870.

Maisons et moulins du 17e et 18e siècles, caractéristiques de Zaandam, sont rassemblés dans le Zaanse Schans, ou redoute zanoise, au nordouest d'Amsterdam. L'ensemble forme un musée de plein air de l'architecture et de l'artisanat d'époques désormais révolues. Le jeune Pierre, devenu le tsar Pierre le Grand de Russie, apprit ici comment les Hollandais construisaient des bateaux capables d'affronter toutes les mers.

Alkmaar est mondialement connue pour ses fromages ronds et ses porteurs de fromage tout de blanc vêtus. La ville possède naturellement un

Op de Zaanse Schans te Zaandam, ten noordwesten van Amsterdam, zijn karakteristieke Zaanse woonhuizen en molens uit de zeventiende en achttiende eeuw samengebracht. Het geheel is een openluchtmuseum voor architectuur en ambachten uit vervlogen tijden. De jonge Peter, de latere tsaar Peter de Grote van Rusland, leerde hier hoe de Hollanders schepen bouwden die alle zeeën konden trotseren.

Alkmaar is wereldberoemd om zijn ronde kaasbollen en de witte kaasdragers. De stad heeft natuurlijk een folkloristische kaasmarkt. De Waag uit 1582, vlakbij de markt, heeft een torentje met carillon en een ruiterspel.

Tussen Kamperduin en Petten in Noord-Holland ligt de Hondsbosse Zeewering, een circa vijf kilometer lang dijkencomplex. Het werd aangelegd na de desastreuse Sint Elisabethsvloed van 1421 en vanaf 1870 vernieuwd.

marché folklorique aux fromages. Le Waag, c'est-à-dire le Poids public, de 1582, près du marché, possède une petite tour avec un carillon et des automates qui participent à un tournoi. Entre Kamperduin et Petten, en Hollande du Nord, se trouve le Hondsbosse Zeewering, un complexe de digues long d'environ 5 kilomètres. Ce complexe a été construit après l'inondation de la Sainte Elisabetn, en 1421, et rénové après 1870.

Case e mulini del XVII e XVIII secolo, tipici di Zaandam, sono raccolti nel Zaanse Schans, a nord-ovest di Amsterdam.

Questo insieme costituisce un museo all'aperto dell'architettura e dell'artigianato di epoche ormai scomparse.
Il giovane Pietro, che sarebbe poi diventato lo zar Pietro il Grande di Russia, proprio qui imparò come gli Olandesi costruivano navi in grado di affrontare qualunque mare.
Alkmaar è conosciuta in tutto il mondo per i suoi formaggi bianchi e per i portatori di formaggio vestiti di bianco. La città possiede un mercato folcloristico del formaggio. La pesa pubblica del 1582, vicino al mercato, possiede un carillon e degli automi che partecipano ad un torneo. Fra Kam-

perduin e Petten, nell'Olanda del Nord, si trova Hondsbosse Zeewering, un complesso di dighe lungo 5 Km che è stato costruito dopo l'inondazione della Santa Elisabetta nel 1421, ed è stato rinnovato dopo il 1870.

No Zaanse Schans em Zaandam, a noroeste de Amesterdão, juntaram-se casas de habitação típicas de Zaandam e moínhos dos séculos XVII e XVIII. Este total forma um museu ao ar livre para mostrar a arquitectura e as artes de tempos passados. O jovem Pedro, mais tarde o Czar Pedro, o Grande da Rússia, aprendeu

aqui a maneira como os Holandeses construiam barcos que podiam navegor em todos os mares. Alkmaar é internacionalmente conhecida pelos seus queijos e os carregadores de queijos vestidos de branco. A cidade tem obviamente um mercado de queijos típico. A Balança (de Waag) de 1582, perto do mercado. tem um torre pequena com carrilhão e jogo de cavaleiros. Entre Kamperduin e Petten no Norte da Holanda encontra-se o Hondsbosse Zeewering, um grupo de diques com cerca de 5 quilómetros de comprimento. Foi construido depois das inundações desastrosas de St.

Elisabeth em 1421 e foi reconstruido a partir de 1870.

Στο Ζαάνσε Σχανς στο Ζαάνταμ, βορειοδυτικά από το Άμστερνταμ, συγκεντρώθηκαν τα χαρακτηριστικά Ζαάνσε σπίτια και οι μύλοι από το δεκατό έβδομο και δέκατο όγδοο αιώνα. Το σύνολο αποτελεί υπαίθριο μουσείο του περασμένου καιρού. Ο μικρός Πέτρος, ο μεταγενέστερος τσάρος ο Μέγας Πέτρος της Ρωσίας έμαθε εδώ πως οι Ολλανδοί κατασκεύαζαν πλοία που μπορούσαν να αντιμετωπίσουν όλες τις θάλασσες. Το Άλκμααρ είναι κοσμοξάκουστο για τα σφαιρικά τυριά του και τους ασπροντυ-

μένους μεταφορείς τυριών. Η πόλη οπωσδήποτε κατέχει λαογραφική αγορά τυριών. Η Βαάχ από το 1582, κοντά στην αγορά, έχει ένα πύργο με κωδωνοστοιχία και αγωνιζόμενους ιππείς. Ανάμεσα στο Κάμπερνταουν και το Πέττεν στο νομό Βόρεια Ολλανδία βρίσκεται το Χόντσμποσσε Ζεέβεριγκ, ένα συγκρότημα φραγμάτων μάκρος περίπου 5 χιλιομέτρων. Χτίστηκε μετά την καταστρεπτική φουσονεριά Αγία Ελίσαμπετ του 1421 και ανανεώθηκε από το 1870.

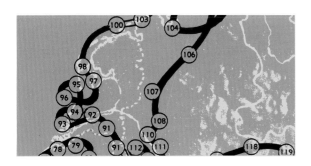

Noord-West Europa heeft één van de grootste natuurgebieden: de Wadden, die zich langs de Noordzee uitstrekken over Noord-Nederland, de Duitse Bocht en Denemar- ken. In zo'n dichtbevolkt en zwaar geïndustrialiseerd gebied is dat een onderwerp van voortdurende zorg. De zeehondencrèche in Pieterburen is daarvan een goed voor-

Nord-vest Europa har et af de største naturområder: Vadehavet, der strækker sig langs med Nordsøen over Nordholland, Den Tyske Bugt og Danmark. I et så tæt befolket og stærkt industriseret område er det et emne, der kræver vedvarende omsorg. Sælhundecentret i Pieterburen er et godt eksempel herpå, og på grund af denne omsorg er sælhunden ikke uddød i dette område. Fra Pieterburen kan man også opleve det sensationelle 'wadlopen', en vandring ved ebbe fra fastlandet til en af vadehavsøerne. Det tilrådes at tage guide med, for havet kan helt uventet stige. Til sidst et billede af landvindingen i Nord Groningen. Havet afsætter slip og trækker sig tilbage.

In Nordwesteuropa gibt es einen der größten Naturparks der Welt, das Wattenmeer, das längs der Nordsee von der niederländischen Nordküste über die Deutsche Bucht bis zur Westküste Dänemarks reicht. In einem so dichtbevölkerten und stark industrialisierten Gebiet ist der Naturschutz von besonderer Dringlichkeit. So hat die Seehundstation in Pieterburen dazu beigetragen, daß diese Meeressäuger hier noch nicht ausgestorben sind. Von Pieterburen aus kann man bei Ebbe eine der Inseln im Watt zu Fuß erreichen – ein eindrucksvolles Erlebnis, bei dem freilich wegen der Gefahr eines plötzlichen Ansteigens des Wassers ortskundige Führung ratsam ist. Abschließend ein Beispiel für die Landgewinnung in Groningen durch die dem Meer neues Nutzland abgerungen wird.

Situated to the North of the Netherlands and extending round Germany to Denmark is one of Northwest Europe's largest nature reserves, the Frisian Islands. In such a densely populated and over-industrialized area, environmental issues give permanent cause for concern. The seal centre in Pieterburen, which has succeded in preventing seals from becoming extinct in this area, is a good example of this environmental awareness. At Pieterburen it is also possible to walk over mudflats at low tide to reach one of the Wadden's islands, but you need an expert guide, as the water can start to rise unexpectedly. Finally, we have a view of land reclamation in Groningen; as the the water recedes the land left behind is reclaimed.

En la Europa del Noroeste, uno de los parques naturales más grandes: los Wadden, que se extienden deesde el Norte de Holanda, la Curva Alemana y Dinamarca. En una zona con tanta densidad de población y tan industrializada este parque es un asunto de cotinua preocupación. La guardería de focas en Pieterburen es un buen ejemplo y gracias a los cuidados la foca no se ha extinguido aquí. Desde Pieterburen se puede experimentar la gran sensación de vadear y llegar a una isla a pie. La compañía de expertos es aconsejable, pues de repente puede subir la marea. Por último una imagen de la lucha contra el Mar en Groninga. El fango del mar se queda y el agua se retira.

L'Europe du Nord-Ouest possède un de ses plus grands parcs naturels: les 'Wadden', qui s'étendent le long de la mer du Nord pour couvrir le Nord des Pays-Bas, la grande baie allemande de la mer du Nord et le Danemark. Dans une région aussi densément peuplée et aussi fortement industrialisée, c'est un objet de préoccupation constante. La crèche aux phoques de Pieterburen en est un bon exemple et c'est grâce à cette précaution que le phoque n'a pas disparu de cette région. A partir de Pieterburen, on peut également éprouver des sensations fortes en franchissant des bas fonds pour atteindre à pied une des îles qui émerge à marée basse. L'accompagnement d'un spécialiste est recommandé car la mer peut survenir de manière tout à fait imprévisible. Enfin une image de terre gagnée sur la mer en Groningue. La vase de la mer se dépose et l'eau se retire.

L'Europa del Nord possiede uno dei più grandi parchi naturali: i 'Wadden' che si estendono lungo il Mare del Nord, coprono il Nord dell'Olanda, la grande baia tedesca del Mar del Nord e la Danimarca. In una regione così densamente popolata e industrializzata, questa è una fonte di preoccupazione costante. L'asilo per le foche di Pieterburen ne è un buon esempio, poichè è grazie a questa istituzione che la foca sopravvive ancora in questa regione.

A partire de Pieterburen si possono avere forti emozioni attraversando il mare a bassa marea per raggiungere a piedi una delle isole che emerge. E' necessaria tuttavia la presenza di un esperto poichè il mare potrebbe improvvisamente risalire. Un'ultima immagine di terra strappata al mare nel Groningen. La melma del mare si deposita e l'acqua si ritira.

O Nordeste da Europa tem um dos maiores terrenos naturais: os Vaus, que se estendem ao longo do Mar do Norte, no Norte de Holanda, a Curva da Alemanha e na Dinamarca. Numa região como esta com grande densidade de população e muito industrializada são estes monumentos naturais uma questão que causa muitos cuidados. A creche para focas em Pieterburen é um bom exemplo e graças a esses bons cuidados as focas ainda não foram extinguidas aqui. Partindo de Pieterburen pode-se gosar a sensação de passar um vau e atingir uma ilha a pé, com maré baixa. A companhia de um especialista é indespensável, pois o mar pode surpreender-nos. Finalmente uma imagem da conquista de terra em Groningen. O lodo do mar deposita-se e a água retira-se.

Η Βορειοδυτική Ευρώπη έχει ένα από τους μεγαλύτερους φυσικούς χώρους, τους Βάντεν,

beeld en dankzij die zorg is de zeehond hier niet uitgestorven. Vanaf Pieterburen kan men ook de sensatie beleven van het wadlopen en een waddeneiland bij eb per voet bereiken. Deskundige begeleiding is wel gewenst, want de zee kan onverwachts opkomen.

Tenslotte een beeld van de landaanwinning in Noord-Groningen. Het slib van de zee zet zich af en het water trekt zich terug.

που εκτείνονται κατά μήκος της Βόρειου Θάλασσας στην Βόρεια Ολλανδία, Γερμανία και Δανία. Σε μια τόσο πυκνοκατοικημένη και βαρειά εκβιομηχανισμένη περιοχή είναι αυτό διχώς άλλο θέμα συνεχούς φροντίδας. Το φωκιοκομείο στο Πήτερνπουρεν είναι καλό παράδειγμα και χάρη της φροντίδας αυτής δεν ξεκληρίστηκε εδώ η φώκια. Από το Πήτερμπουρεν μπορεί κανείς να απολαύσει την αίσθηση του περιπάτου πάνω στα ρηχά και να φτάσει πεζά κατά την άμπωτη σ'ένα Φρεισικό νησί. Ειδικευμένη συνοδεία είναι όμως επιθυμητή, γιατί η θάλασσα μπορεί να σηκωθεί ξαφνικά. Τελικά μια εικόνα της αποξήρανσης εδάφους στο Βόρειο Γκρόνιγκεν. Ο ιλύς της θάλασσας καθιζάνεται και το νερό αποσύρεται.

7
Bundesrepublik
DEUTSCHLAND I

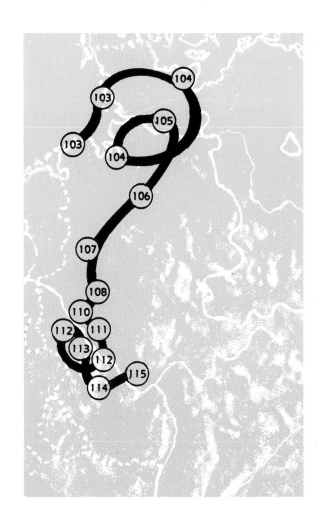

Das nach dem Zweiten Weltkrieg völlig zerstörte, inzwischen aber wieder aufgebaute Helgoland, ein Paradies für Zugvögel, kam erst 1890 an Deutschland. Damals wurde es von England gegen Sansibar eingetauscht. Emden in Ostfriesland wurde während des niederländischen Freiheitskampfes im 16. Jahrhundert zum Bollwerk des Calvinismus und zum Nothafen der Niederländer. Als Seeumschlagshafen hat die Stadt inzwischen allerdings einiges von ihrer früheren Bedeutung eingebüßt.

Helgoland, et paradis for trækfugle, var under den anden verdenskrig en meget stærk tysk flådebase. Den frisisktalende ø blev først tysk i 1890, da England byttede øen med Zanzibar.
Emden, i Østfrisland, var i det 16. århundrede den reformerte protestantismes højborg og et tilflugtsted for hollændere. I dag er det Forbundsrepublikkens fjerde største havn.

Despite being used as a heavily fortified base for the German fleet during both World Wars, Helgoland is a paradise for many species of migratory birds. This island, whose official language is Frisian, was first annexed by Germany in 1890 when England exchanged it for Zanzibar. Emden, in East Friesland, was a stronghold of Calvinism in the 16th century and a haven of refuge for the Dutch. Today it is Germany's fourth largest port.

Helgoland, un paraíso para las aves migradoras, fue durante las guerras mundiales una base naval alemana muy fortalecida. La isla de habla frisona se hizo alemana cuando en 1890 Alemania se la cambió a Inglaterra por Zanzibar.
Emden, en Frisia-Oriental, fue en el siglo XVI un centro del protestantismo reformado y un lugar de refugio para holandeses. Ahora es el cuarto puerto de la Alemania Federal.

Helgoland, un paradis pour les oiseaux migrateurs, fut, pendant les guerres mondiales, une base fortifiée pour la flotte allemande. L'île, de langue frisonne, fut rattachée, en 1890 seulement, à l'Allemagne lorsque l'Angleterre l'échangea contre Zanzibar.
Emden, en Frise Orientale, fut, au 16e siècle, une forteresse du protestantisme réformé et un centre d'accueil pour les habitants des Pays-Bas que avaient fui leur patrie. Aujourd'hui, c'est le 14e port de la République Fédérale d'Allemagne.

Helgoland, un paradiso per gli uccelli migratori, fu durante le guerre mondiali, una base fortificata per la flotta tedesca. L'isola di lingua frisone, fu riunita alla Germania solo nel 1890 quando l'Inghilterra la cedette in cambio di Zanzibar. Emden, nella Frisia Orientale fu, nel XVI secolo, una roccaforte del protestantesimo riformato e un rifugio per gli abitanti dei Paesi Bassi fuggiti dalla loro patria. Oggi è il quarto porto della Repubblica Federale Tedesca.

Helgoland, een paradijs voor trekvogels, was tijdens de wereldoorlogen een zwaar versterkte Duitse vlootbasis. Het Friessprekende eiland kwam eerst in 1890 bij Duitsland toen het door Engeland tegen Zanzibar geruild werd. Emden, in Oost-Friesland, was tijdens de zestiende eeuw een bolwerk van het gereformeerde protestantisme en een vluchthaven voor de Nederlanders. Thans is het de vierde haven van de Bondsrepubliek.

Helgoland, um paraíso para aves de migração, foi durante as guerras mundiais uma base da marinha alemã bastante fortificada. A ilha onde se fala o idioma frísio, passou a ser alemão, quando a Alemanha a trocou com a Inglaterra por Zanzibar.
Emden na Frísia Oriental, foi no século XVI um baluarte do protestantismo reformado e um porto de refúgio para os holandeses. Presentemente é o quarto porto da Alemanha Federal.

Το Χέλγολαντ, παράδεισος για μεταβατικά πουλιά, ήταν κατά τους δυο παγκόσμιους πολέμους μια βαρειά οχυρωμένη ναυτική βάση. Το νησί όπου η ομιλούσα γλώσσα είναι τα Φρεισικά προστέθηκε μόλις το 1980 στη Γερμανία, όταν η Αγγλία το αντάλλαξε με το Ζάνζιμπαρ.
Το Έμπτεν, στην Ανατολική Φρεισία, κατά το δέκατο έκτο αιώνα ήταν προμαχώνας του μεταρρυμιστικού προτεσταντισμού και καταφύγιο για τους Ολλανδούς. Τώρα είναι το τέταρτο λιμάνι της Ομοσπονδιακής Δημοκρατίας.

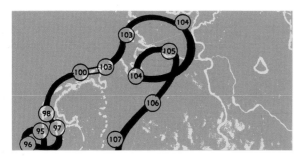

Der Ostseehafen Lübeck war im Mittelalter Drehscheibe der Hanse, eines fast 200 Städte umfassenden Bündnisses, das das Wirtschaftsleben im Nord- und Ostseeraum beherrschte. Dazu gehörten auch Hamburg und Bremen; alle drei Städte bezeichnen sich noch heute offiziell als Hansestadt. Derzeit hat Hamburg den größten und

Østersøhavnen Lübeck ligger nu ved grænsen til DDR, men var engang centrum for de tyske hanseater: fra den Botniske bugt til Holland.
Også Bremen og Hamburg tilhørte dette forbund og de tre byer kalder sig stadig stolt: Hanzestad. Hamburg har nu den største havn og Bremen, med Bremerhaven, er nummer to. Bag Hamburgs havn ser vi Michaeliskirche med dens 132 m høje tårn, der er den største nordtyske bys symbol.

Lübeck is now situated on the border with the GDR. It was, however, once the centre of the German Hanseatic League, which extended from the Gulf of Finland far into the Netherlands. Bremen and Hamburg were also part of the League, and the two cities still call themselves Hanse cities. Today, Hamburg and Bremen are Germany's largest and second largest ports respectively. Behind Hamburg harbour there is the Michaelskirche which, with its 132m white tower is a landmark of Northern Germany's largest city.

El Puerto Oriental de Lübeck se haya ahora en la frontera con la República Democrática Alemana, pero en su tiempo fue el centro del ansa alemana: del golfo finlandés hasta la lejana Holanda.
También Brema y Hamburgo pertenecían al ansa y las tres ciudades con orgullo se llaman aún: Ciudades del Ansa. Hamburgo tien ahora el puerto más grande y Brema, con su puerto, es la número dos. Detrás del puerto de Hamburgo vemos la Iglesia de San Miguel con su alta y blanca torre de 132 metros, el símbolo de la gran ciudad alemana.

Lübeck, port situé sur la Baltique, se trouve à la frontière de la R.D.A., mais fut autrefois le centre de la Hanse allemande qui s'étendait depuis le golfe de Finlande jusque loin aux Pays-Bas. Brême et Hambourg étaient Erattachés à la Ligue hanséatique et les 3 villes s'appellent aujourd'hui encore avec fierté: ville de la Hanse. Hambourg a le port le plus grand, tandis que Brême est numéro deux. Derrière le port de Hambourg, nous voyons la Michaeliskirche, avec sa haute tour blanche de 132 m, le symbole de la plus grande ville du Nord de l'Allemagne.

Lubecca, situata sul Mar Baltico, si trova sul confine della Repubblica Democratica Tedesca, ma è stata un tempo il centro della 'Hanse' tedesca che si estendeva dal Golfo di Finlandia fino ai Paesi Bassi. Brema ed Amburgo appartenevano alla lega anseatica e le tre città si chiamano ancora oggi con orgoglio: città della Hanse. Amburgo ha il porto più grande e Brema le è seconda per importanza. Dietro al porto di Amburgo vediamo la Michaeliskirche, con la grande torre bianca alta 132 metri, simbolo della più grande città del nord della Germania.

O porto do Mar Báltico Lübeck encontra-se actualmente na fronteira com a RDA, mas em tempos foi o foco da Hanze alemã: do Golfo Finlandês até aos Países Baixos. Bremen e Hamburgo tambem faziam parte e as três cidades ainda hoje se chamam com orgulho: as cidades de Hanza. Hamburgo tem presentemente o maior porto e Bremen, com o Porto Bremen, é o segundo. Atrás do porto de Hamburgo vemos a igreja de Micael, com a sua torre branca de 132 m de altura, o símbolo da maior cidade do Norte da Alemanha.

Lübeck ligt aan de DDR-grens, maar was eens het middelpunt van de Duitse Hanze: van de Finse Golf tot ver in de Nederlanden. Ook Bremen en Hamburg hoorden hierbij en de drie steden noemen zich nog steeds trots: Hanzestad. Hamburg heeft nu de grootste haven en Bremen, met Bremerhaven, is nummer twee. Achter de haven van Hamburg zien we de Michaeliskirche, met zijn 132 m hoge witte toren het symbool van de grootste Noordduitse stad.

Η Λυβέκκη στη Βαλτική Θάλασσα βρίσκεται σήμερα στα σύνορα της Ανατολικής Γερμανίας, αλλά άλλοτε ήταν το κέντρο της γερμανικής χανσεατικής ένωσης; από το Φιννικό Κόλπο μέχρι και πέρα στην Ολλανδία. Επίσης η Βρέμη και το Αμβούργο ήταν μέλη της ένωσης αυτής και οι τρείς πόλεις ονομάζονται ακόμα υπερήφανα; Χανσεατικές Πόλεις. Το Αμβούργο σήμερα έχει το μεγαλύτερο λιμάνι και η Βρέμη με το Μπρεμερσχάφεν είναι δεύτερη. Πίσω από το λιμάνι του Αμβούργου βλέπουμε τη Μιχαέλισκιρχε που με το 132μ. ψηλό άσπρο καμπαναριό της είναι το σύμβολο της μεγαλύτερης Βορειογερμανικής πόλης.

Bremen mit Bremerhaven den zweitgröß-
ten Hafen der Bundesrepublik.
Hinter dem Hamburger Hafen erhebt sich
der 132 m hohe patinierte Turm der Michaeliskirche, das Symbol der größten Stadt
Norddeutschlands.

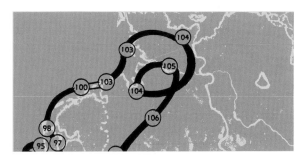

Heute ist Hannover die Hauptstadt des Bundeslandes Niedersachsen, doch bis 1866 war Hannover ein selbständiges Königreich, das von 1714 bis 1839 – unterbrochen durch die französische Besetzung zur Zeit Napoleons – in Personalunion mit England verbunden war. Nach den starken Zerstörungen des Zweiten Weltkriegs wurden viele Gebäude restauriert oder neu errichtet. Ein Opfer des Krieges wurde das Schloß Herrenhausen, dessen berühmte Gärten glücklicherweise erhalten blieben. Auch Münster, die historische Hauptstadt Westfalens, wurde zum größten Teil zerstört. Hier hat man fast die ganze Stadt im ursprünglichen Stil wiederaufgebaut. In neuem Glanz erstrahlt auch der Paulus-Dom, der auf das Jahr 1225 zurückgeht. Unweit des Domplatzes liegt der von Lauben- und Giebelhäusern der Gotik und Renaissance gesäumte berühmte Prinzipalmarkt.

Hannover er i dag Nedersaksens hovedstad, men den var indtil 1866 et selvstændigt kongerige, der fra 1714 til 1839, afbrudt af napoleonstiden, var i personalunion med England. Byen blev for en stor del ødelagt under den anden verdenskrig, men mange monumenter er restaureret eller genopbygget. Desværre gælder det ikke for slottet Herrenhausen, men den berømte Herrenhauser Garten eksisterer heldigvis stadig.
Münster, Westfalens historiske by, blev også for en stor del ødelagt. Byen er dog næsten helt genopbygget i sin oprindelige skikkelse. Og domkirken fra 1225 smykker nu igen byen. Bag Domplatz ligger nu atter det berømte Prinzipalmarkt omgivet af arkader og gotiske renæssancegavle.

Nowadays, Hannover is the capital of Lower Saxony. It was an independent kingdom until 1866, united with England from 1714 to 1839, broken by a short period of French rule. During the Second World War there was extensive damage to the city; however many monuments have been restored or rebuilt. Fortunately the famous Herrenhausen Garten was not badly damaged, but Herrenhausen Castle was not so fortunate. The historical capital of Westphalia, Münster, was also largely destroyed. Virtually the entire city has since been reconstructed in its original style. The cathedral, which dates from 1225, is now once again complete. Behind the Cathedral square surrounded by arcades and Gothic facades is the famous 'Prinzipalmarkt'.

Hannover es ahora la capital de la Baja Sajonia pero hasta 1866 fue un reino independiente que de 1714 a 1839, con una pausa en la época francesa, estuvo unida personalmente con Inglaterra. La ciudad fue destruida en gran parte durante la Segunda Guerra Mundial, pero muchos monumentos han sido restaurados y reconstruidos. Pero no el castillo Herrenhausen ya que esta famosa construcción se salvo.
Münster, la histórica capital de Westfalia, fue destruida casi en su totalidad. Aquí se ha reconstruido prácticamente toda la ciudad en su estilo original. Y la Catedral de 1225, vuelve a adornar la ciudad. Detrás de la Plaza de la Catedral se hayan los famosos soportales y las góticas fachadas renacentistas que rodean el mercado Principal.

Hanovre est aujourd'hui la capitale de la Basse-Saxe, mais jusqu'en 1866, ce fut un royaume autonome qui, de 1714 à 1839, avec comme interruption la période française, fut uni personnellement avec l'Angleterre. La ville fut détruite en grande partie pendant la Seconde Guerre mondiale, mais de nombreux monuments ont été restaurés ou reconstruits. A l'exception, toutefois, du château de Herrenhauser; heureusement, le célèbre jardin de Herrenhauser a subsisté jusqu'aujourd'hui.
Münster, la capitale historique de la Westphalie, fut elle aussi très ravagée. Ici également, on a reconstruit la totalité de la ville dans son style d'origine et le 'Dom', qui date de 1225, orne à nouveau la ville. Derrière la place de la Cathédrale (Domplatz) se trouve le Prinzipalmarkt, célèbre pour ses arcades et les façades renaissance gothiques qui l'entourent.

Το Αννόβερο τώρα είναι η πρωτεύουσα της Κάτω Σαξωνίας, αλλά μέχρι το 1866 ήταν αυτόνομο βασιλείο που από το 1714 μέχρι το 1839, διακοπτούμενο από τη γαλλική εποχή, ήταν ενωμένο με την Αγγλία σε προσωπική ένωση. Ένα μεγάλο μέρος της πόλης καταστράφηκε κατά το δε ύτερο παγκόσμιο πόλεμο, αλλά πολλά μνημεία ανακαινίστηκαν ή ανοικοδομήθηκαν. Όχι όμως ο πύργος Χέρρενχαουσεν, αλλά ευτυχώς ο φημισμένος κήπος του Χέρρενχαουσεν συνεχίζει να υπάρχει.
Το Μύνστερ, η ιστορική πρωτεύουσα της Βεστφαλίας, καταστράφηκε επίσης για ένα μεγάλο μέρος. Εδώ όμως ανοικοδομήθηκε περίπου όλη η πόλη στον αρχικό της ρυθμό. Και ο Καθεδρικός ναός από το 1225 ξανακοσμάει την πόλη. Πίσω από το Ντόμπλατς βρίσκεται πάλι η φημισμένη Πρι ντσιπάλμαρκτ, τριγυρισμένη από στοές και γοτθικές προσόψεις της Αναγέννησης.

Hannover, capitale della Bassa Sassonia, fu un regno indipendente fino al 1866 e dal 1714 al 1839, eccettuato il periodo di dominazione francese, fu unita all'Inghilterra. La città fu quasi interamente distrutta durante la seconda guerra mondiale, ma numerosi monumenti sono stati restaurati o ricostruiti. Fa eccezione il castello di Herrenhausen di cui fortunatamente è rimasto il celebre giardino.
Anche Münster, capitale storica della Vestfalia, fu quasi completamente distrutta e poi ricostruita nel suo stile originario. Il 'Dom', che risale al 1225, ab-

bellisce nuovamente la città. Dietro la Piazza della Cattedrale si trova il Prinzipalmarkt, celebre per le sue arcate e le facciate in stile gotico rinascimentale.

Hannover is nu de hoofdstad van Nedersaksen, maar het was tot 1866 een zelfstandig Koninkrijk, dat van 1714 tot 1839, onderbroken door de Franse tijd, in een personele unie verenigd was met Engeland. De stad werd in de Tweede Wereldoorlog grotendeels verwoest, maar veel monumenten zijn gerestaureerd of herbouwd. Echter niet het kasteel Herrenhausen, maar de beroemde Herrenhaüser Garten bleef gelukkig wel bestaan.
Münster, de historische hoofdstad van Westfalen, werd ook grotendeels verwoest. Hier

heeft men vrijwel de hele stad in oorspronkelijke stijl herbouwd. En de Dom, van 1225, siert nu weer de stad. Achter de Domplatz ligt weer de beroemde met arcaden en gotische renaissancegevels omgeven Prinzipalmarkt.

Hannover é agora a capital da Saxónia de Baixo, mas foi até 1866 um reinado independente, que esteve ligado à Inglaterra por uma união pessoal, com interrupção do período francês. A cidade foi destruída em grande parte, durante a segunda Guerra Mundial, mas muitos monumentos foram restaurados ou reconstruídos. No entanto, não o foi o castelo Herrenhausen; o famoso jardim de Herrenhausen continuou a existir, felizmente.
Münster, a histórica capital da Vestfália, foi tambem destruída em grande parte. Aqui

reconstruiu-se quase toda a cidade no estilo original. E a Sé de 1225, embeleza novamente a cidade. Atrás de Praça da Sé encontra-se o famoso Mercado Principal com arcades a fachadas góticas da Renascência.

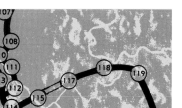

Das Ruhrgebiet in Nordrhein-Westfalen ist mit seinen 4970 Quadratkilometern und 5,7 Millionen Einwohnern das Zentrum der deutschen Schwerindustrie und Steinkoh-lenförderung, was ihm im Volksmund den Beinamen 'Kohlenpott' eingebracht hat. Lange Kernraum der deutschen Wirtschaft, machte das Ruhrgebiet im Gefolge der

Med sine 4970 km2 og 5,7 millioner indbyggere er Ruhrdistriktet i Nordrhein-Westfalen den tyske svær- og kulmineindustris største centrum. I folkemunde hedder distriktet 'Kohlenpott'. På grund af den europæiske kulkrise gennemgår Ruhrdistriktet, der længe ansås for den tyske økonomis pulsåre, også en vanskelig tid. Der hvor floderne Ruhr og Emscher munder ud i Rhinen ligger Duisburg-Ruhrort, der er Europas største indlandshavn.

The Ruhrgebiet in Nordrhein-Westfalia has the greatest concentration of German industry and is Germany's largest coal-mining region, known by the locals as the 'Kohlenpott' (coal cap). As a result of the European coal crisis, the Ruhrgebiet, which has long been the heart of the German economy, is experiencing difficult times. Duisburg-Ruhrort is situated at the mouth of the Ruhr and the Emscher in the Rhine, and is Europe's largest inland harbour.

Con sus 4970 km2 y 5,7 millones de habitantes la región del Rhur, en Nordrhein-Westfalia, el gran centro de la industria pesada alemana y del carbón. En el lenguaje popular la región se llama 'Kohlenpott'. Debido a la crisis europea del carbón la región del Ruhr, que durante mucho tiempo fuera le arteria de la economía alemana, pasa tiempos difíciles. En la desembocadura del Ruhr y del Emscher en el Rin se haya Duisburgo-Ruhrgot, del puerto fluvial más grande de Europa.

Avec ses 4970 km², et ses 5,7 millions d'habitants, la Ruhr, en Rhénanie de Nord-Westphalie, constitue le centre le plus important de l'industrie lourde et de l'industrie minière allemandes. Dans le langage populaire, ce territoire s'appelle le 'Kohlenpott'. La Ruhr connaît elle aussi la crise charbonnière qui a secoué l'Europe et après avoir été longtemps le véritable révélateur de l'économie allemande, elle connaît aujourd'hui des temps difficiles. A l'embouchure de la Ruhr et de l'Emscher on trouve Duisburg-Ruhrort, le plus grand port fluvial d'Europe.

Con una superficie di 4970 Km e 5,7 milioni di abitanti, la Ruhr, nella Renania del nord-Vestfalia, rappresenta il centro più importante dell'industria pesante e di quella del carbone. In linguaggio popolare, questo territorio si chiama il 'Kohlenpott'. Anche la Ruhr è coinvolta nella crisi europea del carbone e quindi, dopo essere stata per decenni il cuore dell'economia tedesca, si trova oggi in crisi. Alla fòce della Ruhr e dell'Emscher si trova Duisburg-Rhurort, il più grande porto fluviale d'Europa.

Met zijn 4970 km2 en 5,7 miljoen inwoners is het Ruhrgebied, in Nordrhein-Westfalen, het grootste centrum van de Duitse zware industrie en steenkoolmijnbouw. In de volksmond heet het gebied 'Kohlenpott'. Met de Europese steenkoolcrisis verkeert ook het Ruhrgebiet, dat lange tijd als slagader van de Duitse economie gold, in een moeilijke tijd. Aan de monding van de Ruhr en de Emscher in de Rijn ligt Duisburg-Ruhrort de grootste Europese binnenhaven.

Com os seus 4970 km2 e 5,7 milhões de habitantes é a região do Rur, no Reno, do Norte-Vestfália, o mair centro de indústria pesada e da exploração de carvão de pedra da Alemanha. Na voz popular chama-se esta região o 'Kohlenpott'. Com a crise europeia de carvão de pedra, encontra-se tambem a Região do Rur, que durante muito tempo foi a artéria principal da economia alemã, num período difícil. Na foz do Rur e do Emscher, no Reno, encontra-se Duisburg-Ruhrort, o maior porto interno da Europa.

Η περιοχή του Ρουρ, στη Νορντράιν-Βεστφαλία, με τα 4970 τετραγωνικά χιλιόμετρα και με τα 5,7 εκατομμύρια κατοίκους είναι το μεγαλύτερο κέντρο της γερμανικής βαρειάς βιομηχανίας και ανθρακωρυχίας.
Στη λαϊκή γλώσσα αυτή η περιοχή λέγεται 'Κώλενποτ'. Με την ευρωπαϊκή κρίση άνθρακα περνάει και το Ρούργκεμπητ, που ισχυούσε για πολύ καιρό ως αρτηρία της γερμανικής οικονομίας, στα πολύ δύσκολα χρόνια. Στην εκβολή του Ρούρ και του 'Εμσερ στο Ρήνο βρίσκεται το μεγαλύτερο εσωτερικό λιμάνι της Ευρώπης· το Ντύσμπεργκ-Ρούρορτ.

europäischen Kohle- und Stahlkrise schwere Zeiten durch, doch wurden inzwischen umfangreiche Maßnahmen zur wirtschaftlichen Sanierung eingeleitet. Duisburg-Ruhrort, der größte Binnenhafen Europas, liegt an der Mündung von Ruhr und Emscher in den Rhein. Er hat seine zentrale Bedeutung nach wie vor behalten.

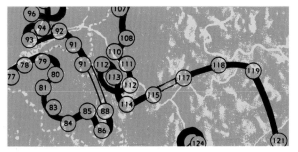

Düsseldorf, die Hauptstadt von Nordrhein-Westfalen, wurde nach den Zerstörungen des Zweiten Weltkriegs rasch wiederaufgebaut und mit seinen modernen Anlagen und luxuriösen Geschäftsstraßen zu einem Inbegriff des deutschen Wirtschaftswunders. Zahlreiche historische Gebäude in der Altstadt sind Zeugnisse einer reichen Ge-

schichte. Leverkusen ist eine blühende Industriestadt mit Rheinhafen. Neben Textil- und Schwerindustrie hat hier auch ein chemisches Unternehmen von Weltruf seinen Sitz: die Farbenfabriken Bayer AG, denen letztlich die erst 1930 durch den Zusammenschluß von vier Gemeinden gebildete Stadt ihre Entstehung und heutige Bedeutung verdankt.

Den efter krigen hurtigt genopbyggede Düsseldorf, hovedstad i Nordrhein-Westfalen, vidner med sine luksuriøse butiksgader og moderne anlæg om det tyske 'Wirtschaftswunder'. I Altstadt kan byens historie endnu aflæses fra de talrige historiske bygninger. I industribyen og rhinhavnen Leverkusen har blandt forskellige jern-, stål- og tekstilfabrikker først og fremmest den kemiske kæmpe af verdensformat Farbenfabriken Bayer A.G. hjemme. Særligt kendt for sine aspirintabletter.

Düsseldorf, capital of Westfalia, with its modern architecture and luxurious shopping streets rebuilt soon after the war, is living proof of the German 'Wirtschaftswunder'. In the Aldstadt the development of the city is visible in the numerous historical buildings. Various iron, steel and textile factories are situated in the industrial city and Leverkusen, its port on the Rhine, but its major industrial enterprise is the gigantic multinational company Farbenfabriken Bayer AG, best known for the.'Asprin'.

Con su construcción moderna y sus modernas calles de tiendas Düsseldorf, la capital de la Rin Septentrional Westfalia, es una muestra de la rápida reconstrucción tras la guerra, la 'wirtschaftswunder' alemana. En la Aldstadt la historia de la ciudad se puede leer en la multitud de edificios históricos. En la ciudad industrial y el puerto al Rin Leverkusen junto a las fábricas de hierro, acero y textiles está establecida sobre todo el gigante de la química Farbenfabriken Bayer A.G. Muy conocida por sus aspirinas.

Avec ses aménagements modernes et ses rues commerçantes luxueuses, Düsseldorf, reconstruit rapidement après la guerre, est la capitale de la Rhénanie de Nord-Westphalie. Elle témoigne du miracle économique allemand. Dans la vieille ville, l'histoire peut encore être lue sur de nombreux bâtiments historiques. Ville industrielle et port sur le Rhin, Leverkusen, abrite outre diverses usines sidérurgiques et textiles le géant de la chimie Farbenfabriken Bayer A.G., une firme de format mondial (qui, en effet, ne connaît pas ses aspirines?).

Con le moderne costruzioni e le vie fiancheggiate di negozi di lusso, Düsseldorf è la prova tangibile del miracolo economico tedesco operatosi dopo la guerra. Nel centro storico, si possono ancora ammirare numerosi edifici, testimoni della lunga storia della città. Leverkusen, città industriale e porto fluviale sul Reno, è sede di numerose industrie siderurgiche e tessili ed è celebre per la presenza dell'industria chimica Farbenfabriken Bayer A.G., nota soprattutto per le sue aspirine.

Met zijn moderne aanleg en luxeuze winkelstraten getuigt het snel na de oorlog herbouwde Düsseldorf, hoofdstad van Nordrhein-Westfalen, van het Duitse 'Wirtschaftswunder'. In de Altstadt is de geschiedenis van de stad nog af te lezen van talrijke historische gebouwen. In de industriestad en Rijnhaven Leverkusen is naast diverse ijzer-, staal- en textielfabrieken vooral de chemische reus van wereldformaat Farbenfabriken Bayer A.G. gevestigd. Vooral bekend van zijn aspirines.

Com a sua construção moderna e ruas de comércio luxuosas testemunha Dusseldorf, capital do Norte do Reno-Vestfália, reconstruída logo a seguir à guerra, o 'milagre da economia alemã'. Em Altstadt reconhece-se a história da cidade pelos inúmeros edifícios históricos. Na cidade industrial e porto do Reno Leverkusen é, alem das fábricas de ferro, aço e texteis, em especial o gigante da química, de formato mundial Farbenfabriken Bayer A.G., de grande importância. Conhecido em especial pelas aspirinas.

Το γρήγορα μετά το πόλεμο ανοικοδομημένο Ντύσσελντορφ, πρωτεύουσα της Νορντράιν-Βεστφαλίας, είναι με τη μοντέρνα κατασκευή και τους πολυτελείς εμπορικούς δρόμους του, μάρτυρας της γερμανικής 'Wirtschaftswunder'. Στην παλαιά πόλη τα ανάριθμα ιστορικά κτίρια διηγούνται την ιστορία της πόλης. Στη βιομηχανική πόλη και στο λιμάνι του Ρήνου Λέβερκουζεν, εκτός από διάφορα χαλυβδουργεία, σιδηρουργεία και εργοστάσια υφασμάτων, είναι εγκατεστημένος ο χημικός γίγαντας πελώριου αναστήματος Farbenfabriek Bayer A.G. ιδιαίτερα γνωστός από τις ασπιρίνες.

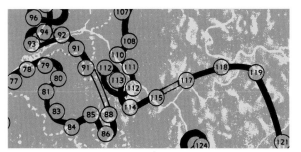

Aachen war seit 794 die Lieblingsresidenz Karls des Großen. Von seinem Palast ist nur die achteckige Pfalzkapelle (heute Kern des Aachener Doms) erhalten, in der von 936 bis 1531 fast alle deutschen Kaiser gekrönt wurden. Bonn wurde im Jahre 1949 die vorläufige Hauptstadt der Bundesrepublik Deutschland und ist es bis heute geblieben.

Fra 794 var Aachen Karl den Stores elskede residens. Fra hans slot er kun det ottekantede Pfalzkapelle tilbage. Fra 936 til 1531 blev alle tyske kejsere kronet her. I 1949 blev Bonn Forbundsrepublikkens midlertidige hovedstad, og det er den stadig. Køln er Rhinlandets største by. Den gamle by, med sin skov af kirketårne, domineres af den enorme gotiske domkirke, der påbegyndtes i 1248.

From 794 Aix-la-Chapelle was the much-loved residence of Charlemagne. The octagonal Pfalzkapelle, where all German emperors were crowned between 936 and 1531, has survived from the original palace. Bonn became the capital of post-war Germany in 1949 and has remained so to the present day. Cologne is the largest city of the Rhineland. The old city, with its forest of church towers, is dominated by its enormous Gothic Cathedral, the construction of which began in 1248.

Aquisgrán fue desde 794 la querida residencia de Carlomagno. De su palacio sólo nos queda la octogonal Pfalzkapelle. De 936 hasta 1531 fueron coronados aquí todos los emperadores alemanes. En 1949 Bonn se convirtió en capital de la República Federal y aún lo sigue siendo. Colonia es la ciudad más grande de la región del Rin. La ciudad antigua, con su bosque de torres, está dominada por la enorme catedral gótica cuya construcción se comenzó en 1248.

Depuis 794, Aix-la-Chapelle était la résidence préférée de Charlemagne. De son palais ne subsiste plus que la Pfalzkapelle, un bâtiment octogonal. De 936 à 1531 c'est dans cette ville que furent couronnés tous les empereurs allemands. En 1949, Bonn devenait la capitale provisoire de la République Fédérale, ce qu'elle est toujours aujourd'hui. Cologne est la plus grande ville de Rhénanie. L'ancienne ville, avec sa forêt de tours d'église, est dominée par l'énorme cathédrale gothique, dont la construction commença en 1248.

Fin dal 794, Aquisgrana era la residenza preferita di Carlomagno. Del suo palazzo è rimasta solo la Pfalzkapelle, un edificio a forma ottagonale. Dal 936 al 1531 tutti gli imperatori tedeschi furono incoronati in questa città. Nel 1949 Bonn divenne la capitale provvisoria della Repubblica Federale tedesca ed essa lo è tuttora. Colonia è la più grande città della Renania. Il centro storico con una selva di torri di chiese è dominato dall'immensa cattedrale gotica, la cui costruzione iniziò nel 1248.

Aken was sedert 794 de geliefkoosde residentie van Karel de Grote. Van zijn paleis rest nog de achthoekige Pfalzkapelle. Van 936 tot 1531 werden hier alle Duitse keizers gekroond. Bonn werd in 1949 de voorlopige hoofdstad van de Bondsrepubliek en is dat nog steeds. Köln is de grootste stad van het Rijnland. De oude stad, met haar woud van kerktorens, wordt beheerst door de enorme gotische Dom, waarvan de bouw in 1248 begon.

Aquisgrano foi desde 794 a residência preferida de Carlos, o Grande. Do seu palácio conservou-se até agora a Pfalzkapelle octogonal. De 936 até 1531 todos os imperadores alemães foram coroados aqui. Bona passou a ser a capital provisória de República Federal Alemã, em 1949, e até agora ainda a é. Colónia é a maior cidade do País do Reno. A cidade antiga, com o seu 'bosque' de torres de igreja, é dominada pela enorme Sé gótica, cuja construção se iniciou em 1248.

Το Άαχεν ήταν από το 794 η αγαπημένη διαμονή του Μεγάλου Καρόλου Από το παλάτι του απέμεινε μόνο η οκτάγωνη Πφάλτσκαπελλε. Από το 936 μέχρι το 1531 εδώ στέφονταν όλοι οι Γερμανοί αυτοκράτορες. Η Βόννη έγινε το 1949 η προσωρινή πρωτεύουσα της Ομοσπονδιακής Δημοκρατίας όπου και ακόμα είναι. Η Κολωνία είναι η μεγαλύτερη πόλη του νομού Ράινλαντ. Η παλαιά πόλη με δάσος από καμπαναριά κυριαρχείται από το πελώριο γοτθικό Καθεδρικό ναό, που το χτίσιμό του άρχισε το 1248.

Die größte Stadt des Rheinlands ist das alt-ehrwürdige Köln, das von einem wahren Wald von Kirchtürmen überragt wird. Das Stadtbild beherrscht der gotische Dom, mit dessen Bau 1248 begonnen wurde. Die Arbeiten wurden freilich immer wieder unterbrochen, und so wurden die beiden mächtigen Türme erst im Jahre 1880 fertiggesellt.

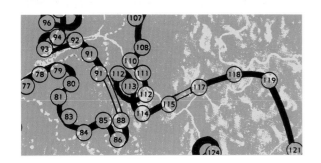

Benediktinerklostret Maria Laach har ligget ved bredden af Laacher See siden 1093. Klosterbiblioteket tæller mere end 120.000 bind.
På Effelsberg i Eifelområdet finder vi det berømte Max Planck Instituts radioteleskop. Cochem ved Moselfloden er en meget yndet turistby.
Koblenz, opstået af en romersk koloni, har fået sit navn på grund af sin beliggenhed på det sted, hvor Rhinen og Mosel flyder sammen, på latin: ad confluentes. På landtungen 'Deutsches Eck' ligger stadig den tyske ordens kommandørbolig fra det 14. århundrede.

Built in 1903, the Benedictine Abbey of Maria Laach is situated on the banks of the Laacher See. The convent library contains more than 120,000 books.
The radio telescope of the celebrated Max Planck Institute can also be found in the Eifel, on the Effelsberg.
Cochem an der Mosel is a very popular town with tourists.
The city of Koblenz had its origins as a Roman settlement, and owes its name to its location on the confluence (in Latin: ad confluentes) of the Rhine and the Mosel. The strip of land called the 'Deutschen Eck' still contains the commander of the Tutonic Order's residence, which dates from the 14th century.

Die Benediktinerabtei Maria Laach am West-ufer des Laacher Sees wurde 1093 gegründet. Die Bibliothek des Klosters umfaßt mehr als 120.000 Bände.
Das Radioteleskop des weltbekannten Max-Planck-Instituts erhebt sich auf dem Effelsberg in der Eifel, einem Teil des Rheinischen Schiefergebirges.

Cochem an der Mosel ist ein malerisches, beliebtes Touristenziel.
Das Römerkastell, aus dem Koblenz hervorgegangen ist, verdankte seinen Namen (ad confluentes) seiner Lage am Zusammenfluß von Mosel und Rhein, der durch eine Landzunge, das 'Deutsche Eck', markiert wird.

A las orillas del Laacher See se encuentra ya desde 1093 la abadía benedictina Maria Laach. La biblioteca del monasterio cuenta con más de 120.000 volúmenes.
También en el Eifel en la Effelsberg encontramos el famoso radiotelescopio del instituto Max Planck.
Cochem an dem Mosel es un lugar preferido de los turistas.
Koblenz, que surgió de un campamento romano y que debe su nombre a su situación en la confluencia, en latín: ad confluentes. del Rin y el Mosela. Ahí, en la lengua de tierra 'Deutsches Eck', se haya la vivienda del comandante de una Orden alemana del siglo XIV.

C'est sur les rives du Laacher See que se dresse depuis 1093 l'abbaye bénédictine de Maria Laach. La bibliothèque du cloître comporte plus de 120000 volumes.
Dans l'Eifel, sur l'Effelsberg, nous trouvons également le radiotélescope du célèbre institut Max Planck.
Cochem, sur la Moselle, est un lieu de villégiature très apprécié.
Coblence, née d'un établissement romain, doit son nom à sa situation au confluent, en latin: ad confluenties, du Rhin et de la Moselle. Sur la langue de terre appelée 'Deutsches Eck' se trouve la maison du commandeur de l'Ordre Allemand qui date du 14e siècle.

Na margem do lago Laacher See está desde 1093 a abadia dos benedictinos Maria Laach. A biblioteca do convento possui mais de 120.000 volumes. Na Eifel encontramos tambem, no monte Effel o radiotelescópio do famoso Instituto Max Planck.
Cochem an dem Mosel é um lugar turístico muito procurado.
Koblenz, originária de uma povoação romana, deve o seu nome à sua posição junto à junção de dois rios: em Latim 'ad confluentes', o Reno e o Mozela. Aí se encontra ainda, na península 'Deutsches Eck', a moradia do comendador da Ordem Alemã, que data do século XIV.

Στις όχθες του Λαάχερζεε υπάρχει κιόλας από το 1093 το αββαείο των Βενεδικτίνων μοναχών. Η βιβλιοθήκη του μοναστηρίου μετράει περισσότερο από 120.000 τομείς. Επίσης στο Άιφελ, πάνω στο Άιφελσμπεργκ, βρίσκουμε το ραδιοτηλεσκόπιο του ξακουστού ινστιτούτου Μαξ Πλανγκ.
Το Κόχεμ αν ντερ Μόζελ είναι αγαπημένη τουριστική πόλη.
Το Κόμπλεντς προήλθε από ρωμαϊκή παροικία και οφείλει το όνομά του στην τοποθεσία που βρίσκεται στη συρροή του Ρήνου και του Μοζέλλα, στα λατινικά: ad confluentes. Εκεί, στη γλώσσα ξηράς 'Ντόιτσες Εκ' από το δέκατο τέταρτο αιώνα βρίσκεται ακόμα η οικία του κυβερνήτη του Τευτονικού Τάγματος.

Sulle rive del Laacher See si trova dal 1093 l'abbazia benedettina di Maria Laach. La biblioteca del monastero conta più di 120.000 volumi.
Nell'Eifel, sull'Effelsberg, si trova anche il famoso radiotelescopia dell'istituto Max Planck, Cochem, sulla Mosella, è una località turistica molto frequentata.
Coblenza, fondata dai Romani, prende nome dalla sua posizione geografica di confluenza di due fiumi: il Reno e la Mosella. Su di una lingua di terra chiamata 'Deutschen Eck' si trova la casa del 'Comandante' dell'Ordine Tedesco, che risale al XIV secolo.

Aan de oevers van de Laacher See staat al sedert 1093 de benedictijnenabdij Maria Laach. De kloosterbibliotheek telt meer dan 120.000 banden.
Ook in de Eifel op de Effelsberg vinden we de radiotelescoop van het beroemde Max Planck Institut.
Cochem an dem Mosel is een zeer geliefde toeristenplaats.
Koblenz, ontstaan uit een Romeinse nederzetting, dankt zijn naam aan zijn ligging aan de samenvloeiing, in het Latijn: ad confluentes, van Rijn en Moezel. Daar staat op de landtong 'Deutsches Eck' nog de commandeurswoning van de Duitse Orde uit de veertiende eeuw.

8
Bundesrepublik DEUTSCHLAND II

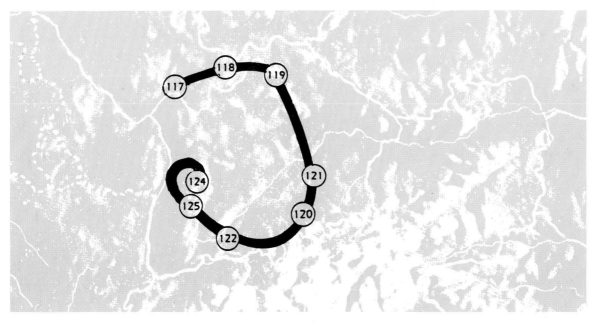

Wegen der das Stadtbild beherrschenden modernen Hochbauten gilt Goethes Geburtsstadt Frankfurt heute als 'amerikanischste' Stadt der Bundesrepublik. Einst Wiege der Rothschilds, ist die Mainmetropole zu einem Finanz- und Wirtschaftszentrum von Weltgeltung geworden. Mit seiner Buchmesse hat es die führende Rolle übernommen, die Leipzig vor dem Kriege hatte. Bedeutend ist auch der Binnenhafen am Main, der nach Fertigstellung des Main-Donau-Kanals sicherlich eine noch größere Rolle in der europäischen Binnenschiffahrt spielen wird.

Med sine moderne skyskrabere gælder Goethes fødeby Frankfurt for at være Tysklands mest 'amerikanske' by. Byen, der engang var Rothschildernes vugge, er et ekønomisk og finansielt centrum. Bogmessen overtog helt den førende rolle som Leipzig havde haft før krigen. Ved floden Main ligger den mest betydningsfulde indlandshavn og med Main-Donaukanalen tilvejebragtes for nylig den forbindelse mellem Nordsøen og Sorte Havet som allerede romerne drømte om.

As a consequence of its modern high-rise buildings, Goethe's birthplace, Frankfurt am Main, has the reputation of being the most Americanised city of the Federal German Republic. Once the home of the Rothschilds, it is now a commercial, financial and major exhibition centre. Its important inland harbour is situated on the River Main; when the Main-Danube Canal is completed, the North Sea and the Black Sea will be connected.

Con sus modernos rascacielos, la ciudad donde nació Goethe es la ciudad más americana de la República Federal. La ciudad, en su día cuna de los Rothschilds, es un centro financiero y comercial. La Buchmesse tomó la dirección que Leipzig tenía antes de la guerra. Al Main se encuentra el importante puerto fluvial y con el canal Main-Donau se realizó recientemente la conexión Mar del Norte-Mar Negro en lo cual ya habían soñado los romanos.

Avec sa tour moderne, la ville natale de Goethe, Francfort, est considérée comme la ville la plus "américaine" de la 'République Fédérale. La ville, qui fut autrefois le berceau des Rothschild, est un centre financier et commercial. La Buchmesse ou Foire du Livre a repris le rôle de leader qu'occupait Leipzig dans ce domaine avant la guerre. Le Main abrite un port fluvial important. Grâce au canal Main-Danube on a réalisé récemment la liaison mer du Nord-mer Noire, dont les Romains rêvaient déjà à leur époque.

Con i suoi moderni grattacieli, Francoforte, città natale di Goethe, è considerata la città più 'americana' della Repubblica Federale. La città, in altri tempi culla dei Rothschild, è un grosso centro finanziario e commerciale. La Buchmesse, o fiera del libro, ha soppiantato Leipzig che aveva un ruolo di primo piano in questo settore da prima della guerra. Sul Reno si trova un importante porto fluviale. Grazie al canale Reno-Danubio si è realizzata recentemente la comunicazione fra Mar del Nord e Mar Nero, di cui già sognavano i Romani.

Met zijn moderne hoogbouw geldt Goethes geboortestad Frankfurt als de meest 'Amerikaanse' stad van de Bondsrepubliek. De stad, eens de bakermat van de Rothschilds, is een financiëel en commercieel centrum. De Buchmesse nam de vooroorlogse leidende rol van Leipzig volledig over. Aan de Main ligt de belangrijke binnenhaven en met het Main-Donau kanaal kwam onlangs de verbinding Noordzee-Zwarte Zee tot stand waarvan de Romeinen al droomden.

Com os seus edifícios altos a cidade onde nasceu Goethe, Franqueforte é considerada a cidade mais 'americana' da República Federal. A cidade, em tempos a pátria dos Rothschilds, é um centro financeiro e comercial. A Buchmesse tomou a seu cargo o papel de chefia que Leipzig tinha antes da guerra. Junto ao Meno encontra-se o importante porto interior e com o canal do Meno e o Danúbio, entre Bamberg e o vale de Altmühl, realiza-se a ligação entre o Mar do Norte e o Mar Negro, do qual já os romanos sonhavam.

Με τα ψηλά της κτίρια η Φραγκφούρτη αμ Μάιν, γενέτειρα του Γκαίτε, ισχύει σαν την πιο 'αμερικανική' πόλη της Ομοσπονδιακής Δημοκρατίας. Η πόλη άλλοτε η κοιτίδα των Ρότσιλντ, είναι χρηματικό και εμπορικό κέντρο. Η Μπούχμεσσε ανέλαβε εντελώς το προπολεμικό ηγετικό ρόλο της Λειψίας. Στο Μάιν βρίσκεται το σημαντικό εσωτερικό λιμάνι και με τη διώρυγα Μάιν-Δούναβις, ανάμεσα στη Βαμβέργη και την κοιλάδα του Άλτμυλ, δημιουργήθηκε πρόσφατα ο σύνδεσμος Βορείου Θάλασσας και Ευξείνου Πόντου που τον ονειρεύονταν ήδη οι Ρωμαίοι.

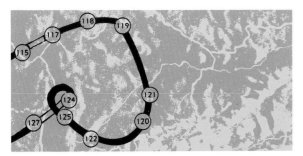

Bamberg ist eine alte fränkische Bischofsstadt mit Dom, Alter Hofhaltung und Rathaus auf einer Insel in der Regnitz. Das Bistum wurde im Jahr 1007 gegründet.

Die Reichsstadt Nürnberg hat trotz schwerer Kriegsschäden viel von ihrem früheren Aussehen zurückgewonnen; Mauern und Türme blieben größtenteils erhalten.

Bamberg, det gamle bayerske bispesæde, hvorfra vi kun nævner domkirken, den Alte Hofhaltung og rådhuset, der ligger på en ø i Regnitzfloden. Trods krigens svære ødelæggelser har Nürnberg, takket være de sparede bymurer og tårne, bevaret meget af sin middelalderlige karakter.
I Oberpfalz gør delstaten Bayern meget for at skaffe arbejde. Ved Schwandorf blev der bygget en aluminiumsfabrik og i Sulzbach-Rosenberg blev Max-Hütten reddet.

Bamberg is the old seat of the bishops of Bavaria, famous for its cathedral, the Alte Hofhaltung, and the Rathaus, which is on an island in the Regnitz. Despite considerable damage during the war, Nürnburg has retained much of its medieval character, largely because the city walls and towers survived. The federal state of Bavaria is trying hard to create employment in Oberpfalz and has built an aluminium factory at Schwandorf, whilst the Max-Hütte in Sulzbach-Rosenberg has now been saved.

Bamberg, la antigua ciudad episcopal de Baviera de la que sólo nombramos la Catedral, el Alte Hofhaltung y el Ayuntamiento, en la isla en el Regnitz. A pesar de los daños de la guerra Nürnberg, gracias a que las murallas y torres se salvaron, ha podido mantener bastante de su carácter.
En la Oberpfalz el estado de Baviera se esfuerza mucho por puestos de trabajo. En Schwandorf se ha fundado una fábrica de aluminio y en Sulzbach-Roseberg se salvo el Max-Hütte.

Bamberg, vieille ville archiépiscopale bavaroise dont nous ne nommerons que la cathédrale, l'Alte Hofhaltung et le Rathaus. Malgré les nombreuses destructions de la guerre, Nuremberg, grâce à ses murailles et à ses tours épargnées, a conservé beaucoup de son caractère.
Dans le Haut-Palatinat, le land de Bavière fait de gros efforts en matière de lutte contre le chômage. Près de Schwandorf, une fabrique d'aluminium a été construite et à Sulzbach-Rosenberg, l'usine sidérurgique de Max-Hütte a été sauvée.

Bamberg, vecchia città arcivescovile della Baviera, di cui ricordiamo solo il Duomo, la Halte Hofhaltung e il Rathaus, su di un'isoletta nel Regnitz. Nonostante i gravi danni subiti durante la guerra, Norimberga conserva il suo carattere grazie alle vecchie mura e alle torri rimaste intatte. Nell'Oberpfalz, il 'Land' di Baviera fa molti sforzi per lottare contro la disoccupazione. Vicino a Schwandorf è stata costruita una fabbrica di alluminio e a Sulzbach-Rosenberg è stata salvata l'industria siderurgica, la Max-Hütte.

Bamberg, de oude Beierse bisschopsstad, waarvan we de Dom, de Alte Hofhaltung en het Rathaus, op een eilandje in de Regnitz, noemen. Ondanks zware oorlogsschade heeft Nürnberg, dankzij de gespaarde stadsmuren en torens, veel van haar karakter behouden. In Oberpfalz doet de deelstaat Beieren veel moeite voor werk. Bij Schwandorf werd een aluminiumfabriek opgericht en in Sulzbach-Rosenberg de Max-Hütte gered.

Bamberg, a velha cidade episcopal da Bavária, da qual só citamos a Dom, Alte Hofhaltung e a Rathaus, numa ilha em Regnitz. Apesar das grandes destruições da guerra, Nurenberga conservou muito do seu carácter, graças ao facto de as suas muralhas e torres terem sido poupadas.
Em Oberpfalz a Bavária faz todos os possíveis para criar trabalho. Perto de Schwandorf foi instalada uma fábrica de alumínio e em Sulzbach-Rosenberg foram acabados de construir os altos-fornos Max-Hütte.

Η Βαμβέργη, το παλαιό επισκοπείο της Βαυαρίας είναι ένα κόσμημα. Από αυτό ονομάζουμε μόνο τον Καθεδρικό ναό, την Άλτε Χόφχαλτουγκ και το Ράτχαους σ' ένα μικρό νησί στο Ρέγνιτς. Παρά τις σοβαρές πολεμικές βλάβες η Νυρεμβέργη, χάρη στα τείχη και τους πύργους που διασώθηκαν, έχει διατηρήσει πολύ από τον χαρακτήρα της. Το ομοσπονδιακό κράτος Βαυαρία καταβάλλει κόπους για να δημιουργήσει απασχόληση στο Ομπερπφάλτς. Στο Σβάντορφ ιδρύθηκε εργοστάσιο αλουμινίου και στο Σούλτσμπαχ-Ρόχενμπεργκ σώθηκε η Μαξ-Χύττε.

Bayern bemüht sich sehr um die wirtschaftliche Stabilisierung der Oberpfalz, so durch ein
Aluminiumwerk bei Schwandorf und die Ret-
tung der Maxhütte in Sulzbach-Rosenberg.

Das am Fuß der Zugspitze gelegene Garmisch-Partenkirchen ist ein beliebter Kur- und Wintersportort. 1936 fanden hier die Olympischen Winterspiele statt.

1972 war die bayerische Hauptstadt München Austragungsort der Olympischen Sommerspiele, für die nordwestlich des Stadtzentrums umfangreiche Anlagen mit Wettkampfstätten und Olympischem Dorf errichtet wurden; überragt werden sie vom Fernsehturm. München ist ein bedeutendes Wirtschafts- und Kulturzentrum und hat die größte Universität der Bundesrepublik. Als Touristenziel ist die Stadt nicht nur während der Oktoberfestzeit weltweit sehr beliebt.

Südlich der Hauptstadt erstrecken sich zahlreiche Voralpenseen, unter ihnen der malerische Ammersee, an dessen Ufern sich einige Meisterwerke deutscher Barockarchitektur finden, aber auch hochmoderne Anlagen wie die hier gezeigte Satelliten-Erdfunkstation bei Raistung mit ihren gewaltigen Antennen-'Schüsseln'.

Garmisch-Partenkirchen es una preferida estación termal y un centro de deportes de invierno muy visitado al pie del Zugspitze. El compositor de ópera alemán Richard Strauss vivió y murió ahí en 1949 en una villa magnífica.

Al nordoeste de la capital de Baviera Munich, está la moderna ciudad olímpica en la que en 1972 se celebraron los Juegos Olímpicos de verano. El deportista entonces más admirado fue el nadador americano Mark Spitz que ganó siete medallas de oro. Esta Olimpiada, sin embargo, fue ensombrecida por al atentado del comando Septiembre Negro contra el equipo de Israel: murieron once niembros de este equipo.

Junta al pequeño y pintoresco lago Ammersee, al sudoeste de Munich, se encuentran famosas maravillas de la arquitectura barroca alemana, como la iglesia Stiftskirche y la iglesia de peregrinacíon en la ciudad Diessen.

Gramisch-Partenkirchen est un centre de cure et de sports d'hiver au pied de la Zugspitze. Le compositeur d'opéras Richard Strauss habitait ici une jolie villa. Il y est décédé en 1949. Au nord-ouest de Munich, capitale de la Bavière, se trouve le village olympique moderne où ont eu lieu les jeux Olympiques d'Eté en 1972. A cette époque, un des sportifs les plus admirés, le nageur américain Mark Spitz avait remporté sept médailles d'or. Pourtant, les jeux Olympiques furent assombris par l'attaque du camp israélien par le commando de Septembre noir; onze membres de cette équipe israélienne y perdirent la vie. Sur le petit lac pittoresque d'Ammersee, au sud-ouest de Munich, on peut admirer les miracles architectoniques du baroque allemand, comme la Stiftskirche et l'église des pélerins à Diessen également.

Garmisch-Partenkirchen è una località di cura e di sport invernali, ai piedi della Zugspitze. Qui visse e morì il compositore tedesco Richard Strauss.

A Nord-Ovest di Monaco, capitale della Baviera si trova il moderno villaggio olimpico in cui si sono svolti i Giochi Olimpici estivi del 1972. In quell'occasione il campione di nuoto americano Mark Spitz vinse sette medaglie d'oro. Purtroppo questi Giochi Olimpici furono sconvolti dall'attentato contro il campo israeliano, ad opera del gruppo terroristico Settembre nero: undici membri dell'equipe israeliana persero la vita.

Sul pittoresco laghetto di Ammersee, a Sud-Ovest di Monaco, si possono ammirare i miracoli architettonici del barocco tedesco, come ad esempio la Stiftskirche e la chiesa dei pellegrini a Diessen.

Garmisch-Partenkirchen is een geliefd kurort en wintersportcentrum aan de voet van de Zugspitze. De Duitse componist Richard Strauss bewoonde hier een riante villa en stierf er in 1949.

Ten noordwesten van de Beierse hoofdstad München ligt het moderne Olympische dorp, waar in 1972 de Olympische zomerspelen plaatsvonden. Toen was de meest bewonderde sportman de Amerikaanse zwemmer Mark Spitz die maar liefst zeven gouden medailles in de wacht sleepte. Toch werden deze Olympische spelen overschaduwd door de aanslag van de Zwarte September-bende op het Israëlische kamp; elf leden van deze equipe verloren hierbij het leven.

Aan het kleine en pittoreske meer, Ammersee, ten zuidwesten van München, bevinden zich beroemde architectonische wonderen van de Duitse barok zoals de Stiftskirche en de bedevaartskerk te Diessen.

Garmisch-Partenkirchen é um lugar de termas apreciado e centro de desportos de inverno no sopé de Zugspitze. O compositor alemão Richard Strauss viveu aqui numa mansão aprazível e nela morreu em 1949.

A nordoeste da cidade bávara de Munique está situada a moderna cidade olímpica onde, em 1972, se deram os Jogos Olímpicos de Verão. O desportista então mais admirado foi o nadador americano Mark Spitz que obteve nem mais nem menos de 7 medalhas de ouro. No entanto estes jogos foram ensombrados pelo ataque do grupo Black September ao campo israelita onde pereceram 11 membros da equipa do Israel. À beira do lago pequeno e pitoresco, Ammersee, a sudoeste de Munique, encontram-se as maravilhas arquitectónicas famosas de barroco alemão tais como, Stiftskirche e a igreja de peregrinação em Diessen.

Garmisch-Partenkirchen er et yndet kursted og vintersportscentrum beliggende ved foden af Zugspitze. Den tyske operakomponist Richard Strauss boede her i en kæmpevilla, hvor han døde i 1949.

Nordvest for den bayerske hovedstad München ligger den moderne olympiske by, hvor de olympiske sommerlege fandt sted i 1972. Den mest beundrede sportsmand ved disse lege var den amerikanske svømmer Mark Spitz, der vandt ikke mindre end syv guldmedaljer. Alligevel overskyggedes disse olympiske lege af attentatet på den israelske lejr, der udførtes af den Sorte September-gruppe; elleve medlemmer af den israelske gruppe mistede livet ved dette overfald.

Ved den lille pittoreske sø, Ammersee, sydvest for München, ligger nogle berømte arkitektoniske vidundere fra den tyske barok såsom Stiftskirche og Pelgrimskirken i Diessen.

Situated at the foot of the Zugspitze, Garmisch-Partenkirchen is a favourite health resort and winter sports centre. Richard Strauss, lived here until his death in 1949.

Munich's Olympic Village, scene of the 1972 Olympic Games, lies to the Northwest of the Bavarian capital. At those Olympic Games the American swimmer, Mark Spitz, won 7 gold medals. The Games were overshadowed by the Black September Movement's attack on the Israeli quarters, in which eleven Israeli athletes lost their lives.

The Ammersee is a small, picturesque lake to the Southwest of Munich, where there are several famous examples of German Baroque architecture, such as the Stiftskirche and the Pilgrim's Church in Diessen.

München, Ammersee

Το Γκάρμις-Πάρτενχιρχεν στους προπόδες της Τσούγκσπιτσε είναι αγαπημένη λουτρόπολη και κέντρο χειμερινού σπορ. Ο Γερμανός συνθέτης όπερας Ρίχαρντ Στράους κατοικούσε εδώ σε μια ευρύχωρη, άνετη βίλα και πέθανε το 1949. Νοτιοδυτικά από την πρωτεύουσα της Βαυαρίας Μόναχο βρίσκεται το μοντέρνο ολυμπιακό χωριό που το καλοκαίρι του 1972 έγιναν οι Ολυμπιακοί αγώνες. Τότε ο πιο θαυμαστός αθλήτης ήταν ο Αμερικανός κολυμβητής Μαρκ Σπιτς που κέρδισε όχι λιγώτερα από εφτά χρυσά μετάλλια. Οι ολυμπιακοί αγώνες αυτοί όμως επισκιάστηκαν από τη βίαια επίθεση της συμμορίας του Μαύρου Σεπτεμβρίου κατά της ισραηλιτικής ομάδας· εφτά μέλη της ομάδας έχασαν τη ζωή τους. Στη μικρή και γραφική Άμμερζεε, νοτιοδυτικά από το Μόναχο, βρίσκονται τα φημισμένα αρχιτεκτονικά θαύματα του γερμανικού Μπαρόκ, όπως η Στίφτσκιρχε και ο ναός προσκυνήματος στο Ντήσσεν.

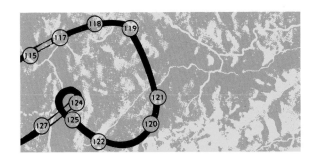

Das auf einer Insel im Bodensee liegende Lindau gehört erst seit 1805 zu Bayern, vorher war es seit 1230 freie Reichsstadt. Eine Straßen- und eine Eisenbahnbrücke stellen die Verbindung zum Festland her. Südlich von Lindau grenzt Österreich mit der Stadt Bregenz an den Bodensee; das am Horizont sichtbare Ufer gehört zur Schweiz. Das Dreiländereck lockt zahlreiche Touristen an.

Den lille historiske by Lindau på en ø i Bodensøen, også kaldet Konstantzersøen, er via en bro og en jernbanedæmning forbundet med det bayeriske fastland, hvorunder byen hører siden 1805. Mellem 1230 og 1805 var Lindau en fri rigsstad. Ved siden af Lindau, ved søen, ligger det østrigske Bregenz og på den anden side ligger Schweiz. Der er ingen tvivl om, at turismen her er meget vigtig.

The historical town of Lindau was a free 'Reichstadt' from 1230 to 1805, since when it has been part of Bavaria. Situated on an island in Lake Boden, also known as Lake Constance, it is connected with the mainland of Bavaria by both a bridge and railway dam. Bregenz, in Austria, lies next to Lindau on the banks of the lake, and across from it is Switzerland. This area's most important industry is tourism.

La histórica ciudad Lindau, en la isla en el Bodenmeer, también conocida como Konstanz, está unida por un puente y un dique ferroviario con la tierra firma de Baviera, a la que pertenece desde 1805. Antes, de 1230 a 1805, fue una ciudad-reino libre. Junto a Lindau, al lago, se encuentra la austríaca Begrenz y al otro lado está Suiza. No cabe duda de que el turismo aquí es enorme.

La petite ville historique de Lindau, située sur une île du lac de Constance, appelé également Bodensee, est reliée, par un pont et une digue surmontée d'une voie ferrée, à la Bavière à laquelle elle appartient depuis 1805. A côté de Lindau, sur le lac, se trouve la ville autrichienne de Bregenz, tandis que la Suisse est de l'autre côté du lac. Il ne fait pas de doute que le tourisme est très important dans cette région.

La storica cittadina di Lindau, su di un'isola del lago di Costanza, è collegate alla Baviera, a cui appartiene dal 1805, per mezzo di un ponte e di una diga su cui passa una ferrovia. Dal 1230 al 1805 essa fu una città indipendente. Vicino a Lindau, sul lago, si trova la città austriaca di Bregenz, mentre dalla parte opposta si trova la Svizzera. Il turismo è molto importante in tutta questa zona.

Het historische stadje Lindau op een eiland in het Bodenmeer, ook Meer van Konstanz genoemd, is door een brug en een spoorwegdam verbonden met het vaste land van Beieren, waartoe het sedert 1805 behoort. Daarvoor was het van 1230-1805 een vrije rijksstad. Naast Lindau, aan het meer, ligt het Oostenrijkse Bregenz en aan de overkant is Zwitserland. Dat het toerisme hier erg belangrijk is lijdt geen twijfel!

A vila histórica de Lindau, numa ilha no lago Bodem, tambem chamado o lago de Constância, tem ligação, por meio de uma ponte e um dique para a via férrea, com a Bavária à qual pertence desde 1805. Antes dessa data, de 1230 a 1805, foi uma cidade imperial livre. A lado de Lindau, à margem do lago, encontra-se a Bregenza austríaca e na outra banda a Suíça. De que o turismo aqui é de grande importância não há dúvida.

Η ιστορική πόλη Λίνταου σε νησί στη λίμνη Κωνσταντία, συνδέεται με γέφυρα και σιδηροδρομικό φράγμα με τη στεριά της Βαυαρίας στην οποία ανήκει από το 1805. Από το 1230 - 1805 ήταν ελεύθερη αυτοκρατορική πόλη. Δίπλα στο Λίνταου στη λίμνη βρίσκεται το Αυστριακό Μπρέγκεντς και στην απέναντι πλευρά βρίσκεται η Ελβετία. Δεν αμφισβητείται πως ο τουρισμός εδώ είναι πολύ σημαντικός.

Der Stuttgarter Fernsehturm ist das Wahrzeichen der Hauptstadt von Baden-Württemberg. Das stark exportorientierte Bundesland steht mit seiner Wirtschaftskraft in der Bundesrepublik an erster Stelle. Der Wohlstand seiner Bevölkerung spiegelt sich im Bild der historischen Stadt. Auf dem Zollernberg bei Hechingen finden wir das Stammhaus der einst mächtigen Hohenzollern-Dynastie. Von der ursprünglichen Burg ist nur die romanische Michaelskapelle erhalten. Im vorigen Jahrhundert wurde die Burg im neugotischen Stil wieder aufgebaut. Seit 1952 birgt sie das Hohenzollernmuseum, und im gleichen Jahr wurden die sterblichen Überreste Friedrich Wilhelms I. und Friedrichs II. in die Burg überführt.

Stuttgarts fjernsynstårn er blevet til et symbol for Baden-Wurttembergs hovedstad. Denne delstats økonomiske styrke rager langt over gennemsnittet for Forbundsrepublikken, hvilket skyldes tilstedeværelsen af eksportprodukter af meget høj kvalitet. Den moderne velfærd er synlig i den historiske by.
Ved Hechlingen på Burgberg finder vi den tidligere så mægtige fyrsteslægt Hohenzollerns stamslot. Fra den gamle borg resterer kun Michaelskapelle. Slottet blev genopbygget i det forrige århundrede i senromantisk stil og huser nu Hohenzollernsches Landesmuseum.

Stuttgart's television tower has become a symbol of the capital of Baden-Württemberg. Supported by the high quality of its exported goods, the economic strength of this area is far greater than the national average. Modern-day prosperity clearly shows itself in this historic city. The original castle of the powerful aristocratic family, the Hohenzollern, can be found near Hechlingen on the Burgberg, but only the Michaelskapelle has survived from the original building. The castle was rebuilt in the 19th century and now houses the Hohenzollernsches Landesmuseum.

La torre de televisión de Stuttgart se ha convertido en un símbolo de la capital de Baden-Wurtemberg. Este estado cuya economía está sobre el nivel medio de la República Federal, tiene además muchos productos de exportación de alta cali-

dad. La prosperidad moderna se puede ver en la histórica ciudad.
En Hechlingen en la montaña Burgberg se encuentra el castillo de la, en su tiempo, poderosa familia Hohenzollern. Del antiguo castillo queda sólo la Michaelskapelle. El Castillo ha sido reconstruido en el giglo pasado en un estilo romántico tardío y acoge ahora el Hohenzollernsches Landesmuseum.

La tour de télévision de Stuttgart est devenue le symbole de la capitale du Bade-Würtemberg. Land dont la puissance économique se situe loin audessus de la moyenne de la République Fédérale, car il peut s'appuyer sur des exportations à haute valeur ajoutée. Le bien-être moderne se retrouve dans la ville historique. Près de Hechlingen, sur le Burgberg, nous trouverons le château à l'origine des Hohenzollern, une famille princière autrefois très puissante. De l'ancien château il ne reste plus aujourd'hui que la Michaelskapelle. Le chateau, recon-

struit au siècle précédent dans un style post-romantique, abrite actuellement le Hohenzollernsches Landesmuseum.

La torre della televisione di Stoccarda è diventata il simbolo della capitale del Baden-Württemberg. La regione gode di una prosperità economica molto al disopra della media nazionale, poichè trae vantaggio dall'esportazione di prodotti di alta qualità. Il benessere moderno si può osservare nel centro storico.
Vicino a Hechlingen, sul Burgberg, troviamo il castello di origine degli Hohenzollern, un'aristocratica famiglia anticamente molto potente. Del vecchio castello rimane oggi solo la Michaelskapelle. Il castello ricostruito nel secolo scorso in uno stile post-romantico, ospita oggi il Museo Nazionale degli Hohenzollern.

De televisietoren van Stuttgart is tot een symbool van de hoofdstad van Baden-Württemberg geworden. De deelstaat waarvan de econo-

mische kracht ver boven het gemiddelde van de Bondsrepubliek ligt, daarbij gesteund door hoogwaardige exportprodukten. De moderne welvaart is de historische stad aan te zien.
Bij Hechlingen op de Burgberg vinden we het stamslot van het eertijds machtige vorstelijke geslacht Hohenzollern. Van de oude burcht rest slechts de Michaelskapelle. Het kasteel is in de vorige eeuw in laat-romantische stijl herbouwd en huisvest nu het Hohenzollernsches Landesmuseum.

A torre da televisão tornou-se um símbolo da capital de Baden-Württemberg. O sub-estado, cujo poder oconómico está a um nível superior ao nível médio da República Federal, apoiado na exportação de produtos de alta qualidade. A riqueza moderna nota-se bem na cidade histórica.
Próximo de Hechlingen, em cima do monte Burg, encontra-se o castelo da dinastia Hohenzollern, que em tempos

teve aqui grande potência. Do velho castelo restou apenas a capela de Michael. No século passado foi ele resconstruído em estilo post-romântico e nele funciona agora o Muzeu Nacional de Hohenzollern.

Ο τηλεοπτικός πύργος της Στουτγάρδης έγινε σύμβολο της πρωτεύουσας του Μπάντεν-Βύρτεμπεργκ. Η οικονομική δύναμη του ομοσπονδιακού κράτους αυτού υπερβαίνει πολύ το μέσο όριο, ενισχυμένη από εξαγωγικά προϊόντα υψηλής ποιότητας. Η ιστορική πόλη δείχνει την ευπορία αυτή. Στο Χεχλίγκεν στο Μπούργκμπρεγκ βρίσκουμε τον πύργο της άλλοτε εξουσιαστικής δυναστείας Χόεντσολλερν. Από το παλαιό φρούριο απέμεινε μόνο η Μίχαελσκαπελλε. Ο πύργος ανοικοδομήθηκε τον περασμένο αιώνα σε ρομαντικό ρυθμό και τώρα φιλοξενεί το Χόεντσολλερνσες Λαντεσμουσέουμ.

9
FRANCE I

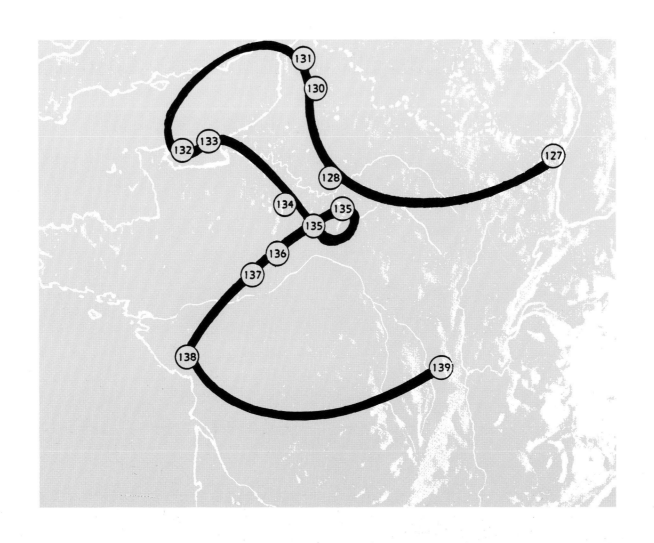

L'Alsace et sa capitale revinrent à Louis le Germanique lors du partage du royaume de Lotharingie. Toute la région, depuis la mer du Nord jusqu'à la Méditerranée et l'Adriatique, allait être pendant des siècles le siège de nombreux conflits européens. En 1949, Strasbourg devint le siège du Conseil de l'Europe, aujourd'hui organe consultatif de 21 pays européens. C'est dans le Palais de l'Europe que se réunit également le Parlement européen des 12 pays de la Communauté européenne.

Elzas med hovedstaden Strasbourg kom ved delingen af Lothars rige i Tyske Ludvigs besiddelse. Hele området, fra Nordsøen til Middelhavet og Adriaterhavet, skulle i århundreder blive indsatsen i adskillige europæiske konflikter. I 1949 blev Strasbourg sæde for Europarådet, der nu tjener som forhandlingsorgan for 21 europæiske stater. Europaparlamentet, der udgøres af de 12 EF-lande, afholder også deres møder i Palais de l'Europe.

Als die Enkel Karls des Großen 843 das Reich teilten, fiel das Elsaß mit seiner Hauptstadt Straßburg an Ludwig den Deutschen. Nach dem Westfälischen Frieden (1648) kam das Land bis 1681 nach und nach in Besitz der französischen Krone, blieb aber lange ein Zankapfel zwischen Deutschen und Franzosen. Heute ist Straßburg eine europäische Stadt: Seit 1949 ist es Sitz des Europarats, und im modernen Palais de l'Europe tagt das Europäische Parlament der zwölf Staaten der Europäischen Gemeinschaft.

When the Lotharingian Empire was divided up, the Alsace and its capital were apportioned to Louis the German. This region, which stretches from the North Sea to the Mediterranean and the Adriatic Sea, has been fought over in numerous European conflicts. In 1949, Strasbourg became the seat of the Council of Europe, now a consultative body for 21 European countries. The European Parliament, composed of the 12 Member States of the EC, also assembles here.

La Elzas y su capital, en la división del reino de Lotario, quedó en manos de Luis el Alemán. Toda la zona, desde el Mar del Norte hasta el Mediterráneo y el Mar Adrático sería el centro de multitud de conflictos europeos. En 1949 se fijó en Estrasburgo el Consejo de Europa, ahora un órgano de consejo de 21 países europeos. En Palais de l'Europe se reúne también el Parlamento Europeo de los doce países miembros de la CEE.

Nella suddivisione del Regno di Lotaringia, l'Alsazia e la sua capitale furono assegnate a Luigi il Germanico. L'intera zona, dal Mar del Nord fino al Mediterraneo e all'Adriatico, sarebbe stata, per secoli, teatro di numerosi conflitti europei. Nel 1949 Strasburgo divenne sede del Consiglio d'Europa, oggi organo consultivo di 21 paesi europei. Nel Palazzo d'Europa si riunisce anche il Parlamento Europeo dei 12 paesi membri della Comunità Europea.

De Elzas en zijn hoofdstad kwam bij de verdeling van het rijk van Lotharius aan Lodewijk de Duitser. Het hele gebied, vanaf de Noordzee tot aan de Middellandse en de Adriatische Zee, zou eeuwenlang de inzet zijn van tal van Europese conflicten. In 1949 werd Straatsburg de zetel van de Raad van Europa, nu een overlegorgaan van 21 Europese landen. In het Palais de l'Europe vergadert ook het Europese Parlement van de 12 landen van de Europese Gemeenschap.

A Elzas e a sua capital passaram a pertencer ao imperador Luiz, o Alemão, por ocasião da divisão do império de Lotharius. Toda a região, desde o Mar do Norte até ao Mediterâneo e ao Adriático foi, durante muitos séculos, a razão de muitos conflitos europeus. Em 1949 passou Estrasburgo a ser a sede do Conselho da Europa, presentemente um orgão de deliberação de 21 países europeus. No palácio dá Europa reune-se o Parlamento dos 12 países membros da Comunidade Europeia.

Όταν μοιράστηκε το κράτος του Λοθάριου, η Αλσατία και η πρωτεύουσά της ήρθαν στα χέρια του Λουδοβίκου του Γερμανού. Όλη η περιοχή, από τη Βόρειο Θάλασσα μέχρι τη Μεσόγειο και την Αδριατική Θάλασσα, θα ήταν για αιώνες το θέμα πολλών συγκρούσεων. Το 1949 έγινε το Στρασβούργο η έδρα του Ευρωπαϊκού Κοινοβουλίου, τώρα το διασκεπτήριο σώμα 21 ευρωπαϊκών χωρών. Στο Παλαί ντε λ'Ερώπ συνεδριάζει επίσης η Ευρωπαϊκή Βουλή των 12 χωρών της Ευρωπαϊκής Κοινότητας.

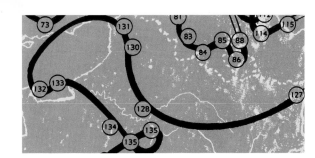

Le berceau de Paris est situé dans une boucle de la Seine, l'île de la Cité, avec la cathédrale Notre-Dame qui date du début du 13e siècle. En haut, à droite, nous voyons un monument de 1977, le Centre National d'Art et de Culture Georges Pompidou. Napoléon fit construire son Arc de Triomphe et le nom de Charles de Gaulle fut ajouté à la place de l'Étoile qui l'entoure.

I et knæk på floden Seine ligger Paris vugge, l'ile de la Cité, med Notre-Dame fra begyndelsen af det 13. århundrede. Øverst til højre ser vi et monument fra 1977, Centre national d'art et de culture George-Pompidou.
Napoleon byggede sin l'arc de Triomphe og pladsen, Etoile, der omkranser triumfbuen, fik tilføjet Charles de Gaulles navn.

Auf einer Insel in der Seine, der Ile de la Cité, liegt das Herz von Paris mit der Kathedrale Notre-Dame aus dem frühen 13. Jahrhundert. Am Bildrand rechts oben erhebt sich das 1977 errichtete Centre National d'Art et de Culture Georges Pompidou, das supermoderne Kulturzentrum.
Den Triumphbogen ließ Napoleon errichten; die Place de l'Etoile, auf der er sich erhebt, wurde inzwischen nach Charles de Gaulle umbenannt.

L'île de la Cité, the cradle of Paris, is situated on a bend in the River Seine. There we can find the Notre-Dame, which dates from the 13th century. In the top right hand corner of the photograph there is the Pompidou Centre, which was built in 1977. The Arc de Triomphe was erected by Napoleon in honour of the victories of his Grande Armeé. In more recent times the Etoile, the square surrounding it, was renamed after Charles de Gaulle.

En una curva del Sena se haya la cuna de París, l'île de la Cité, con el Notre-Dame del s. XIII. Arriba a la derecha vemos un monumento de 1977, el Centro Nacional de Arte George Pompidou.
Napoleón hizo construir el Arco del Triunfo y a la plaza que lo rodea, Etoile, se la dio el nombre Charles de Gaulle.

Il cuore di Parigi è situato in un'ansa della Senna, l'île de la cité, con la cattedrale di Notre-dame, che risale al XIII secolo. In alto a destra, vediamo un monumento del 1977, il Centro Nazionale d'Arte e Cultura Georges Pompidou. Napoleone fece costruire il suo arco di trionfo e il nome di Charles de Gaulle fu aggiunto alla Piazza dell'Etoile che circonda l'Arco.

In een bocht van de Seine ligt de wieg van Parijs, l'île de la Cité, met de Notre-Dame uit het begin van de dertiende eeuw. Rechtsboven zien we een monument uit 1977, het Centre national d'art et de culture Georges-Pompidou.
Napoléon liet zijn l'arc de Triomphe bouwen en aan het plein, Etoile, eromheen werd de naam van Charles de Gaulle toegevoegd.

Na curva do Sena está o 'berço' de Paris, a île de la Cité, com a Notre-Dame, do pricípio do século XIII. À direita, em cima, vemos um monumento de 1977, o Centro Nacional da Arte e da Cultura Georges-Pompidou.
Napoleão mandou construir o seu Arco do Triumfo, na Praça d'Etoile; à volta dele foi adicionado o nome de Charles de Gaulle.

Σε μια στροφή του Σηκουάνα βρίσκεται η κούνια του Παρισιού, Λιλ ντε λα Σιτέ, με τη Νοτρ Νταμ από τις αρχές του δέκατο τρίτου αιώνα. Απάνω δεξιά βλέπουμε ένα μνημείο από το 1977, το Εθνικό Κέντρο τέχνης και πολιτισμού Ζωρζ Πομπιντού.
Ο Ναπολέων έχτισε την Αψίδα του Θρίαβου και γύρω στην πλατεία Ετουάλ δόθηκε το όνομα του Σάρλ ντε Γκώλ.

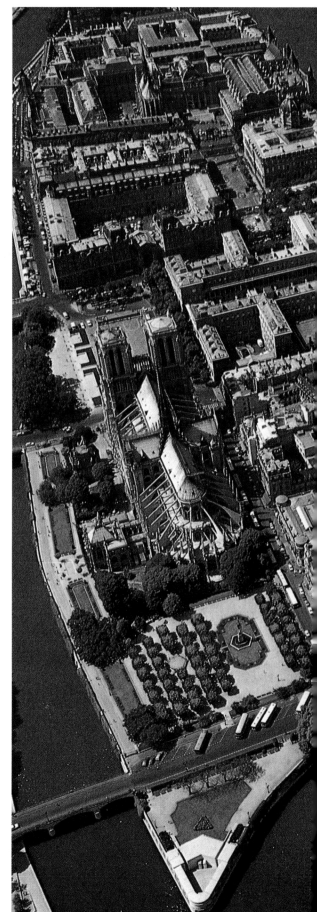

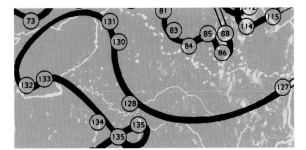

preserved here for the last thousand years, but the abbey dedicated to him has disappeared and the town no longer bears his name.

Kassel, la ciudad en la colina en el Flandés francés. El molino, que había estado ahí desde 1564, fue víctima de un incendio. Pero desde 1948 se encuentra de nuevo en la Kassel-

berg. Y en la fiesta nacional de Francia, el 14 de julio, Kassel celebra desde entonces su fiesta del molino.
Arras ya no es conocida por sus tapices y porcelanas. Aún es la

capital, pero no más de Artois, sino del Paso de Calais. Pero Arras es sobre todo conocida por sus plazas con galerías. Dentro del cinturón de defensa, construido por Vauban, se

Cassel, ville sur une colline de la Flandre française. Le moulin qui surmontait cette colline depuis 1564 avait été la proie des flammes en 1911. Mais depuis 1948, il domine à nouveau le mont Cassel. Et le jour de la fête nationale, le 14 Juillet, Cassel célèbre sa fête depuis le moulin. Arras n'est plus connu pour ses tapis, ni ses faïences. C'est encore une capitale, non plus celle de l'Artois, mais bien celle du Pas-de-Calais. Arras, toutefois, est surtout connue par ses places avec galeries.

Bergues est enserrée par une ceinture d'ouvrages défensifs dus à Vauban. La verte montagne est à l'origine de la petite ville et dans le français, nous reconnaissons encore le 'berg' flamand. Les saintes reliques de saint Winok y sont conservées depuis 1000 ans, mais l'abbaye qui portait son nom a disparu, ainsi que du nom français et de l'appellation officielle de la ville.

Cassel, byen på en bakke i Fransk-Flanderen. Den mølle, der havde stået der fra 1564, var i 1911 blevet flammernes bytte. Men siden 1948 står der atter en mølle på Cassel-bjerget. Og siden da fejrer Cassel den franske nationaldag, 14 juli, med en møllefest.
Arras kendes ikke mere for sine vægtæpper og keramik. Det er stadig en hovedstad, men ikke mere for Artois, men for Pas-de-Calais. Arras er dog først og fremmest kendt for sine pladser med gallerier.
Bag sit bælte af forsvarsværker, anlagt af Vauban, ligger Bergues. Det grønne bjerg var oprindelsen til den lille by, og i det franske navn, Bergues, genkender vi endnu det flamske berg. Sint-Winoks hellige knoglerester opbevares her allerede i tusind år, men det efter ham opkaldte kloster er forsvundet ligesom hans navn i byens officielle franske navn.

Auf einer Anhöhe im französischen Flandern liegt die Stadt Cassel. Die 1564 gegründete Mühle, die 1911 den Flammen zum Opfer fiel, wurde 1948 wieder aufgebaut. Seither wird in Cassel am 14. Juli, dem Nationalfeiertag, das Mühlenfest gefeiert. Der Ruhm von Arras als Zentrum von Bildwirkerei und Keramik ist längst verblaßt, doch immer noch locken seine von Bogengängen gesäumten herrlichen

Plätze viele Besucher an. Die historische Hauptstadt des Artois ist inzwischen zum Hauptort des Departements Pas-de-Calais abgestiegen. Der Anhöhe (flämisch 'berg'), auf der es liegt, verdankt das Städtchen Bergues seinen Namen. Es ist von einem Festungsgürtel umschlossen, den Vauban errichtet hat. Seit tausend Jahren birgt es die Gebeine des heiligen Winok, doch die nach ihm benannte Abtei ist ebenso verschwunden wie der Name des Heiligen aus dem offiziellen französischen Namen des Städtchens.

Cassel is the name of this town on a hilltop in French Flanders. The mill, which had been standing since 1564, was reduced to ashes in a fire in 1911. However, in 1948 another mill was built on the Kasselberg. From that time, Cassel has celebrated its annual Festival of the Mill on the French national anniversary, 14 July. Although once famous for its tapestries and earthenware, Arras, once the capital city of Artois, is perhaps now better known as the capital of the Pas de Calais and is renowned for its squares and arcades. Bergues, built by Vauban, is situated within a ring of fortifications. The town was originally established on a green mountain which its French name still echoes. The relics of St. Winok have been

encuentra Bergues. La montaña verde formó el origen de la ciudad y en el francés encontramos la palabra flamenca 'berg'. La reliquia de San Winok se guarda ya desde hace siglos, pero la abadía a él nombrada ha desaparecido así como su nombre en el nombre francés y oficial de la ciudad.

Cassel, ciudad su di una collina della Fiandra francese. Il mulino che dominava questa collina fin dal 1564, era stato distrutto da un'incendio nel 1911. Dal 1948 esso domina di nuovo il Mont de Cassel e il 14 luglio, festa nazionale, Cassel celebra le sua festa dal mulino.

Arras non è più conosciuta per i tappeti e le maioliche. Essa è ancora una capitale, non più dell'Artois, ma del Pas-de-Calais. Arras è famosa soprattutto per le sue piazze con i loggiati. Bergues è racchiusa da una cerchia di fortificazioni, opera di Vauban. La verde collina è all'origine della cittadina e nella parola francese ritroviamo il 'Berg' fiammingo. Le sante reliquie di Saint-Winok sono conservate da 1000 anni, ma il convento che portava il suo nome è scomparso, sia dal nome francese che dal nome ufficiale della città.

Kassel, de stad op een heuvel in Frans-Vlaanderen. De molen, die er sedert 1564 had gestaan, was in 1911 ten prooi gevallen aan de rode haan. Maar sinds 1948 staat er weer een op de Kasselberg. En op de nationale Franse feestdag, 14 juli, viert Kassel sindsdien zijn molenfeest.

Atrecht is niet meer bekend om zijn tapijten en zijn aardewerk. Het is nog wel een hoofdstad, niet meer van Artois, maar van het Pas-de-Calais. Maar vooral is Atrecht bekend door zijn pleinen met galerijen.
Binnen zijn gordel van verdedigingswerken, door Vauban aangelegd, ligt Bergues. De groene berg vormde de oorsprong van het stadje en in het Frans herkennen we nog het Vlaamse berg. Het heilig gebeente van Sint-Winok wordt er al duizend jaar bewaard, maar de naar hem genoemde abdij is verdwenen evenals zijn naam in de Franse en officiële naam van de stad.

Cassel, a cidade em cima de uma colina, na Flândria francesa. O moínho, que lá estava desde 1564, foi sacrificado pelo galo vermelho. Mas desde 1948 está outra vez um, no monte de Cassel. E no dia da festa nacional, 14 de julho, realiza Cassel a sua festa do moínho. Arras já não de Artois, mas sim de Pas de Calais. Mas Arras, sobre tudo, é conhecida pelos seus tapetes e pela sua loiça. É ainda uma capital, não é conhecida pelas suas praças com arcadas.
Dentro da orla das suas marulhas, mandadas construir por Vauban, encontra-se o Bergues. O monte verde foi a origem da vila e na língua francesa reconhece-se ainda 'o monte Flamengo'. Os restos mortais de St. Winok são lá conservados à mil anos, mas a abadia, com o seu nome, já não existe, assim como o seu nome desapareceu do nome francês e oficial da vila.

Η πόλη Κάσσελ επάνω σε λόφο στη Γαλλική Φλάντρα. Ο μύλος που υπήρξε εκεί από το 1564 έγινε παρανάλωμα του πυρός το 1911. Αλλά από το 1948 υπάρχει ξανά ένας μύλος στο Κάσσελμπεργκ. Μαζί με την εθνική γαλλική γιορτή της 14 Ιουλίου γιορτάζει το Κάσσελ και τη γιορτή του μύλου. Η Αρράς δέν είναι πιά διάσημη για τους ταπήτες και την κεραμική της. Είναι μέν η πρωτεύουσα του νομού Πα-ντε-Καλαί, αλλά όχι πια του Αρτουά. Προπαντώς όμως είναι η Αρράς γνωστή για τις πλατείες της με στόες.
Μέσα στη ζώνη από αμυντικά έργα, χτισμένα από τον Βωμπάν, βρίσκεται το Βέργυες. Το πράσινο βούνο αποτελεί η γένεση της μικρής πόλης και το γαλλικό όνομα θυμίζει ακόμα το φλαμανδικό 'μπεργκ'. Το

άγιο λείψανο του Σιντ-Βίνοκ φυλάγεται εκεί κιόλας χίλια χρόνια, αλλά το αββαείο με το δικό του όνομα έχει εξαφανιστεί όπως εξαφανίστηκε το όνομά του από την επίσημη ονομασία της πόλης.

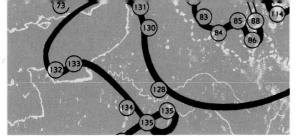

Dans la Manche, dans la baie qui sépare la Bretagne de la Normandie, la différence de niveau entre la marée montante et la marée descendante est particulièrement importante puisqu'elle est d'une quinzaine de mètres. C'est donc là un lieu idéal pour la centrale marémotrice de la Rance, près de Saint-Malo, grâce à laquelle la France qui pour son approvisionnement en électricité compte fermement sur les centrales atomiques, fournit une contribution élémentaire à un approvisionnement en énergie alternatif et propre. Non loin de là nous trouvons un autre exemple de l'influence qu'exercent les marées sur le niveau de la mer. La célèbre abbaye du Mont-Saint-Michel, depuis des siècles aux limites entre terre et eau est, depuis le début de ce siècle, dotée d'une digue qui relie l'île et la terre ferme. Cet accès aisé a provoqué de nos jours un afflux massif de touristes. On essaye aujourd'hui de freiner quelque peu celui-ci de façon à ce que les visiteurs d'aujourd'hui puissent prendre conscience du calme et du repos recherchés ici autrefois par les pèlerins.

Rance at St. Malo which is making a fundamental contribution to the alternative and ecologically compatible generation of energy in a country greatly dependent on nuclear energy. Not far away is the famous abbey of Mont St. Michel, which has stood on the boundary between mainland and sea for hundreds of years. Since the beginning of the century, a dam has connected the island with the mainland. This ease of accessibility has resulted in a massive increase in tourism, and attempts are now being made to slow down this development, so that visitors may be able to experience some of the peace and tranquillity once sought by pilgrims.

En el Canal entre la bahía entre Bretaña y Normandía hay una gran diferencia entre la marea alta y baja, unos quince metros. Un lugar ideal, pues, para la central de energía de mareas en el Rance cerca de St. Malo, con la que Francia, que depende en mucho de sus centrales nucleares, ofrece una alternativa y limpia de suninistración de energía.
No lejos de aquí encontramos otro ejemplo de diferencia de marea. La famosa abadía de Mont St. Michel, que ya desde hace siglos se haya en el límite entre tierra y agua y que desde principios de este siglo tiene un dique para unir la isla con tierra firme. Este fácil acceso ha ocasionado una atracción ma-

siva de turistas. Esto se intenta frenar en la actualidad para que los visitantes puedan notar algo del silencio y tranquilidad que en otras épocas buscaban los peregrinos aquí.

Nella Manica, nella baia che separa la Bretagna dalla Normandia, la differenza fra alta e bassa marea è molto alta (15 metri circa). Un luogo ideale por la centrale elettrica di Rance vicino a Saint Malo, grazie a cui la Francia che per il proprio fabbisogno di elettricità si serve delle centrali atomiche, dà il proprio apporto in energia alternativa e pulita.
Non lontano da qui troviamo un altro esempio dell'influsso che le maree esercitano sul livello del mare. La celebre abbazia di Mont St. Michel, da secoli al confine fra la terra e l'acqua è dall'inizio di questo secolo provvista di una diga che unisce l'isola con la terraferma. Questo facile accesso ha provocato un enorme afflusso di turisti. Si cerca attualmente di porre un freno a questo fenomeno in modo che i visitatori dei nostri tempi possano prendere coscienza della quiete e del riposo che i pellegrini di un tempo cercavano in questo luogo.

In Het Kanaal bij de inham tussen Bretagne en Normandië is het tijverschil, tussen eb en vloed dus, bijzonder groot en wel zo'n vijftien meter. Een ideale plaats dus voor de getijdenkrachtcentrale in de Rance

bij St. Malo, waarmee Frankrijk, dat voor zijn electriciteitsvoorziening sterk op atoomkrachtcentrales is aangewezen, een elementaire bijdrage levert in de alternatieve en schone energievoorziening. Niet ver hier vandaan vinden we nog een ander voorbeeld van het getijverschil. De beroemde abdij van Mont St. Michel, al eeuwen op de grens van land en water en sinds het begin van deze eeuw voorzien van een dijk die het eiland en verbinding met het vaste land gaf. De gemakkelijke toegang heeft in onze dagen een massale toevloed van toeristen veroorzaakt. Men poogt dit wat af te remmen, zodat de bezoekers van vandaag ook weer iets gewaar kunnen worden van de stilte en de rust die pelgrims hier vroeger zochten.

No Canal, junto ao golfo entre a Bretanha e a Normândia, a diferença de marés, portanto a diferença entre a maré alta e a baixa, é muito grande; às vezes à volta de quinze metros. Um lugar ideal, pois, para uma central eléctrica de maré em Rance, próximo de St. Malo, com o que a França, que depende da energia atómica para dá uma contribuição elementar a sua produção alternativa de energia sem poluição. Não muito longe de aqui encontramos mais um exemplo da diferença de marés. A celebre abadia de St. Michel, à séculos no limite entre a água e a terra e desde o princípio

deste século provida de um dique, que liga a ilha com o continente. Esta acessibilidade causou nos nossos dias uma invasão de turista. Presentemente tenta-se evitar isto um pouco, de maneira que os visitantes possam sentir algo do sossego, que os peregrinos, antigamente, procuravam aqui.

Στον κόλπο της Μάγχης, ανάμεσα στην Βρετάνη και τη Νορμανδή, είναι η παλιρροϊκή διαφορά, δηλάδη η διαφορά ανάμεσα σε άμπωτη και πλυμμιρίδα, πολύ μεγάλη και μάλιστα περίπου δεκαπέντε μέτρα. Ένας ιδανικός τόπος λοιπόν για τον παλιρροϊκό ηλεκτροπαραγωγικό σταθμό στο Ραν στο Σαιν Μαλό. Με αυτόν τον τρόπο η Γαλλία που για την παροχή ηλεκτρισμού βασίζεται πολύ στους πυρηνικούς ηλεκτροπαραγωγικούς σταθμούς, δίνει στοιχειώδη συνεισφορά στην άλλη και καθαρή παροχή ηλεκτρικής ενέργειας.
Όχι μακριά από εδώ βρίσκουμε κι' άλλο ένα παράδειγμα της παλιρροϊκής διαφοράς. Το διάσημο αββαείο του Μον Σαιν Μισέλ, αιώνες κιόλας στα σύνορα στεριάς και νερού και από τις αρχές του αιώνα μας εφοδιασμένο με ένα φράγμα που συνδέει το νησί με τη στεριά. Αυτή η ευπροσιτότητα στα χρόνια μας προκάλεσε μαζικής συρροή τουρισμού. Τώρα προσπαθούν να νιώθουν πάλι τη γαλήνη και την ηρεμία που αναζητούσαν οι άλλοτε χατζήδες.

I Kanalen ved bugten mellem Bretagne og Normandiet er tidevandssforskellen, altså forskellen mellem ebbe og flod, særdeles stor, helt op til 15 meter. Tidevands-kraftværket i Rance ved St. Malo ligger således særdeles gunstigt, og Frankrig, der er meget afhængig af atomkraftværker, yder på denne måde et elementært bidrag til den alternative og rene energiforsyning.
Ikke langt herfra finder vi et andet eksempel på tidevandsforskellen. Mont St. Michels berømte kloster har allerede i århundreder ligget på grænsen mellem land og vand, men ved dette århundredes begyndelse anlagdes et dige, der har givet øen en forbindelse til fastlandet. Denne lette adgang har i vore dage forårsaget en massiv turiststrøm. Man forsøger nu at bremse denne udvikling noget, således at vor tids besøgende igen kan opleve den ro og hvile som pilgrimmene tidligere søgte her.

In der Bucht zwischen der Bretagne und der Normandie ist der Tidenhub des Ärmelkanals mit nahezu 15 Metern besonders groß. Um die dadurch erzeugten Energien zu nutzen, hat man in der Rance bei Saint-

Malo ein Gezeitenkraftwerk errichtet. Damit leistet Frankreich, das in der Energieversorgung den Kernkraftwerken den Vorzug gibt, auch einen wesentlichen Beitrag zu einer sauberen alternativen Energiegewinnung.
Wie sehr sich an dieser Küste der Wasserstand zwischen Ebbe und Flut verändert, können wir unweit von Saint-Malo am Mont-Saint-Michel mit seinem prächtigen, im Jahr 966 gegründeten Benediktinerkloster beobachten. Seit 1879 ist der vor der Küste aufragende Granitblock durch einen Damm mit dem Festland verbunden, doch bei Ebbe kann man den Klosterfelsen auch zu Fuß über die trockengefallenen Dünen erreichen. Wenn Flut herrscht, branden die Meereswogen rings um das altehrwürdige Kloster, das zu den beliebtesten Touristenzielen in der Bretagne gehört.

The difference between high and low tide in the bay between Brittany and Normandy in the English Channel is approximately 15 metres. This makes it an ideal location for the tidal power station in the

Chartres possède avec sa cathédrale Notre-Dame un des plus beaux monuments d'Europe: l'architecture, la sculpture et les vitraux y sont représentatifs de la maîtrise atteinte par les artisans d'alors.

Orléans est une jolie ville sur la Loire avec une imposante cathédrale en style gothique ornée de deux tours. D'un point de vue historique, elle est une des villes de France les plus célèbres: le 8 mai 1429, Jeanne d'Arc libéra la ville occupée par les Anglais et, par cette victoire, permit un renouvellement du sentiment national français. Jeanne fut "la Vierge d'Orléans" et le 8 mai est encore un jour férié en France.

Le château de Fontainebleau fut construit au 16e siècle par François 1er et agrandi ensuite par les Valois et les Bourbons. Napoléon y fit ses adieux, en 1814, à ses grognards (membres de la Garde) dans la célèbre cour des Adieux.

The Notre-Dame Cathedral in Chartres is one of Europe's most fascinating buildings: the architecture, sculpture and stained glass windows are masterpieces of skill and craftsmanship.

Orléans, a proud city on the River Loire, boasts a magnificent Late Gothic cathedral with two towers. Historically, Orléans is famous for the liberation of the city from the English on 8 May 1429 by Joan of Arc. Joan of Arc become known as the "Maid of Orléans", and 8 May is still a day of national festivities.

Fontainebleau was built in the 16th century for François I, and was later extended by the Valois and the Bourbon kings. In 1814, Napoleon bade farewell to his "grognards" (Members of the Guard) here in the celebrated "Cour des Adieux".

La Catedral Notre-Dame en Chartres es uno de los monumentos más fascinantes de Europa: la arquitectura, la escultura y las vidrieras son verdaderas obras maestras. Orléans es una orgullosa ciudad al Loire con una enorme catedral de dos torres de estilo gótico tardío. Desde el punto de vista histórico es la ciudad más memorable de Francia: el 8 de mayo de 1429 Santa Juana de Arco libertó entonces ocupada por los ingleses y esta victoria causó el renacimiento de la conciencia del sentimiento patriótico francés. Juana es conocida como la Doncella de Orleans y el 8 de mayo es día festivo en Francia.

El castillo de Fontainebleau fue construido en el s. XVI para Francisco I y más tarde ampliado por los reyes de Valois y Borbón. En 1814 Napoleón se despidió ahí de sus 'grognards' (miembros de la guardia).

La cattedrale di Notre-Dame di Chartres è uno dei più bei monumenti d'Europa: l'architettura, la scultura e le vetrate rappresentano esempi grandiosi della maestria raggiunta dagli artigiani di quei tempi.

Orléans è una graziosa città sulla Loira con una maestosa cattedrale in stile gotico a due torri.

Dal punto di vista storico, essa è una delle città più famose di Francia: l'otto maggio 1429, Giovanna d'Arco liberò la città occupata dagli inglesi e ciò resuscitò il sentimento nazionale francese. Giovanna è ricordata come la 'Vergine di Orléans' e l'otto maggio è ancora oggi festa nazionale.

Il castello di Fontainebleau fu costruito nel XVI secolo da Francesco I e in seguito fu ingrandito dai Valois e dai Bourbons. Nelle celebre 'Corte degli addii' Napoleone si congedò, nel 1814, dai suoi 'Grognards' (membri della guardia).

Chartres bezit met zijn Notre-Dame-kathedraal een der schitterendste monumenten van Europa: arcitectuur, beeldhouwkunst en glas in loodramen vormen hoogtepunten van ambachtelijk kunnen.

Orléans is een trotse Loire-stad met een machtige laatgotische kathedraal met twee torens. Historisch is ze een van Frankrijks meest gedenkwaardige steden: op 8 mei 1429 ontzette Jeanne d'Arc de door de Engelsen bezette stad en bracht door deze overwinning een heropstanding van het Franse nationale gevoel. Jeanne werd 'de Maagd van Orléans' en 8 mei is nog steeds een feestdag in Frankrijk.

Het kasteel van Fontainebleau werd in de zestiende eeuw gebouwd voor François I en later uitgebreid door de Valois- en de Bourbonkoningen. Napoleon nam er in de bekende 'Cour des adieux' in 1814 afscheid van zijn 'grognards' (leden van de Garde).

Chartres possui com a sua catedral Notre Dame um dos mais belos monumentos da Europa: a arquitetura, escultura e janelas são o auge do poder artístico.

Orleães é uma cidade orgulhosa do Loire com uma catedral magnífica de estilo gótico recente. Historicamente esta cidade é uma das mais notáveis: em 8 de Maio de 1429 Joana d'Arc livrou a cidade então ocupada pelos ingleses, tendo com esta vitória acordado o espírito patriótico de povo francês e levá-lo à revolta. Joana ficou a ser conhecida pela 'Virgem de Orleães' e o dia 8 de Maio ainda é um dia de festa em França. O castelo de Fontainebleau foi construido no séc. XVI por François I e mais tarde foi ampliado pelos reis de Valois e de Bourbon. Napoleão fez a sua despedida dos seus 'grognards' (veteranos da Guarda) no famoso 'Cour des adieux' em 1814.

Med Notre-Dame-Katedralen besidder Chartres et af Europas mest strålende monumenter: arkitektur, skulptur og glasarbejde udgør højdepunkter indenfor håndværkmæssig kunnen.

Orléans er en stolt Loire-by med en pragtfuld sengotisk katedral med to tårne. Historisk er den en af Frankrigs mest mindeværdige byer: den 8. maj 1429 kom Jeanne d'Arc den af englænderne besatte by til undsætning. Denne sejr førte til en ny vækkelse af den franske nationalfølelse. Jeanne blev til 'Jomfruen fra Orléans' og den 8. maj er stadig en festdag i Frankrig.

Fontainebleau blev bygget i det 16. århundrede til Frans d. I og senere blev det udvidet af Valois og Bourbonkongerne. I den bekendte 'Cour des adieux' tog Napoleon i 1814 afsked med sine 'grognards' (gardere).

Eines der schönsten Bauwerke Europas erhebt sich in Chartres: die gotische Kathedrale Notre-Dame. Das Gotteshaus mit seiner reichen Innenausstattung zählt zu sein Meisterwerken europäischer Kunst.

Eine bedeutende gotische Kathedrale (Sainte-Croix) finden wir auch in Orléans, der stolzen Stadt an der Loire. Im Hundertjährigen Krieg zwischen Frankreich und England vermochte hier 1429 Jeanne d'Arc, die 'Jungfrau von Orléans', das Kriegsglück zugunsten der Franzosen zu wenden. Ihr Fest am 8. Mai wird noch heute in ganz Frankreich gefeiert.

Das Königsschloß Fontainebleau wurde 1527 unter Franz I. begonnen und später durch Herrscher aus den Häusern Valois und Bourbon großzügig erweitert. Auf dem berühmten Abschiedshof des Schlosses verabschiedete Napoleon 1814 vor seiner Verbannung auf die Insel Elba seine 'Grognards' (Gardisten), doch das Ende seiner Herrschaft führte erst die Niederlage bei Waterloo (1815) herbei.

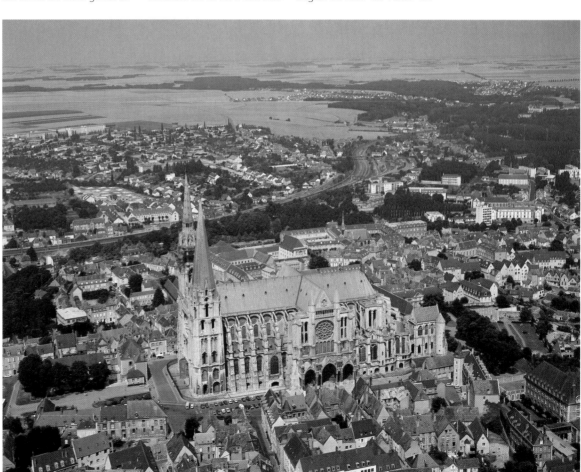

Fontainebleau

Ο Καθεδρικός ναός Νοτρ-Νταμ στην πόλη Σάρτρη είναι ένα από τα πιο εξαίρετα μνημεία της Ευρώπης· η αρχιτεκτονική, η γλυπτική και τα υαλογραφήματα είναι τα αποκορυφώματα επαγγελματικής τέχνης.

Η Ορλεάνη υπερήφανη για το μεγαλοπρεπή φλογωτό Καθεδρικό ναό με δύο καμπαναριά, είναι πόλη στο Λιγήρα. Ιστορικά είναι μια από τις πιο αξιομνήμευτες πόλεις της Γαλλίας· στις 8 Μαΐου 1429 απελευθέρωσε η Jeanne d'Arc την από τους Άγγλους καταλημένη πόλη και με τη νίκη αυτή χάρισε στη Γαλλία αναβίωση εθνικών αισθημάτων. Η Jeanne ονομάστηκε η παρθένα της Ορλεάνης και η 8 Μαΐου γιορτάζεται ακόμα στη Γαλλία.

Ο πύργος του Φονταινμπλώ χτίστηκε το δέκατο έκτο αιώνα από τον Φραγκίσκο Α΄ και εκτάθηκε αργότερα από τους Βασιλείς των οίκων Βουρβόν και Βαλουά. Ο Ναπολέων στο φημισμένο Ίκουρ ντε Αντιέ' αποχαιρέτησε τους 'grognards' του [μέλη της Φρούρας].

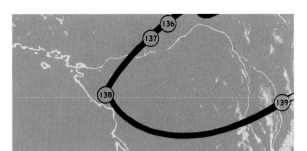

Qu'y a-t-il de plus éloquent que ces photos pour parler des châteaux de la Loire, tel celui de Chambord, et de ses affluents, comme le Cher avec le château de Chenonceaux?

Hvad kan bedre beskrive slottene langs med floden Loire, som her Chambord, og bifloderne, som Cher og slotte Chenonceaux, end disse fotografier?

Weit mehr als Worte sagen Bilder über die prächtigen Schlösser an der Loire und ihren Nebenflüssen aus. Wir zeigen hier Chambord an der Loire und Chenonceaux am Cher.

These pictures of the châteaux on the Loire and its tributaries are more eloquent than any words. Shown here are Chambord on the Loire and Chenonceaux on the Cher.

¿Qué puede decir más de los castillos al Loira, como aquí el de Chambord, y sus afluyentes como el Cher y el castillo Chenonceaux, que estas foto?

Queste foto sono il modo più eloquente per parlare dei castelli della Loira; vediamo ad esempio quello di Chambord e dei suoi affluenti, e lo Cher con il castello di Chenonceaux.

Wat zegt meer over de kastelen langs de Loire, zoals hier Chambord, en de zijrivieren, zoals de Cher en het kasteel Chenonceaux, dan deze foto's?

O que é que pode ser mais explícito sobre os castelos ao longo do Loire, como este de Chambord, e dos afluentes, como o castelo Chenonceaux, do que estas fotografias?

Τι λέει περισσότερα για τους πύργους του Λιγήρα, όπως, εδώ το Σαμπόρ και τους παραπόταμους όπως το Σερ και τον πύργο Σενονσώ, από αυτές τις φωτογραφίες;

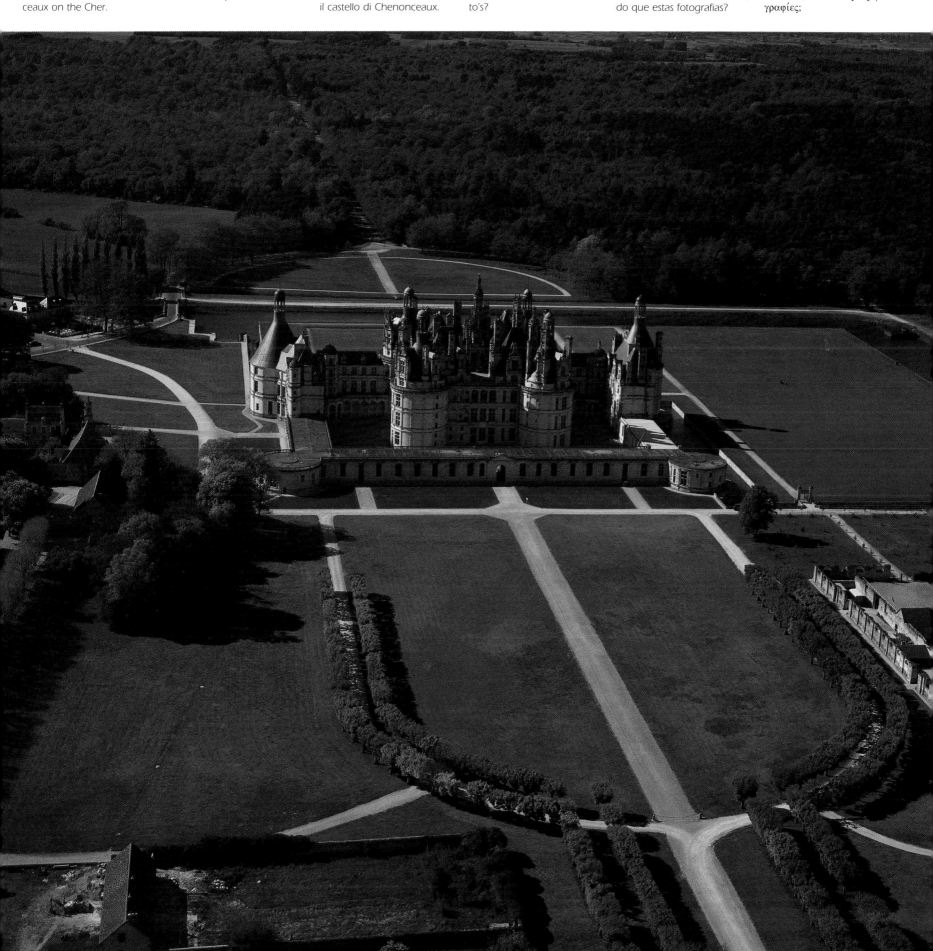

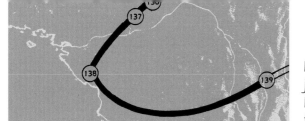

Les horreurs de l'histoire ne sont pas toujours perceptibles sur de jolies photos. A la Rochelle, 25 000 personnes moururent de faim lorsque le cardinal de Richelieu décréta de 1625 à 1628 le blocus total de ce qui était alors un foyer protestant. Une ville intacte tomba entre ses mains.

Le département de la Haute-Loire, fait partie du Massif central, avec Le Puy et le rocher Saint-Michel. C'est un ancien plateau volcanique.

Historiens uhyrligheder kan ikke altid ses på de smukke fotografier. I La Rochelle sulte-de 25.000 mennesker til døde da kardinal Richelieu fra 1625-1628 ledede den totale blokade af dette tidligere protestantiske arnested. Byen faldt ubeskadiget i hans hænder.
Departementet Haute Loire, en del af Massif Central med Le Puy og Rocher St. Michel. Et gammelt vulkanagtigt plateau.

Die schöne Ansicht von La Rochelle läßt nichts mehr von den Tragödien erahnen, die sich einst hier abgespielt haben. So verhungerten während der Blockade, die Kardinal Richelieu 1625 bis 1628 über die damalige Hochburg des Protestantismus verhängte, mehr als 25 000 Bewohner – der Preis dafür, daß die Stadt den katholischen Truppen kampflos in die Hände fiel.
Das Departement Haute-Loire ist Teil des vulkanischen Zentralmassivs mit dem Puy-de-Dôme und dem Rocher Saint-Michel.

When Cardinal Richelieu ordered a total blockade of the Protestant stronghold of La Rochelle between 1625 and 1628, 25000 people starved to death. This photograph of the town today however reveals no evidence of this atrocity.

The second photograph shows Le Puy and Rocher St. Michel in the Department of Haute Loire in the Massif Central, which was formerly a volcanic area.

Las crueldades de la historia no se pueden ver siempre en hermosas fotos. En La Rochelle murieron de hambre 25.000 personas cuando el Cardenal Richelieu organizó un bloqueo total de 1625 e 1628 en este nido protestante. Una ciudad intacta le cayó en manos.

El Departamento Haute Loire, una parte del Macizo Central, con Le Puy y Rocher St. Michel. Una antigua meseta vulcánica.

Non si possono sempre comprendere le tristi vicende della storia attraverso belle fotografie. A La Rochelle, 25.000 persone morirono di fame quando il cardinale Richelieu decretò il blocco totale delle città che era in quei tempi un focolaio protestante. Una città intatta cadde nelle sue mani. Il dipartimento della Haute-Loire fa parte del Massiccio Centrale insieme a Le Puy e al Rocher St. Michel. Si tratta di un antico altipiano vulcanico.

De gruwelen van de geschiedenis zijn niet altijd aan de mooie foto's af te zien. In La Rochelle verhongerden 25.000 mensen toen kardinaal Richelieu van 1625-1628 de totale blokkade leidde van dit eertijds protestantse broeinest. Een onbeschadigde stad viel in zijn handen.

Het departement Haute Loire, een onderdeel van het Massif Central, met Le Puy en Rocher St. Michel. Een oud vulkanisch plateau.

As atrocidades da história não se podem avaliar por belas fotografias. Em La Rochelle morreram 25.000 pessoas de fome quando o cardinal Richelieu, de 1625 e 1628, fez um bloqueio total àquele 'ninho' de protestantes. Assim tomou ele posse de uma cidade intacta.

O departamento Houte Loire, uma parte do Planalto Central, com Le Puy e Rocher St. Michel. Um antigo planalto vulcânico.

Τα κακουργήματα της ιστορίας δεν φαίνονται πάντα στις ωραίες φωτογραφίες. Στο Λαποσέλ λιμοκτόνησαν 25.000 άτομα όταν ο καρδινάλιος Ρισελιέ από το 1625-1628 ηγήθηκε τον πλήρη αποκλεισμό της αλλοτινής εστίας των καλβινιστών. Μια απείραχτη πόλη έπεσα στα χέρια του. Ο νομός Ω Λουάρ, ένα κομμάτι του Μασσίφ Σεντράλ, με το Λε Πουί και το Ροσέ Σαιν Μισέλ, ένα παλαιό υφαιστειογενές οροπέδιο.

10
FRANCE II

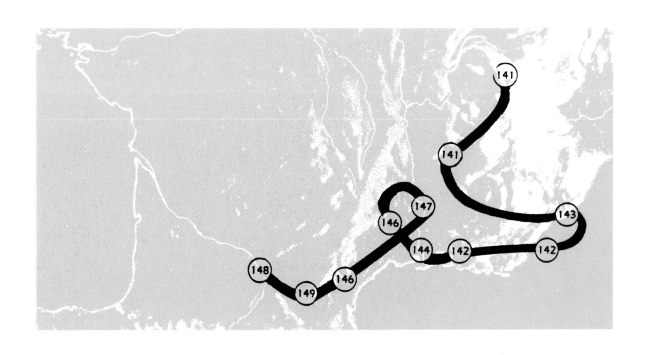

En 1786, deux habitants de Chamonix, Balmat et Paccard, réussirent à atteindre le sommet du mont Blanc. La plus haute montage d'Europe de 4810 m était vaincue, l'alpinisme était né, le caractère majestueux du mont Blanc n'en a pas été affecté pour autant. La ville la plus importante des Alpes françaises est Grenoble, magnifiquement situées au carrefour de plusieurs vallées et entourée de montagnes. Il s'agit naturellement d'un lieu voué aux sports d'hiver mais qui, à l'évidence, est aussi bien plus que cela!

I 1786 lykkedes det to indbyggere fra Chamonix, Balmat og Paccard, at nå op til toppen af Mont Blanc. Hermed var Europas højeste bjerg, 4810 m, overvundet og alpinsporten født. Det majestætiske ved det Hvide Bjerg var ikke blevet berørt heraf. Den vigtigste by i de franske alper er Grenoble, pragtfuldt beliggende der, hvor flere dale mødes og omkranset af bjerge. Naturligvis et vintersportssted, men også tydeligt mere end det.

1786 gelang es zwei Bewohnern von Chamonix, Balmat und Paccard, erstmals den Montblanc zu ersteigen, den mit 4810 m höchsten Berg Europas. Das war die Geburtsstunde des heute weltweit beliebten Alpinismus. Der Majestät des 'Weißen Berges' hat die Bergsteigerei keinen Abbruch getan. Die größte Stadt der französischen Alpen ist Grenoble, wunderschön am Ausgang mehrerer Täler und von hohen Bergen umrahmt. Der Wintersportort ist freilich auch administratives, wirtschaftliches und mit einer alten Universität geistiges Zentrum.

In 1876, Balmat and Plancard, two citizens of Chamonix, succeeded in reaching the summit of Mont Blanc, the highest mountain in Europe (4810 metres). This success marks the beginning of Alpine mountaineering. Magnificently situated where valleys meet, and surrounded by mountains Grenoble is the foremost city of the French Alps. It is, of course, best known for its winter sports, but is much more than a winter resort.

Dos habitantes de Chamonix alcanzaron la cima del Mont Blanc en 1786: Balmat y Paccard. La montaña más alta de Europa, 4810 metros, había sido dominada, había nacido el alpinismo, aunque la majestuosidad de la Montaña Blanca sigue intocable. La ciudad más importante de los Alpes Franceses es Grenoble, situada hermosamente en un cruce de valles y rodeada por montañas. Naturalmente un lugar de deportes de invierno, pero claramente de muchas otras cosas.

Nel 1786, due abitanti di Chamonix, Balmat e Paccard, riuscirono la cima del Monte Bianco, le più alta montagna europea con i suoi 4810 m. L'alpinismo era nato, ma la maestosità del Monte Bianco è rimasta da allora inalterata. La città più importante delle Alpi francesi è Grenoble, situata alla confluenza di numerose vallate e circondata di montagne. Si tratta di un luogo celebre per gli sport invernali e per molte altre ragioni.

Twee inwoners van Chamonix slaagden er in 1786 in om de top van de Mont Blanc te bereiken: Balmat en Paccard. De hoogste berg van Europa, 4810 m, was bedwongen, het alpinisme was geboren, de majestueusiteit van de Witte Berg is er niet door aangetast. De belangrijkste stad van de Franse Alpen is Grenoble, prachtig gelegen in een kruispunt van dalen en omringd door bergen. Natuurlijk een wintersportplaats, maar ook duidelijk meer dan dat!

Dois moradores de Chamonix conseguiram atingir o topo do Mont Blanc, em 1786: Balmat e Paccard. O monte mais alto da Europa, 4810 m, foi conquistado; o alpinismo teve o seu início, mas a masjestuosidade do Monte Blanco nada sofreu com isso. A cidade mais importante dos Alpes franceses é Grenoble, situada magnificamente num cruzamento de vales e rodeada por montes. Naturalmente é um local excelente para desportos de inverno, mas é indubitavelmente mais que isso!

Δύο κάτοικοι του Σαμονί πέτυχαν το 1786 να φτάσουν στη κορυφή του Λευκού Όρου, ο Μπαλμά και ο Παγκάρ. Το ψηλότερο βουνό της Ευρώπης, 4810μ., είχε υπερνικηθεί και ο αλπινισμός γεννήθηκε, αλλά το μεγαλείο του Λευκού Όρου δεν μολύνθηκε. Η σημαντικότερη πόλη των Γαλλικών Αλπέων είναι το Γκρενόμπλ που βρίσκεται θαυμάσια σ' ένα σταυροδρόμι από κοιλάδες και τριγυρίζεται από βουνά. Οπωσδήποτε τόπος για χειμερινό σπορ, αλλά επίσης νοητό περισσότερο από αυτό.

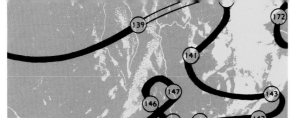

Marseille, fondée par les Grecs, est le port le plus important de France. A l'avant-plan, la basilique Notre-Dame-de-la-Garde, date du milieu du siècle précédent. C'est également à cette époque que les touristes anglais mirent la Côte d'Azur à la mode.
Jusqu'à cette époque, celle-ci était une oasis de paix et de calme, comme l'est encore

Marseille, oprindeligt anlagt af grækerne, er Frankrigs vigtigste havneby. I forgrunden basilikaen Notre-Dame-de-la-Garde fra midten af det forrige århundrede. På den tid kom Côte d'Azur også på mode hos de engelske turister. Indtil da var det en roens og stilhedens oase, ligesom nu klostret St. Honorat på den lille ø med samme navn lige ud for Cannes. På azurkysten, men ikke i Frankrig, ligger også fyrstendømmet Monaco.

Marseille, established by the Ancient Greeks, is the most important of all French ports. In the foreground there is the basilica of Notre-Dame-de-la-Garde, which dates from the middle of the last century. Even at that time, the Côte d'Azur was a popular holiday resort for English tourists, before this it had been a haven of peace and quiet, as is the monastery of St. Honorat, situated on the small island with the same name, just off the coast from Cannes. The sovereign state of Monaco is also situated on the, Côte d'Azur though, of course, it does not form part of French territory.

Das um 600 v. Chr. von Griechen und Phokäern gegründete Marseille ist die bedeutendste Hafen Frankreichs. Im Vordergrund sehen wir die um 1860 erbaute Wallfahrtskirche Notre-Dame-de-la-Garde. Um jene Zeit begann der Ansturm englischer Touristen auf die Côte d'Azur, einst eine Oase der Ruhe, wie man sie heute noch im Kloster Saint-Honorat auf der gleichnamigen Insel vor Cannes spüren kann. Ebenfalls an der Côte d'Azur liegt das politisch nicht zu Frankreich gehörende Fürstentum Monaco mit dem Luxusbadeort Monte Carlo.

Marsella, ya fundada por los griegos, es el puerto más importante de Francia. En primer plano la basílica Notre-Dame-de-la-Garde de mediados del siglo pasado. Igualmente en ese tiempo sugió la moda de los turistas ingleses en la Costa Azul. Hasta esas fechas esta zona era un oasis de calma y tranquilidad, como ahora aún lo es el monasterio de St. Honorat en la isla del mismo nombre, cerca de Cannes. También en la Costa Azul, pero no en Francia naturalmente, el Principado de Monaco.

Marsiglia, fondata dai Greci, è il porto più importante di Francia. In primo piano, la Basilica di Notre-Dame de la Garde risale alla metà del secolo scorso. Nelle stesso periodo gli inglesi resero alla moda la Costa Azzurra quale luogo di turismo. Fino a quel momento, la Costa Azzurra era stata un'oasi di pace e di calma, come lo è ancora oggi il chiostro di St. Honorat, situato sull'omonimo isolotto di fronte a Cannes. Ancora sulla Costa Azzurra, ma al di fuori della Francia, troviamo il Principato di Monaco.

Marseille, al door de Grieken gesticht, is de belangrijkste havenstad van Frankrijk. Op de voorgrond de baseliek Notre-Dame-de-la-Garde uit het midden van de vorige eeuw. Eveneens in die tijd kwam bij de Engelse toeristen de Côte d'Azur in zwang. Dat was tot aan die tijd een oase van rust en kalmte, zoals nu nog het klooster St. Honorat op een gelijknamig eilandje vlak voor Cannes. Ook aan de azuren kust, maar niet in Frankrijk natuurlijk, het Prinsdom Monaco.

Marselha, fundada já pelos gregos, é a cidade portuária mais importante da França. No primeiro plano vê-se a basílica de Notre-Dame-de-la-Garde, que data do meio do século anterior. Tambem nesse período começou Côte d'Azur a ser muito procurada pelos turistas ingleses. Ela foi até essa altura um oase de sossego e tranquilidade, como é agora ainda o mosteiro de St. Honorat, numa ilha com o mesmo nome, próximo de Cannes. Tambem na Costa Azul, mas não na França, claro, está o Principado do Mónaco.

Η Μασσαλία που είχε ιδρυθεί από τους Έλληνες, είναι το σημαντικότερο λιμάνι της Γαλλίας. Στα προσκήνια η βασιλική Νοτρ Νταμ ντε λα Γκάρντε από τα μέσα του περασμένου αιώνα. Επίσης στην εποχή αυτή έγινε της μόδας για τους Άγγλους τουρίστες η Κυανή Ακτή που μέχρι την εποχή αυτή υπήρξε μια όαση από γαλήνη και ηρεμία, όπως τώρα ακόμα το μοναστήρι Σαιν Ονορά στο συνονόματο νησί κοντά και μπροστά στις Κάννες. Επίσης στην κυανή ακτή, αλλά όχι στη Γαλλία ασφαλώς, το πριγκιπάτο Μονακό.

aujourd'hui le cloître Saint-Honorat, situé sur un îlot du même nom en face de Cannes. Sur la Côte d'Azur également, mais en dehors de la France bien évidemment, la Principauté de Monaco.

La Camargue, un territoire protégé de quelque 13 500 ha, domaine des chevaux sauvages, abrite de nombreux sites naturels. Juste à côté, la "Nouvelle Floride française", née des années soixante.

Camargue, 13.500 ha beskyttet landskab, de vilde hestes og meget anden naturs domæne. Tæt ved 'Nouvelle Floride française' fra tresserne.

Camargue ist ein 13500 ha umfassendes Naturschutzgebiet mit charakteristischer Flora und Fauna. Einen krasser Gegensatz dazu bildet das supermoderne 'französische Neu-Florida' ganz in der Nähe.

The Camargue is 13500 hectares of protected countryside, the home of wild horses and an virtually untouched nature reserve. Nearby is 'Nouvelle Floride Française', which dates from the 1960s.

Camargue, 13.500 hectáreas de paisaje protegido, territorio de caballos salvajes y mucha otra naturaleza. Cerca de ahí la 'Nouvelle Floride française' de los años sesenta.

La Camargue, un territorio protetto di circa 13.500 ettari, dominio di cavalli selvaggi e ricco di angoli incantevoli. Vicinissima la 'Nuovelle Floride Fransaise, nota negli anni 60'.

Camargue, 13.500 ha beschermd landschap, domein van wilde paarden en veel andere natuur. Vlak daarbij 'Nouvelle Floride française' uit onze jaren zestig.

Camargue, 13.500 ha de terreno protegido, o domínio de cavalos selvagens e de mais natureza. Próximo daí a 'Nouvelle Floride Française', da nossa década dos sesenta.

Το Καμάργ, 13.500 στρέμματα προστατευόμενο τοπίο, είναι η επικρατεία των άγριων αλόγων όπου υπάρχει και πολλή άλλη φύση. Κοντά βρίσκεται η 'Νουβέλ Φλορίντ φρανσέσε' από τη δεκαετία του εξήντα μας.

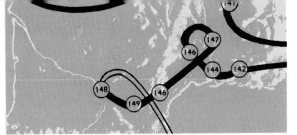

Le port de Narbonne perdit sa fonction de port en 1320 en raison d'une modification soudaine du cours de l'Aude. La ville, qui avait une longue histoire derrière elle puisque celle-ci avait commencé vers 500 av. Jésus-Christ, s'endormit. Pour ne se réveiller, comme la Belle au bois dormant, qu'au cours de ce siècle seulement, grâce au commerce du vin. Les Romains étaient également bien présents à Nîmes. Les arènes sont l'un des amphithéâtres romains les mieux conservés et peuvent accueillir 21 000 personnes. Nombre d'autres monuments romains se retrouvent également ici. Le célèbre Pont d'Avignon, de la fin du 12e siècle, où, selon la chanson, on pouvait si bien danser, surplombe encore le Rhône du haut des trois arches qui lui restent. Le paysage urbain de l'antique Avignon qui a, elle aussi, une histoire romaine est dominé par le palais des Papes. C'est ici que les papes résidèrent pendant leur période de bannissement, au 14e siècle.

In 1320, Narbonne lost its important status as a port when the River Aude suddenly changed its course. The city, which dates from about 500 B.C., fell into decline, only to awaken at the beginning of this century due to the development of a prosperous wine industry.

Nîmes also bears evidence of its Roman occupation, having one of the best preserved Roman amphitheatres which can accommodate 21000 spectators. There are numerous other Roman monuments in this town including the late 12th century Pont d'Avignon with its remaining three arches

still partly bridging the Rhône. The old city of Avignon, also an historical Roman site, is dominated by the Palais des Papes, the residence of the Popes during their exile in the 14th century.

El puerto de Narbona perdió su función en 1320, por un repentino cambio del curso del Aude. La ciudad, que ya en 500 a.C. tenía una larga historia, se durmió. Para despertar como la bella durmiente en nuestro siglo, gracias al comercio vinícola. Los romanos también estuvieron en Nîmes. El Arènes es uno de los amfiteatros que mejor se conservan,

con una capacidad de 21.000 personas. Aún se pueden ver muchos otros monumentos romanos.

El famoso Puente de Aviñón, de finales del s. XII, sobre el que según la canción tan bien se puede bailar, se mantiene en parte con tres arcos sobre el Ródano. La imagen de la antigua Aviñón, también con su historia romana, está dominada por el Palacio de los Papas que residieron ahí durante su exilio en el s. XIV.

Il porto di Narbonne perse completamente la sua funzione di porto nel 1320, in seguito ad un improvviso cambia-

mento del corso dell'Aude. La città che risaliva al 500 a.C., cadde in letargo e si risvegliò solo nel nostro secolo grazie al commercio del vino. I Romani furono presenti anche a Nîmes. Les Arènes è uno degli anfiteatri romani meglio conservati e può contenere 21.000 persone.

Nella zona si trovano numerosi altri monumenti romani. Del famoso Ponte di Avignone, che risale alla fine del XII secolo, e su cui si poteva così facilmente ballare, come dice la celebre canzone, rimangono ancora tre arcate.

L'immagine del centro storico di Avignone è dominata dal

Narbonnes havn mistede i 1320 sin betydning på grund af en pludselig ændring af floden Audes løb. Byen, der dengang allerede fra 500 f.kr. havde en lang historie bag sig, sov ind. For først i vort århundrede, takket være vinhandelen, at vågne op fra sin tornerose søvn. Også i Nîmes har romerne tydeligvis været tilstede. Arenaen er et af de bedst bevarede romerske amfiteatre med plads til mere til 21.000 mennesker. Der findes i øvrigt talrige andre romerske monumenter.

Den berømte Pont d'Avignon, fra slutningen af det 12. århundrede, hvor man ifølge sangen så godt kan danse, står der stadig delvist med tre buer i floden Rhone. Det gamle Avignons bybillede, der også har en romersk historie, domineres af Palais des Papes (Paveslottet). Paverne residerede her under deres fangeskab i det 14. århundrede.

Als die Aude 1320 ihren Lauf änderte, verlor der Hafen von Narbonne seine Bedeutung; die schon um 500 v. Chr. gegründete geschichtsreiche Stadt verfiel in einen Dornröschenschlaf. Erst in unserem Jahrhundert erwachte sie durch den Weinhandel zu neuem Leben. Daß Nîmes schon in römischer Zeit in hoher Blüte stand, beweisen die 'arènes', eines der besterhaltenen römischen Amphitheater, das bis zu 21.000 Besucher aufnehmen konnte, aber auch viele weitere römische Bauten. Solche finden wir auch in Avignon mit seiner berühmten, vielbesungenen Rhone-Brücke aus dem späten 12. Jahrhundert. Das die Stadt beherrschende Bauwerk ist freilich der mächtige, festungsgleich wirkende Papstpalast, in dem die Päpste von 1309 bis 1376 die sogenannte 'babylonische Gefangenschaft der Kirche' überstanden, nachdem sie aus Rom vertrieben worden waren. Bis 1797 blieb Avignon in päpstlichem Besitz. Den Päpsten hat die Stadt viele ihrer schönsten Bauwerke zu verdanken.

Palazzo dei Papi. Esso fu la residenza dei papi, nel periodo del loro esilio nel XIV secolo.

De haven van Narbonne verloor in 1320, door een plotselinge wijziging van de loop van de Aude, zijn functie. De stad, die toen al een vanaf ca. 500 v. Chr. lange geschiedenis achter zich had, sliep in. Om eerst in onze eeuw, dankzij de wijnhandel, als een schone slaapster wakker te worden. De Romeinen waren ook overduidelijk aanwezig in Nîmes. De Arènes is één der best bewaarde Romeinse amfitheaters met plaats voor 21.000 mensen. Ook tal van andere

Romeinse monumenten zijn hier nog te vinden.
De beroemde Pont d'Avignon, van het eind van de twaalfde eeuw, waarop men volgens het liedje zo goed dansen kan, staat nog gedeeltelijk, met drie bogen, in de Rhône. Het stadsbeeld van het oude Avignon, dat ook al een Romeinse geschiedenis heeft, wordt gedomineerd door het Palais des Papes. De pausen resideerden hier tijdens hun ballingschap in de veertiende eeuw.

O porto de Norbonne perdeu em 1320 a sua função, devido a uma modificação inesperdada da corrente do Aude. A cidade, que nessa altura já tinha uma história iniciada em 500 a.c., adormeceu. Para, apenas no nosso século se acordar, como uma formosa sonhadora, graças os comércio do vinho.
Os romanos estiveram tambem em Nîmes, como facilmente se pode constatar. O Arènes é um dos anfiteatros romanos mais bem conservados, com lugar para 21.000 pessoas. Muitos outros monumentos romanos podem ser admirados aqui.

A famosa Pont d'Avignon, do fim do século XII, sobre a qual se pode dançar bem, como diz a cantiga conhecida, está ainda parcialmente, com três arcos sobre o Rhône. A imagem da cidade, que tambem tem um passado romano, é dominada pelo Palais des Papes. Os papas tiveram aqui a sua residência, durante o seu exílio, no século XIV.

Το λιμανί του Ναρμόν έχασε το 1320 από ξαφνική αλλαγή της ροής του Ωντ τη θέση του. Η πόλη που τότε είχε κιόλας μακρόχρονη ιστορία από το 500 προ Χριστού, αποκοιμήθηκε για να ξυπνήσει στο δικό μας αιώνα σαν την κοιμισμένη καλλονή χάρη στο εμπόριο κρασιού.
Οι Ρωμαίοι ολοφάνερα ήταν παρόντες στο Μιμ. Το Αρέν είναι ένα από τα καλύτερα συντηρημένα ρωμαϊκά αμφιθέατρα που προσφέρει θέσεις σε 21.000 ανθρώπους. Μπορείτε να βρείτε και πολλά άλλα ρωμαϊκά μνημεία. Το φημισμένο Πον ντ'Αβινιόν από τα τέλη του δωδέκατου αιώνα, που πάνω του μπορεί κανείς να χορέψει τόσο καλά, όπως λέει και το τραγούδι, υπάρχει ακόμα μερικώς με τρεις καμάρες στο Ροδανό.
Η μορφή της παλαιάς πόλης Αβινιόν που επίσης έχει ρωμαϊκή ιστορία, κυριαρχείται από το Παλαί ντε Παπ. Οι πάπηδες διέμειναν εδώ το δέκατο τέταρτο αιώνα κατά τον εξορισμό τους.

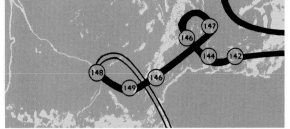

Toulouse connut également un grand développement à l'époque romaine. Elle possède aujourd'hui une industrie extrémement variée, surtout dans les domaines de pointe axés sur l'aéronautique et l'astronautique. Avec Carcassonne, nous cloturons la série des villes romaines antiques. Cette ville est surtout connue par sa double enceinte.

Toulouse er sydvest-frankrigs vigtigste by, og den blomstrede allerede under romerne. Byen har nu en varieret og frem for alt avanceret industri, bl.a. tilpasset luft- og rumfarten. Med Carcassonne slutter vi rækken af gamle romerske byer. Byen er mest berømt for sin dobbelte mur.

Eine römische Gründung ist Toulouse, die bedeutendste Stadt in Südwestfrankreich, in der heute hochmoderne Industrie (vor allem Luft- und Raumfahrt) angesiedelt ist. Die letzte Römerstadt die wir zeigen wollen ist Carcassonne, umschlossen von einem riesigen Mauerkomplex mit wuchtigen Türmen. Dank großer Restaurationsarbeiten im vergangenen Jahrhundert hat die Stadt ihr mittelalterliches Bild bewahrt.

Toulouse, which dates from Roman times, is the most important city in Southwest France. It has now developed as a centre for aviation and space technology.
Carcassonne, with its twin walls of fortification, ends our tour of ancient Roman cities.

Toulouse es la ciudad más importante del sudoeste de Francia y ya en la época romana fue muy floreciente. Tiene ahora una industria variada y avanzada, sobre todo dirigida a la navegación aérea y espacial. Con Carcassone cerramos la lista de antiguas ciudades romanas. La mayor fama la tiene está ciudad por sus dobles murallas.

Anche Toulouse ebbe un grande sviluppo in epoca romana. Oggi essa possiede un'industria avanzata, in particolar modo nel campo dell'areonautica e dell'astronautica. Con Carcassonne terminiamo la serie delle antiche città romane.
Questa città è conosciuta soprattutto per la sua doppia cerchia di mura.

Toulouse is de belangrijkste stad van Zuidwest-Frankrijk en kwam ook al in de Romeinse tijd tot grote bloei. Het heeft nu een gevarieerde en ook een geavanceerde industrie, onder andere afgestemd op lucht- en ruimtevaart. Met Carcassonne sluiten we de rij van oude Romeinse steden. De grootste faam heeft deze stad door de dubbele ommuring.

Tolosa é a cidade mais importante do Sul da França e gosou tambem, no tempo dos romanos, de um grande desenvolvimento. Tem agora uma indústria variada e, em especial, avançada, entre outras, adaptada è aeronáutica e aos fogetões espaciais. Com Carcassonne chegamos ao fim da lista das cidades antigas romanas. A maior fama tem esta cidade pelas suas muralhas duplas.

Η Τουλούζη είναι η πιο σημαντική πόλη της νοτιοδυτικής Γαλλίας και άκμαζε κιόλας στη Ρωμαϊκή εποχή. Τώρα κατέχει διάφορες και προχωρημένες βιομηχανίες, μεταξύ άλλων στον τομέα αεροναυτικής και διαστημικής. Με το Καρκασόν κλείνουμε την ουρά από παλαιές ρωμαϊκες πόλεις. Η μεγαλύτερη φήμη έχει η πόλη αυτή από το διπλό εντοιχισμό.

11 ESPAÑA

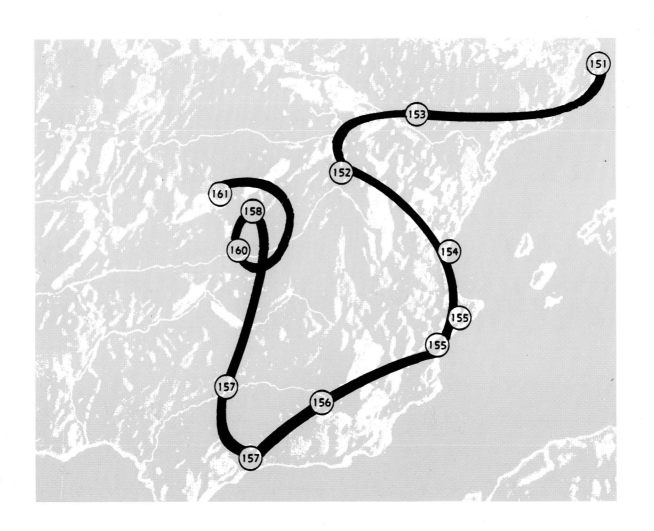

En Tossa de Mar, en la Costa Brava, se hace visible la milenaria historia de Cataluña. Las murallas de la edad media están intactas y el museo tiene hallazgos romanos y también un Chagall original.
La costa más brava en Lloret de Mar se encuentra en los clubs y discotecas.

På Costa Brava, den vilde kyst, kan man se kataloniens 1000-årige historie i Tossa de Mar. Middelaldervolden er intakt og på museet findes der fund fra romertiden og en ægte Chagall.
Det vildeste på kysten i Lloret de Mar drejer sig frem for alt om natklubberne og diskotekerne.

The city of Tossa de Mar on the Costa Brava ('the wild coast') reflects a thousand years of Catalonian history. Its medieval walls have remained intact, and its museum contains archeological treasures which date back to Roman times, as well as a painting by Chagall. The present-day 'wild coast' is perhaps best experienced in its numerous nightclubs and discos.

La millenaria storia della Catalogna è visibile a Tossa del Mar, sulla Costa Brava.
Le cerchia di mura di epoca medioevale è intatta e nel museo sono conservati oggetti romani ed un autentico Chagall.
Lloret de Mar, le più selvaggia della costa, fa spicco per i club notturni e le discoteche.

Na Costa Brava, nota-se a história milénia da Catalunha, em Tossa de Mar. As marulhas medievais estão intactas e o museu possui achados romanos e... tambem um verdadeiro Chagall.
A bravura da costa em Lloret de Mar reflete-se tambem nos diversos boîtes noturnos e nas discotecas.

Der jahrhundertealten Geschichte Kataloniens begegnet man an der Costa Brava, der 'wilden' Küste in Tossa de Mar: mittelalterliche Stadtmauern bergen ein Museum mit römischen Funden, aber auch mit einem echten Chagall. Wild wie die Küste ist das Treiben in den Nachtklubs und Diskotheken des vielbesuchten Seebads Lloret de Mar.

L'histoire millénaire de la Catalogne est bien visible à Tossa de Mar, sur la Costa Brava ou côte sauvage. L'enceinte médiévale est intacte et le musée abrite des objets romains, ainsi qu'un véritable Chagall.
Mais ce qu'il y a de plus sauvage sur la côte de Lloret de Mar se retrouve surtout dans les night-clubs et les discothèques.

Aan de Costa Brava, de wilde kust, is de 1000-jarige geschiedenis van Catalonië in Tossa de Mar zichtbaar. De middeleeuwse omwalling is intact en het museum heeft Romeinse vondsten en ook een echte Chagall.
Het wildste van de kust in Lloret de Mar slaat vooral op de nachtclubs en discotheken.

Στην Κόστα Μπράβα, την άγρια ακτή, η 1000-χρονη ιστορία της Καταλωνίας είναι ορατή στην Τόσσα ντε Μαρ. Τα μεσαιωνικά τείχη είναι απείραχτα και στο μουσείο βρίσκονται Ρωμαϊκά ευρύματα και ένα αληθινό Σαγκάλ.
Στην ακτή της Λορέτ ντε Μαρ κυριαρχεί η ζωηρότητα προπαντώς στα νυχτερινά κέντρα και στις ντισκοτέκ.

El paisaje de Calatayud nos muestra la secana meseta de Aragón. Sólo en la cuenca del Ebro es posible una agricultura de irrigación. Zaragoza fue en el pasado la capital del Reino de Aragón hasta 1833, fecha en que dejó de existir esa denominación. Y desde entonces es la capital de la provincia del mismo nombre. Una ciudad tan histórica e importante que casi no superó la época francesa. Un sitio de unos tres meses costó la vida a 50.000 habitantes en 1809; apenas 10.000 habitantes lo sobrevivieron.

Calatayuds landskab viser os Aragoniens tørre højslette. Kun i Ebrobækkenet er kultivering af afgrøder mulig gennem et omfattende vandingssystem. Zaragoza var tidligere kongeriget Aragoniens hovedstad, der med navn ophørte med at bestå i 1833. Og siden da er det hovedstaden i provinsen med samme navn. Den gamle historiske og vigtige by ved Ebro overlevede med nød og næppe den franske tid. En belejring på knap tre måneder kostede i 1809 50.000 indbyggere livet, og kun 10.000 indbyggere overlevede.

Das karge Hochland Aragoniens zeigt uns diese Landschaft bei Calatayud. Fruchtbar ist dank eines ausgedehnten Bewässerungssystems nur das Tal des Ebro. Saragossa war einst Hauptstadt des Königreichs Aragonien, das bis 1833 bestand; seither ist es Provinzhauptstadt. Die von den Römern gegründete Stadt hatte unter den Napoleonischen Kriegen schwer zu leiden: Eine dreimonatige Belagerung durch die Franzosen überlebten nur knapp 10 000 der 60 000 Einwohner, doch blieben viele der alten Bauten erhalten.

The countryside around Calatayud is characterised by the high arid plains of Aragon. The Ebro basin is the only place where it is possible to cultivate crops, thanks only to extensive irrigation. Zaragoza was the capital city first of the kingdom of Aragon, and subsequently became the capital of the region that bears the same name. This city on the banks of the River Ebro barely survived the period of French rule, when in 1809, a short but severe three month siege claimed the lives of 50000 of its citizens.

Le paysage des environs de Calatayud nous fait voir les hauts plateaux arides de l'Aragon. Ce n'est que dans le bassin de l'Ebre que la croissance des plantes cultivées est possible grâce à une irrigation extensive des terres arables. Autrefois, Saragosse était la capitale du royaume d'Aragon dont l'existence a cessé en 1833. Et depuis, Aragon est la capitale de la province du même nom. Cette ville ancienne sur l'Ebre avait survécu à grand-peine à l'occupation française. Celle-ci qui dura trois mois seulement dut être achetée par la mort de 50 000 habitants en 1809.

Il paesaggio dei dintorni di Catalayud ci mostra gli altipiani aridi dell'Aragona. Solo nel bacino dell'Ebro è possibile la crescita di piante coltivate e ciò in virtù di una irrigazione estesa delle terre coltivabili. Saragozza è stata un tempo la capitale del regno d'Aragona che non esiste più dal 1833. Da allora, Aragona è la capitale della provincia omonima. L'antica città sull'Ebro è sopravvisuta con difficolta all'occupazione francese. Un assedio di soli tre mesi costò la vita a 50.000 abitanti nel 1809; solo 10.000 persone sopravvissero.

Het landschap bij Calatayud toont ons de dorre hoogvlakte van Aragon. Alleen in het Ebrobekken is er met een uitgebreide landbouwirregatie cultivatie van gewassen mogelijk. Zaragoza was vroeger de hoofdstad van het koninkrijk Aragon, dat in naam in 1833 ophield te bestaan. En sindsdien is het de hoofdstad van de gelijknamige provincie. De historisch oude en belangrijke stad aan de Ebro had de Franse tijd nauwelijks overleefd. Een beleg van amper 3 maanden moest door 50.000 inwoners in 1809 met de dood bekocht worden.

A paîsagem dos arredores de Calatayud apresenta-nos o planalto árido de Aragão. Apenas com auxílio de ampla irrigação é possível a cultura agrícola na bacia do Ebro. Saragoça foi em tempos a capital do reino de Aragão, o qual deixou de existir em nome em 1833. E a partir de então passou a ser a capital da província com o mesmo nome. A cidade histórica e de grande importância nas margens do Ebro sobreviveu dificilmente o período francês. Um assídio de 3 meses custou a vida a 50.000 habitantes em 1809 e apenas uns 10.000 sobreviveram.

Το τοπίο του Καλαταγιούντ μας δείχνει το άγονο υψόπεδο της Αραγωνίας. Μόνο στην κοιλάδα του Έβρου υπάρχουν δυνατότητες με εκτεταμένη γεωργική άδρευση να καλλιεργούνται φυτά. Η Σαραγόσα ήταν στα παλιά η πρωτεύουσα του βασιλείου Αραγωνίας που το όνομα του βασιλείου σταμάτησε να υπάρχει από το 1833. Και από τότε είναι η πρωτεύουσα του συνονόματου νομού. Η ιστορική, παλαιά και σπουδαία πόλη στις όχθες του Έβρου μόλις που επέζησε τη Γαλλική εποχή. Μια πολιορκία τριών μηνών στοίχισε τη ζωή σε 50.000 κατοίκους.

Valencia, la cuarta ciudad de España, tiene una plaza de toros. Antes que los romanos, estuvieron ahí los griegos, los cartagineses y después los visigodos y los musulmanes. Siendo ciudad musulmana el héroe español El Cid la reconquistó en 1094. La región se hizo un principado independiente y en el siglo XV fue incorporada a Aragón y Castilla. La Costa Blanca, con sus playas de Alicante y Benidorm, es la costa de Europa más visitada por los turistas que adoran el sol. Millones de turistas de la Europa del norte y de Gran Bretaña toman ahí el sol en verano. Para la generación más mayor, Alicante y Benidorm es una atracción para escapar en el invierno del frío y nebuloso norte.

Eine wechselvolle Geschichte hat Valencia, die viertgrößte Stadt Spaniens. Vor den Römern siedelten hier schon Griechen und Karthager, und später kam die Stadt in westgotischen und maurischen Besitz. Den Mauren entrissen wurde sie 1094 durch den spanischen Nationalhelden, El Cid. Zunächst Hauptstadt eines unabhängigen Teilkönigtums, fiel Valencia im 13. Jahrhundert an Aragonien, bis dieses 1497 mit Kastilien vereinigt wurde.
Zu den beliebtesten Touristenzielen in Spanien zählen die sonnigen Strände der Costa Blanca mit den modern ausgebauten Seebädern Alicante und Benidorm, die besonders in der kälteren Jahreszeit viele Besucher aus nördlichen Gefilden anlocken, weil sie dort dem unfreundlichen Winterklima ihrer Heimatländer entfliehen können.

Valence, la quatrième ville d'Espagne en superficie, possède une arène. Avant les Romains, les Grecs et les Carthaginois et, après les Romains les Visigoths et les Maures occupèrent longtemps la ville. Le héros espagnol El Cid s'em-para de la ville, occupée par les Maures, en 1094. La région fut principauté indépendante et rattachée, au 15e siècle, à l'Aragon et à la Castille.
La Costa Blanca possède avec ses plages d'Alicante et de Benidorm, la plus grande concentration de touristes par mètre carré d'Europe. Des millions de touristes du Nord de l'Europe et de Grande-Bretagne viennent y lézarder au soleil de l'été. Pour les plus âgés, Alicante et Benidorm constituent des endroits privilégiés à l'abri des hivers froids et brumeux du Nord.

Valencia, la quarta città più grande i Spagna, possiede un'arena. Prima dei Romani, Cartaginesi e i Greci, e dopo i Romani, i Visigoti e i Mori, occuparono a lungo la città. L'eroe spagnolo, El Cid, conquistò la città, occupata dai Mori, nel 1094. La regione fu un principato indipendente e fu poi unita, nel XV secolo, all'Aragona e alla Castiglia. La Costa Blanca, con le spiagge di Alicante e Benidorm, costituisce la più grande concentrazione di turisti per metro quadrato d'Europa. Milioni di turisti del Nord Europa e della Gran Bretagna vengono qui a go-dersi il sole dell'estate. Per le persone anziane, Alicante e Benidorm costituiscono località privilegiate, lontane dagli inverni e dalle nebbie del Nord.

Valencia, in grootte de vierde stad van Spanje, bezit een arena. Voor de Romeinen waren er reeds Grieken, Carthagers en na hen Visigoten en Moren die de plaats met een langdurige aanwezigheid vereerden. De Spaanse held El Cid veroverde de stad in 1094 op de Moren. Het gebied werd een onafhankelijk vorstendom en in de vijftiende eeuw bij Aragon en Castilië gevoegd.
De Costa Blanca bezit met zijn stranden te Alicante en Benidorm de grootste concentratie van zonnetoerisme per vierkante meter in Europa. Miljoenen toeristen uit Noord-Europa en Groot-Brittannië komen zich hier in de zomer koesteren aan de zon. Voor de oudere generatie zijn Alicante en Benidorm begeerde trekpleisters om het kille en mistige Noorden in de winter te ontvluchten.

Valência, em tamanho é a quarta cidade de Espanha e tem uma arena. Antes dos Romanos, já tinham honrado com a sua longa permanência os Gregos, os Cartagineses, os Visigodos e os Mouros. Foi o herói espanhol El Cid que conquistou a cidade aos Mouros em 1094. Esta área tornou-se reino independente que foi agregado a Aragão e Castilha, no séx. XV.
A Costa Blanca com as suas praias em Alicante e Benidorm possui a maior concentração de turismo por metro quadrado da Europa. Milhões de turistas vindos do Norte da Europa e da Grã-Bretanha vêm aqui para se deixarem afagar pelo sol. Para a geração mais velha Alicante e Benidorm são lugares cobiçados de atracção turística quando querem fugir do inverno nos países frios e nublados do Norte.

Valencia, Spaniens fjerdestørste by, har en arena. Valencia blev allerede før romerne bæret med et længere varende besøg af grækere og kartagere og efter romerne kom visigoterne og maurerne. Den spanske helt El Cid erobrede byen fra maurerne i 1094. Området blev et selvstændigt fyrstedømme og i det 15. århundrede blev det indlemmet i Aragonien og Castillien.
Med sine strande ved Alicante og Benidorm har Costa Blanca Europas højeste koncentration af solturisme per kvadratmeter. Milioner af turister fra Nordeuropa og Stor-Britanien kommer dertil om sommeren for at varme sig i solen. For den ældre generation er Alicante og Benidorm yndede overvintringssteder med henblik på at undslippe Nordens kolde og tågede vintre.

Valencia, Spain's fourth largest city has been home for many invaders: the Greeks and Carthaginians, and then the Romans, followed by the Visigoths and Moors, all of whom left vestiges of their presence. In 1094, El Cid, the Spanish national hero, defeated the Moors and liberated the city. The area became an independent principality, until in the 15th century it was annexed to Aragon and Castile Here we see the bull-fighting arena in Valencia, Spain's fourth largest city.
The Costa Blanca, with its famous beaches in Alicante and Benidorm, has the largest concentration of sun-worshipping tourists per square metre in Europe. Millions of visitors from Northern Europe gather here each summer to bask in the sun. Alicante and Benidorm are also favourite resorts for senior citizens trying to escape the cold Northern winters.

Alicante, Benidorm

Η Βαλένσια, σε μέγεθος η τέταρτη κατά σειρά πόλη της Ισπανίας, διαθέτει αρένα. Πριν από τους Ρωμαίους, είχαν έρθει οι Έλληνες και Καρχιδόνιοι και μετά αυτούς ήταν οι Βησιγότθοι και Μαυριτανοί που τιμούσαν την πόλη με μια μακροπρόθεσμη παρουσία τους. Ο Ισπανός ήρωας, Ελ Σιντ, κατάκτησε την πόλη από τους Μαυριτανούς το 1094. Ο τόπος έγινε ανεξάρτητος πριγκιπάτο και το δέκατο πέμπτο αιώνα προστέθηκε στην Αραγωνία και Καστίλλη.

Η Κόστα Μπλάγκα με τις παραλίες της στην Αλικάντε και στο Μπένιδορμ δέχεται τη μεγαλύτερη συγκέντρωση ηλιοτουρισμού ανά τετραγωνικό μετρό στην Ευρώπη. Εκατομμύρια τουρίστες από τη Βόρεια Ευρώπη και τη Μεγάλη Βρεταννία μαζεύονται εδώ το καλοκαίρι για να απολαύσουν τον ήλιο. Για τους ηλικιωμένους είναι η Αλικάντε και το Μπένιδορμ επιθυμητοί τόποι για να αποφύγουν το χειμώνα τον κρύο και την ομίχλη του βορρά.

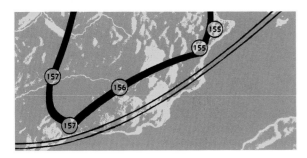

Justo el mismo año en que Colón descubrió América (1492) cayó definitivamente el califato de Córdoba. La reconquista se había acabado y Andalucía era española. Málaga cayó en 1487 y es conocida fundamentalmente como el centro de la Costa del Sol. Como un aviso de la Sierra Nevada nos encontramos la Alhambra en Granada, el último bastión de los moros en la Península. La ciudad de Córdoba ya había caído en manos españolas mucho antes, en 1236. La ciudad, hermosamente situada al Guadalquivir, sigue teniendo un inconfundible carácter moro.

hambra, the last bastion to fall, is situated in the foothills of the Sierra Nevada. Cordoba had already fallen into Spanish hands in 1236, the capital of Andalusia it is magnificently situated on the banks of the Guadalquivir and to this day retains a Moorish character.

L'année où Colomb découvrit l'Amérique pour le compte de l'Espagne (1492) fut également l'année où tomba le calife de Cordoue. La reconquête était achevée et l'Andalousie était espagnole. Málaga, qui tomba en 1487 est surtout connue comme le centre de la Costa del Sol.
Sur un contrefort de la Sierra Nevada, on trouve l'Alhambra de Grenade, la dernière forteresse maure à tomber.
La ville de Cordoue elle-même était déjà devenue espagnole beaucoup plus tôt c'est-à-dire en 1236. La cité, qui occupe une situation magnifique sur le Guadalquivir, possède toujours un caractère indubitablement maure.

Nell'anno in cui Colombo scoprì l'America (1492) cadde il califfato di Cordoba. La riconquista era terminata e l'Andalusia era spagnola. Malaga che cadde nel 1487 è conosciuta soprattutto come il centro della Costa del Sol.
Su di un contrafforte della Sierra Nevada si trova l'Alhambra di Granada che fu l'ultima fortificazione dei Mori a cadere. La città di Cordoba era già diventata spagnola molto tempo prima, nel 1236. Cordoba che è splendidamente situata sul Guadalquivir, ha ancora oggi un carattere tipicamente moro.

In het jaar dat Columbus voor Spanje Amerika ontdekte (1492) viel ook het kalifaat van Córdoba. De reconquista was voltooid en Andalusië was Spaans. Malaga viel in 1487 en is nu vooral bekend als het centrum van de Costa del Sol.
Op een uitloper van de Sierra Nevada ligt het Alhambra in Granada, het laatste Moorse bolwerk dat toen viel.

De stad Córdoba zelf was al veel eerder, in 1236, in Spaanse handen gevallen. De stad, schitterend gelegen aan de Guadalquivir, heeft nog steeds een onmiskenbaar Moors karakter.

No ano em que Christovão Colombo descubriu a América, para a Espanha (1492), deu-se tambem a queda do Califado de Córdoba. A reconquista estava completa e a Andaluzia passou a ser espanhola. Málaga caiu em 1487 e agora é conhecida, em especial, como o centro da Costa do Sol.
Sobre um ramal da Sierra Nevada encontra-se o Alhambra, em Granada, o último forte mouro que caiu.
A cidade de Córdoba tinha já caído em mãos espanholas, em 1236. Córdoba, situada magnificamente à margem do Guadalquivir tem ainda um carácter genuïnamente mouro.

Τη χρονιά που ο Κολόμβος ανακάλυψε την Αμερική εκ μέρους της Ισμανίας, έπεσε και το χαλιφάτο Κόρδοβα. Η επανακατάκτηση ολοκληρώθηκε και η Ανδαλουσία έγινε Ισπανική. Η Μάλαγα έπεσε το 1487 και σήμερα είναι προπαντώς γνωστή σαν το κέντρο της Κόστα ντελ Σολ.
Σε λοφίσκο της Σιέρα Νεβάδα, στη Γρανάδα, βρίσκεται η τελευταίος Μαυριτανικός προμαχώνας που τότε έπεσε.
Η πόλη Κόρδοβα η ίδια είχε πέσει πολύ πριν, το 1236, στα Ισπανικά χέρια. Κόρδοβα, που βρίσκεται θαυμάσια χτισμένη στις όχθες του Κουαδαλκιβίρ, έχει ακόμα ολοφάνερο Μαυριτανικό χαρακτήρα.

I det år da Columbus opdagede Amerika for Spanien faldt også kalifatet i Cordoba. Reconquistaen (generobringen) var afsluttet og Andalusien var nu spansk. Malaga faldt i 1487 og kendes nu først og fremmest som Costa del Sols centrum. På en udløber fra Sierra Nevada ligger i Granada Alhambra, det sidste mauriske bolværk der faldt.
Selve byen Cordoba var allerede meget tidligere (1236) faldet i spanske hænder. Cordoba, der ligger smukt ved Guadalquivir, har stadig et umiskendeligt maurisk præg.

Im gleichen Jahr, in dem Kolumbus die Neue Welt entdeckte (1492), fiel auch das Kalifat von Córdoba als letzte Bastion der Mauren. Damit war die Reconquisa (Rückeroberung) Spaniens vollendet. Malaga war bereits 1487 zurückerobert worden; heute ist es weltweit als Zentrum der Costa del Sol bekannt.
Am längsten hielten sich die Mauren in Granada, dessen prächtige Alhambra auf einem Ausläufer der Sierra Nevada liegt. Schon viel früher, 1236, war Córdoba von den Spaniern zurückerobert worden. Ihr maurisches Stadtbild hat die am Gudalquivir gelegene stadt bis heute bewahrt.

In 1492, the year in which Columbus discovered America, the 'reconquista' was accomplished with the overthrowing of the Caliph, and Andalusia came under Spanish rule. The city of Malaga had fallen earlier in 1487 and is now best known as the centre of the Costa del Sol. The famous Al-

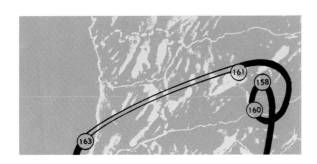

Madrid, la orgullosa capital de España, en la meseta de Castilla la Nueva. Sólo mostramos el Palacio Real acabado en 1764 en el lugar en que en 1734 se había incendiado el Alcázar moro.

Madrid, Spaniens stolte hovedstad på Ny-Castilliens tørre højslette. Vi viser kun det kongelige slot (Palacio Real), der blev færdigt i 1764 på det, hvor det mauriske Alcazar i 1734 var gået op i flammer. På Plaza Maijor (1619) finder vi endnu noget af det gamle Madrid.

Madrid, die stolze Hauptstadt Spaniens, liegt im Herzen der Neukastilischen Meseta (Hochebene). Wir zeigen hier den Stadtpalast der spanischen Könige, der 1764 an der Stelle des 1734 abgebrannten maurischen Alkazars errichtet wurde. Alte Bauten gliedern sich um die 1619 angelegte Plaza Major.

Madrid, the capital of Spain, is situated on the high arid plains of Castilla la Nueva. The Palacio Real (Royal Palace) is of special interest. It was completed in 1764 on the site of the Moorish Alcazar, which burned down in 1734. Parts of the old city of Madrid are still to be found at the Plaza Major, which dates from 1619.

Madrid, fière capitale espagnole sur un haut plateau de Nouvelle-Castille. Nous ne montrerons que le Palais Royal (Palacio Real) qui fut teminé en 1764 à l'endroit même où l'Alcazar maure avait été détruit par les flammes en 1734. Aux alentours de la Plaza Mayor (1619), nous retrouvons encore des parties de l'ancienne Madrid.

Madrid, orgogliosa capitale della Spagna, sull'arido altipiano della Nuova Castiglia. Mostreremo soltanto il Palazzo Reale la cui costruzione fu ultimata nel 1764 nello stesso luogo in cui l'Alcazar dei Mori era stato distrutto da un incendio nel 1734. Nei dintorni di Plaza Major (1619) troviamo ancora alcune parti dell'antica Madrid.

Madrid, een trotse hoofdstad van Spanje op de droge hoogvlakte van Nieuw-Castilië. We tonen slechts het Koninklijk Paleis (Palacio Real) dat in 1764 gereed kwam op de plaats waar het Moorse Alcazar in 1734 in vlammen was opgegaan. Bij de Plaza Maijor (uit 1619) vinden we nog gedeelten van het oude Madrid.

Madrid é a capital orgulhosa da Espanha, situada no planalto árido da Nova Castilha. Mostramos apenas o Palácio Real que se acabou de construir em 1764, no local onde o Alcazar Moro foi destruído pelas chamas em 1734. Junto à Plaza Mayor (de 1619) encontramos ainda restantes da Madrid antiga.

Η Μαδρίτη, η υπερήφανη πρωτεύουσα της Ισπανίας, στο άγονο υψόπεδο της Νέας Καστίλλης, κατέχει πολλά κυβερνητικά κτίρια από τη δεκαετία του 20 του αιώνα μας, αλλά ασφαλώς και πολλά άλλα πράματα. Σας δείχνουμε μόνο τα Ανάκτορα [Παλάσιο Ρεάλ] που το χτίσιμό τους τελείωσε το 1764, εκεί που το 1734 κάηκε το μαυριτανικό Αλκαζάρ. Στην Πλάθα Μαγιόρ σώζονται μέρη της παλαιάς Μαδρίτης.

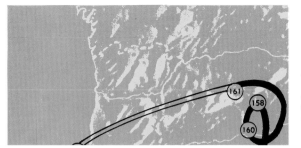

Toledo era hasta 1561 la capital de España y sigue siendo la sede del arzobispo. La ciudad, sobre una roca al Tajo, tiene una hermosura especial.

Felipe II hizo construir El Escorial, un monasterio-palacio. El enorme complejo de 206 x 61 m. se acabó en 1584 y cuenta con una rica colección de cuadros muy especial. Desde su lecho de muerte Felipe II pudo asistir a la Misa en el coro. Aquí fue enterrado al igual que casi todos los otros reyes españoles.

Toledo var indtil 1561 Spaniens hovedstad og ærkebiskoppen har fortsat sæde her. Byen, der ligger på en klippe ved floden Taag, er endnu meget velbevaret.
Kloster-paladset El Excorial blev opført af Filip II. Det enorme kompleks på 206 x 61 m blev færdigt i 1584, og det rummer en meget værdifuld malerisamling. Fra sit sygeleje kunne Filip II følge messen i hovedkoret. Han blev begravet her ligesom næsten alle andre spanske konger.

Toledo war bis 1561 die Hauptstadt Spaniens; heute residiert hier nur noch ein Erzbischof. Die auf felsiger Anhöhe über dem Tajo gelegene Stadt ist reich an historischen Bauten.
Den Escorial ließ Philipp II. als königliche Residenz errichten. Der gewaltige Baukomplex mit einer Grundfläche von 206 x 161 m wurde 1584 vollendet; sie umfaßt das Laurentiuskloster, eine Kirche, den Königspalast und ein Mausoleum. Unter dem Altar der Kirche liegt das Pantheon, die reichgeschmückte Grabstätte aller spanischen Könige seit Karl V.

El Escorial

Toledo was the capital of Spain until 1561, and it is still the seat of the Archbishop. Built on rock near the River Tajo, the city has survived remarkably without blemish to the present day. The monastery in the El Escorial (the Palace) was built by Philip II who was able to follow the Mass from the choir while lying ill in bed in the Palace, and was buried here following the tradition of the Spanish kings. This gigantic complex has an area of 206 x 61 m2 and was completed in 1584. The building houses a particularly fine collection of paintings by old masters.

Jusqu'en 1561, Tolède a été la capitale de l'Espagne. Aujourd'hui, elle est toujours le siège de l'archevêché. La ville, située sur un rocher au bord du Tage, est restée particulièrement bien conservée.
C'est Philippe II qui fit bâtir le cloître-palais de l'Escurial. Ce complexe de 206 x 61 m fut terminé en 1584 et compte une collection de peintures particulièrement riche. Depuis son lit de mort, Philippe II pouvait assister à la messe dans l'annexe principale. C'est ici qu'il fut enterré, comme d'ailleurs pratiquement tous les autres rois d'Espagne.

Fino al 1561 Toledo è stata la capitale della Spagna ed è ancora oggi sede dell'arcivescovado.
La città, costruita su di una roccia in riva al Tago, è rimasta ancora oggi quasi intatta. Filippo II vi fece costruire il convento-palazzo El Escorial. L'enorme complesso di 206 x 61 metri fu terminato nel 1584 e comprende una collezione di quadri molto ricca. Dal suo letto di morte, Filippo II potè seguire la Messa nel coro principale. Egli fu seppellito qui, così come quasi tutti i regnanti di Spagna.

Toledo was tot 1561 de hoofdstad van Spanje en is nog steeds de zetel van de aartsbisschop. De stad op een rots aan de Taag is nog bijzonder gaaf.
Filips II liet het klooster-paleis El Escorial bouwen. Het enorme complex van 206 x 61 m kwam in 1584 gereed en telt een bijzonder rijke schilderijencollectie. Vanaf zijn ziekbed kon Filips II de mis in het hoofdkoor volgen. Hij werd hier begraven, evenals vrijwel alle andere Spaanse koningen.

Toledo foi em 1561 a capital de Espanha e é agora ainda a sede episcopal. A cidade erguida sobre um rochedo à margem do Tejo está ainda em bom estado. Filipe II mandou construir o convento-palácio El Escorial. O enorme complexo de 206 x 61 m foi acabado de construir em 1584 e possui uma importante colecção de pinturas. Filipe II assistia à missa na nave principal, na cama onde se encontrava enfermo. Ele foi lá supultado, assim como quase todos os outros reis espanhois.

Το Τολέδο ήταν μέχρι το 1562 η πρωτεύουσα της Ισπανίας και είναι ακόμα και τώρα η έδρα του Αρχιεπισκόπου. Η πόλη είναι χτισμένη σε βράχο του Τάγου και διατηρείται ακόμα σε πολύ καλή κατάσταση.
Ο Φίλιππος Β΄ έχτισε εκεί το μοναστήρι-ανάκτορο Ελ Εσκουριάλ. Το πελώριο συγκρότημα με διαστάσεις 206 χ 61 μ. τελείωσε το 1584 και κατέχει πολύ πλούσια πινακοθήκη. Από το ασθενικό κρεβάτι του μπορούσε ο Φίλιμμος Β΄ να παρακολουθεί τη λειτουργία στον κύριο χορό. Εδώ θάφτηκε, όπως περίπου όλοι οι Ισμανοί βασιλείς.

12
PORTUGAL

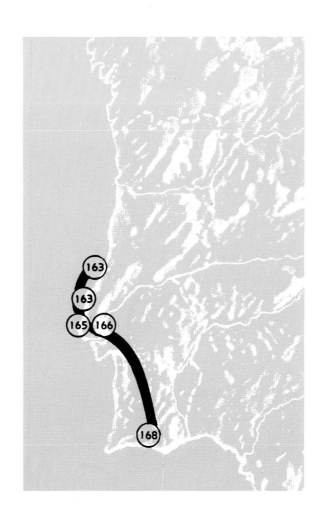

Os palácios e os parques de Sintra libertam os sentimentos poéticos. Os mortais simples podem alegar que o mesmo já se deu com literários ilustres, como o Lord Byron. Este falava então de: A Glorious Eden. Em Obidos, nas ameias, sonha-se de um passado glorioso.

Sintras slotte og parker åbner for poetiske følelser. Almindelige dødelige kan påberåbe sig berømte litterære forgængere som lord Byron, der udtrykte sig således: A glorious Eden. Fra Obidos brystværn kan man drømme om en strålende fortid.

Sintra, einst Sommerresidenz der portugiesischen Könige, ist eine der schönsten Städte des Landes. Eindrucksvollstes Bauwerk ist der großartige Palácio Nacional.
Das am Rio de Vargem gelegene mauerumschlossene Obidos mit einem Kastell aus dem 13. Jahrhundert hat sein mittelalterliches Aussehen noch weitgehend bewahrt.

The palaces and gardens of Sintra have been a great source of poetic inspiration. Lesser mortals can find themselves in the distinguished company of such illustrious predecessors as Lord Byron who wrote os Sintra: "A glorious Eden/Aloft the battlements of Obidos/One dreams of so glorious a past."

Los palacios y parques de Sintra hacen que se suelte el sentimiento poético. Ciudadanos sencillos podemos evocar ilustres nombres de la literatura, como Lord Byron. El llegó incluso a decir: 'A glorious Eden. En las almenas de Obidos podemos imaginarnos su glorioso pasado.

Les palais et les parcs de Sintra engendrent la poésie. Le commun des mortels peut faire appel ici à d'illustres prédécesseurs littéraires tels que lord Byron, qui parla même d'un 'Glorious Eden'.
A Obidos, sur les créneaux, on peut rêver d'un glorieux passé.

I palazzi e i parchi di Sintra generano poesia nell'anima dell'uomo. Chiunque qui può richiamarsi a illustri predecessori letterari, ad esempio Lord Byron, che qui parlò di 'A glorious Eden'.
Sui merli di Obidos si può sognare di un glorioso passato.

De paleizen en parken van Sintra maken poëtische gevoelens los. Gewone stervelingen kunnen zich daarbij beroepen op illustere literaire voorgangers, zoals Lord Byron. Die zelfs sprak van: A glorious Eden.
In Obidos op de kantelen kan men dromen van een glorieus verleden.

Τα παλάτια και πάρκα της Σίντρας δημιουργούν ποιητικά αισθήματα. Κοινοί Θνητοί μπορούν να προσφύγουν σε διάσημους λογοτεχνικούς πρωτοπόρους, όπως ο Λόρδος Βύρων. Ακόμα κι 'αυτός μίλησε για: A glorious Eden.
Στον Οβιδό, στην έπαλξη, μπορεί κανείς να ονειρευτεί το λαμπρό παρελθόν.

di costruttori hanno lavorato per portare e
termine questo edificio che fu poi terminato
a spese di Napoleone fra il 1805 e il 1809.

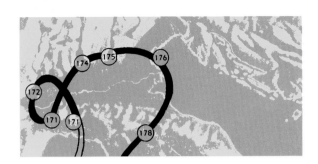

Il centro turistico di Sirmione si trova su di una penisola a Sud del lago di Garda, nell'Italia del Nord. Il Lago di Garda è il più grande lago di questa regione. Esso conosce, come tutti gli altri laghi alpini, il curioso fenomeno detto 'sessa': se il vento si alza o si abbassa rapidamente, l'acqua, a nord, sale di 30 cm, mentre a sud scende di 30 cm. Verona sull'Adige, è una città splendida, dominata da un anfiteatro romano del 1° secolo dopo Cristo. Questo anfiteatro può contenere 22.000 spettatori: in estate vi si rappresentano opere classiche.

Verona è anche la città in cui nacque l'amore fra Giulietta e Romeo ed è la città natale del celebre pittore italiano Veronese.

El centro de turismo Sirmione se encuentra en una península en la ribera sur del lago de Garda de la Italia septentrional. Este lago es el más grande de la región. Así como los otros lagos de los Alpes, el lago Garda experimenta el fenómeno 'sessa': el viento a veces viene y se para tan rápidamente que hace subir el agua en el norte hasta 30 cm y bajando en el sur otro tanto.

Verona, en el Adige, es una ciudad maravillosa dominada por un coliseo romano del siglo I. Este anfiteatro ofrece sitio a 22.000 espectadores: en el verano se dan representaciones de ópera. Verona es también la ciudad en la que Romeo y Julieta se confesaron su juvenil amor y, además, es el lugar de nacimiento del famoso pintor Veronese, que quiere decir: de Verona.

which dates from the 1st century. This amphitheatre can seat 22000 spectators, in summer opera is still performed here. Verona is also the town of the celebrated lovers, Romeo and Juliet, and the birthplace of the famous painter, Veronese.

Le centre touristique de Sirmione est situé sur une presqu'île au sud du lac de Garde, en Italie du Nord. Le lac de Garde est le plus grand lac de cette région. Il connaît, comme les autres lacs des Alpes, le phénomène curieux des seiches: le vent se levant ou tombant rapidement, l'eau, au nord, monte de 30 cm pour descendre de 30 cm au sud. Vérone, sur l'Adige, est une ville splendide, dominée par un amphithéâtre romain du 1er siècle après Jésus Christ. Cet amphithéâtre peut accueillir 22 000 spectateurs. Des opéras y sont représentés en été. Vérone est également la ville où l'amour naquit entre Roméo et Juliette, ainsi que la ville natale du célèbre peintre italien Véronése.

Het toeristencentrum Sirmione ligt op een schiereiland aan de zuidrand van het Garda-meer in Noord-Italië. Het Gardameer is het grootste meer in deze streek. Het kent, evenals andere Alpenmeren, het merkwaardige fenomeen van de 'sessa': door snel opkomende en vallende wind wordt het water in het noorden tot 30 cm opgestuwd en in het zuiden tot 30 cm verlaagd. Verona, aan de Adige, is een schitterende stad, beheerst door een Romeins colosseum uit de eerste eeuw na Christus. Dat amfitheater biedt plaats aan 22.000 toeschouwers; 's zomers hebben er operavoorstellingen plaats. Verona is ook de stad waar Romeo en Julia elkaar hun prille liefde bekenden en tevens de geboortestad van de beroemde schilder Veronese, wat wil zeggen: van Verona.

O centro de turismo Sirmione está situado na península na borda meridional do lago Garda, no Norte da Itália. O lago Garda é o maior deste território. Tal como outros lagos dos Alpes também este lago conhece o fenómeno 'sessa' em que, devido à elevação rápida e abaixamento do vento a água é elevada até 30 cm no Norte e abaixa até 30 cm no Sul.

Verona, no Adige, é uma cidade magnífica, dominada por um coliseu romano do século primeiro antes de Cristo. Este anfiteatro oferece lugar a 22.000 espectadores; no verão existem apresentações de ópera. Verona é também a

cidade onde Romeu e Julieta confessaram o seu amor de jovens e ao mesmo tempo é a cidade onde nasceu o famoso pintor Veronese, que quer dizer: de Verona.

Το τουριστικό κέντρο Σιρμιόνη βρίσκεται σε χερσόνησο στη νότια πλευρά της λίμνης Γκάρδα στη Βόρεια Ιταλία. Η λίμνη Γκάρδα είναι η μεγαλύτερη λίμνη της περιοχής αυτής. Γνωρίζει, όπως όλες οι αλπικές λίμνες, το περίεργο φαινόμενο 'Σέσσα': ο άνεμος, που γρήγορα πιάνει και πέφτει, ανεβάζει το νερό στη βόρεια πλευρά 30 πόντους και κατεβάζει ταυτόχρονα το νερό στη νότια πλευρά 30 πόντους.

Η Βερόνα, μια θαυμάσια πόλη χτισμένη στις όχθες του Αδίγη, κυριαρχείται από το Ρωμαϊκό Κολοσσαίο που χτίστηκε τον πρώτο αιώνα μετά Χριστού. Το αμφιθέατρο αυτό περιέχει θέσεις για 22.000 θεατές. Το καλοκαίρι διοργανώνονται προβολές όπερας. Η Βερόνα είναι επίσης η πόλη που ο Ρωμαίος και η Ιουλιέττα έζησαν τον μεγάλο τους έρωτα. Στη Βερόνα επίσης γεννήθηκε ο διάσημος Ιταλός ζωγράφος Βερονέζε, δηλαδή: από τη Βερόνα.

Turistcentret Sirmione ligger på en halvø ved sydkanten af Gardasøen i Norditalien. Gardasøen er den største sø i dette område. Ligesom ved andre alpesøer, forekommer fænomenet 'sessa' også ved Gardasøen: på grund af hurtigt stigende og faldende vinde presses vandet indtil 30 cm op i søens nordlige del, mens vandstanden i den sydlige del sænkes med 30 cm.

Verona ved floden Adige er en strålende by domineret af et colosseum fra det første århundrede før kristus. Amfiteatret har plads til 22.000 tilskuere; om sommeren opføres der her operaforestillinger. Verona er endvidere den by, hvor Romeo og Julia følte deres første spæde kærlighed og også fødeby for den berømte maler Veronese, hvilket betyder 'fra Verona'.

Auf einer Halbinsel im Süden des norditalienischen Gardasees liegt das beliebte Touristenzentrum Sirmione mit seinen interessanten mittelalterlichen Wehranlagen.

Eine der schönsten Städte Italiens ist das am Ausgang des Etschtals in der Poebene gelegene Verona, eine ursprüng-

lich rätisch-keltische Siedlung, die von den Römern prachtvoll ausgebaut wurde. Das eindrucksvollste Bauzeugnis aus der Römerzeit ist das das Stadtbild beherrschende Kolosseum, ein Amphitheater, das 22 000 Besucher zu fassen vermag und noch heute allsommerlich für Opernfestspiele genutzt wird. Verona war auch die Heimat von Romeo und Julia, deren tragisches Schicksal viele Dichter inspiriert hat, und des nach seiner Geburtsstadt benannten Malers Veronese, der eigentlich Paolo Caliari hieß.

The tourist centre of Sirmione is situated on a peninsula on the Southern bank of Lake Garda in Northern Italy. Lake Garda is the largest in the region. Like the other Alpine lakes, it experiences the phenomenon known as the 'sessa': this is caused by a wind which rises with great rapidity then blows down over the mountains; in the North the water rises by as much as 30 cm. due to this effect and in the South it drops by a corresponding 30 cm. Verona, a very beautiful town on the River Adige, is dominated by its Roman colosseum

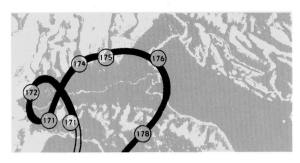

Su 118 isolette collegate fra di loro da 400 ponti sorge la città storica di Venezia, costruita su di una laguna. In Canal Grande si snoda attraverso la città e il Ponte Rialto

(1592) con i suoi negozietti sembra rialzarsi per lasciare passare le gondole. Piazza S.Marco, con i Palazzi dei Dogi è il cuore della città. Di qui Marco Polo partì nel XIII

Den historiske laguneby Venedig flyder på Adriaterhavet på 118 øer, der bindes sammen af 400 broer. Kanal Grande snor sig herigennem og Rialtobroen (1592) med sine små butikker synes at rette sig op for at lade gondolerne sejle under. Piazza San Marco med Dogepaladset er byens hjerte. Herfra rejste Marco Polo i det 13. århundrede ud på sine historiske rejser til det fjerne østen. Under fangenskabet i Genua nedskrev han sin rejseberetning.

Am Rande der Adria liegt Venedig auf 118 Inseln, die durch rund 400 Brücken miteinander verbunden sind. Durchzogen wird sie vom Canal Grande, über den sich seit 1592 die Rialtobrücke mit den kleinen Läden spannt. Das Zentrum Venedigs ist der Markusplatz mit der kuppelgekrönten Markuskirche, dem Campanile und dem Dogenpalast. Auf den übrigen Seiten wird der Platz von den Alten und Neuen Prokuratorien eingefaßt. Von Venedig aus brach Marco Polo zu seiner Reise in den Fernen Osten auf, über die er dann in genuesischer Gefangenschaft einen aufsehenerregenden Bericht verfaßte.

Built on 118 small islands, linked together by 400 bridges, Venice lies in a lagoon of the Adriatic Sea. The Grand Canal flows through the city, and the Ponte di Rialto (1592), with its quaint little shops, seems to raise slightly, as if to allow the gondolas to pass through. The Piazza San Marco, with the Doge's Palace, forms the heart of the city. It was from here that Marco Polo departed in the 13th century on his historic voyages to the Far East. He wrote an account of his voyages during his imprisonment by the Genoese.

En el Mar Adriático, sobre 118 islotes encadenados por 400 puentes flota la histórica ciudad de la laguna, Venecia. El Canal Grande atraviesa serpenteando la ciudad y el Ponto Rialto (1592) con sus tiendecitas parece enderezarse para dejar pasar a las góndolas. La Plaza de San Marco con el Palacio Ducal forma el centro de la ciudad. Marco Polo zarpó desde aquí en el siglo XIII para su histórico viaje al Lejano Oriente. Durante su prisión en Génova pudo hacer una informe de su viaje.

Sur 118 îlots, reliés par 400 ponts, la ville historique de Venise, bâtie sur une lagune, continue à vivre intensément au bord de l'Adriatique. Le Grand Canal serpente à travers la ville et le pont du Rialto (1592), avec ses petits magasins, semble se relever pour laisser passer les gondoles. La place Saint-Marc, avec le palais des Doges est le cœur de la ville. C'est d'ici que Marco Polo est parti au 13e siècle pour ses voyages historiques à destination de l'Extrême-Orient. C'est pendant sa captivité chez les Génois qu'il put rédiger le récit de ses voyages.

Op 118 eilandjes met 400 bruggen aaneengetekend drijft de historische lagunestad Venetië in de Adriatische Zee. Het Canal Grande slingert er zich doorheen en de Ponto Rialto (1592) met zijn winkeltjes lijkt zich even op te richten om de gondels doorgang te verlenen. De Piazzo San Marco met het Dogenpaleis vormt het hart. Marco Polo vertrok vanhier in de dertiende eeuw voor zijn historische reizen naar het Verre Oosten. Tijdens zijn gevangenneming door Genua kon het reisverslag opgetekend worden.

Sobre 118 ilhas ligadas por 400 pontes, fluctua a cidade histórica na laguna de Veneza, no Mar Adriático. O Canal Grande serpenteia através dela e a Ponte Rialto (1592), com as suas lojas parece erguer-se para deixar passar as gôndolas. A Praça de San Marco, com o Palácio dos Doges forma o seu centro. Marco Polo partiu daqui, no século treze, para a sua viagem histórica ao Oriente. Durante o seu internamento em Génua, poude ele descrever a sua viagem.

Με τα 118 νησάκια της, αλυσοδεμένα με τις 400 γέφυρες, πλέει η Βενετιά, η ιστορική αυτή πόλη στη λιμνοθάλασσα της Αδριατικής. Το Κανάλ Γκράντε διαρρέει την πόλη και η Πόντο Ριάλτο [1592] με τα μικρά καταστήματα φαίνεται να υψώνεται για λίγο για να περνάνε οι γόνδολες. Η Πιάτσα Σαν Μάρκο με το παλάτι των Δόγηδων αποτελεί την καρδιά της πόλης. Ο Μάρκο Πόλο ξεκίνησε από εδώ, το δέκατο τρίτο αιώνα, για το ιστορικό του ταξίδι στην Άπω Ανατολή. Κατά τη φυλάκισή του στη Γένουα καταγράφτηκε το ημερολόγιο των ταξιδιών του.

secolo per i suoi storici viaggi in Estremo Oriente. Nel periodo della sua prigionia presso i Genovesi egli potè redigere il racconto dei suoi viaggi.

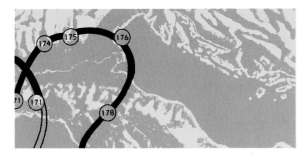

E' impossibile descrivere Firenze in poche righe. Questa città, capitale del Rinascimento, è uno dei centri artistici più importanti d'Italia. Il Duomo (Sante Maria dei Fiori) con la cupola di tegole rosse domina la città. La torre del Palazzo Vecchio, con l'amministrazione comunale, si innalza nel cielo. I ponti storici sono stati distrutti nel corso della Se-

Det er umuligt på nogle få linier at beskrive Florens. Denne hovedstad fra renæssancen er ét af de mest betydningsfulde kunstcentre. Domkirken (Santa Maria del Fiori) dominerer med sit kuppeltag af røde tagsten. Men Palazzo Vecchios tårn med byrådet stikker brutalt ovenover. De historiske broer blev under den anden verdenskrig sprængt i luften, men heldigvis blev 'broen' over Amo-floden sparet. For det gik selv tyskerne for vidt.

Florenz, das Zentrum der Renaissance, ist eine der bedeutendsten Kunststädte der Welt. Der prächtige Dom (Santa Maria del Fiore) wird von einer mächtigen Kuppel gekrönt, doch höher noch ragt der Turm des Palazzo Vecchio, des Sitzes der Stadtverwaltung, dem die Loggia dei Lanzi gegenüberliegt. Eine einzigartige Sammlung florentinischer Kunst bergen die Uffizien. Viele historische Brücken fielen dem Zweiten Weltkrieg zum Opfer, doch die älteste von allen, der Ponte Vecchio aus dem 14. Jahrhundert, ist unversehrt geblieben.

Il est impossible de décrire Florence en quelques lignes. Cette ville de la Renaissance est l'un des centres artistiques les plus importants. Le Dôme (Santa Maria dei Fiori) domine avec sa coupole de tuiles rouges. Mais la tour du Palazzo Vecchio, avec l'administration communale, se dresse brutalement dans le ciel. Les ponts historiques ont été détruits au cours de la Seconde Guerre mondiale, mais le 'pont' sur l'Arno a heureusement été épargné. Même cela était de trop pour les Allemands.

Florence beschrijven in enkele regels is een onmogelijkheid. Deze hoofdstad van de renaissance is één van de belangrijkste kunstcentra. De Dom (Santa Maria del Fiori) met zijn koepeldak van rode dakpannen domineert. Maar de toren van het Palazzo Vecchio, met het stadsbestuur, priemt daar brutaal overheen. De historische bruggen werden in de Tweede Wereldoorlog opgeblazen, maar 'de brug' over de Arno bleef gelukkig gespaard. Want dat ging ook de Duitsers te ver.

It is impossible to describe the beauty of Florence in just a few lines. It was the capital of Renaissance Italy, and is still one of the world's greatest centres of art. The Duomo (Santa Maria del Fiori) dominates the skyline with its dome and terracotta tiled roof, while the striking tower of the Palazzo Vecchio, the seat of the municipality, impudently soars above it. The historic bridges were destroyed during the Second World War, but fortunately the Ponte Vecchio across the Arno was saved by the Allied Forces after the Germans had mined it as they retreated.

Describir Florencia en unas pocas líneas es una tarea imposible. Esta capital del Renacimiento es uno de los centros de arte más importantes. La Catedral (Sante Maria del Fiori) con su cúpula de tejas rojas domina la ciudad. Pero la torre del Palacio Viejo, con el ayuntamiento, se alza sobre ella. Los puentes históricos fueron volados en la Segunda Guerra Mundial, pero el 'puente' sobre el Arno se salvó. Esto ya era demasiado, también para los alemanes.

Descrever Florência em poucas linhas é impossível. Esta capital da Renascência é um dos mais importantes centros artísticos. A Catedral (Santa Maria del Fiori) com a sua cúpula de telhas vermelhas domina o ambiente. Mas as torres do Pallazzo Vecchio, com a administração de cidade, sobressaiem orgulhosamente. As pontes históricas foram destruídas durante a Segunda Guerra Mundial, mas felizmente 'a ponte' sobre o Arno foi poupada. Os alemães não se atreviram a destruí-la.

Να περιγράψει κανείς τη Φλωρεντία με λίγες λέξεις είναι αδύνατο. Αυτή η πρωτεύουσα της Αναγέννησης είναι ένα από τα πιο σπουδαία κέντρα Τέχνης. Το Δουόμο [Σάντα Μαρία ντελ Φιόρι], κυριαρχεί με το θόλο του από κόκκινα κεραμίδια. Αλλά ο πύργος του Παλάτσιο Βέκιο με το δημοτικό του συμβούλιο ορθώνεται επιβλητικά. Οι ιστορικές γέφυρες ανατινάχτηκαν κατά το Δεύτερο Παγκόσμιο Πόλεμο, αλλά 'η γέφυρα' πάνω από τον Άρνο έμεινε ευτυχώς απείραχτη, γιατί θα υπέρβαινε τα όρια και για τους Γερμανούς.

conda Guerra mondiale, ma il 'ponte' sull-
'Arno è rimasto miracolosamente intatto.

14
ITALIA II

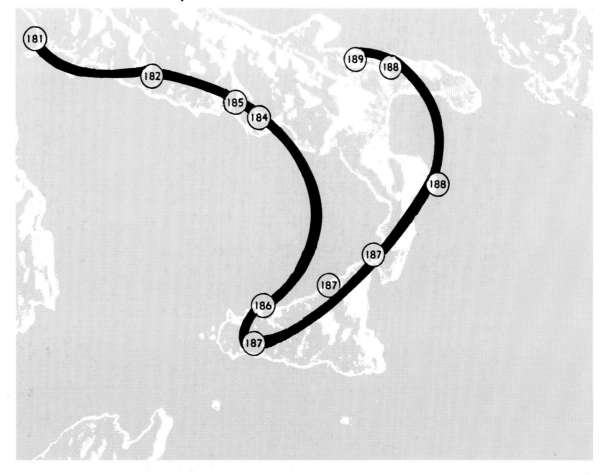

L'abitante più celebre dell'esola d'Elba, Napoleone, fu esiliato qui dal maggio 1814 al febbraio 1815. Non si può negare che vi siano luoghi di vacanza meno piacevoli di questo! La sua residenza era al Palazzo dei Mulini a Portoferraio, ma disponeva anche di una piccola villa, Villa San Martino. A sud, sopra il Golfo Stella, troviamo Capoliveri.

Elbas mest kendte indbygger, Napoleon, levede her i eksil fra maj 1814 til februar 1815. Og man kan let forestille sig et ringere feriested! Foruden residensen Palazzo dei Mulini i Portoferràio havde han også et landsted kaldet Villa San Martino. På øens sydlige del højt over Golfo Stella finder vi Capoliveri.

Napoleon, the most famous resident of Elba, was exiled here from May 1814 to February 1815, living in the Palazzo dei Mulini in Portoferraio, and the Villa San Marino. The island is also one of the most agreeable holiday resorts that one could imagine. The town of Capoliveri is situated high above the Golfo Stella.

L'habitant le plus célèbre de l'île d'Elbe, Napoléon, y fut banni de mai 1814 à février 1815. Et il faut dire qu'il existe des lieux de vacances plus désagréables que celui-ci! Outre sa résidence au Palace dei Mulini à Portoferraio, il possédait encore une petite villa, la villa San Martino. Au Sud, loin au-dessus du Golfo Stella, nous trouvons Capoliveri.

O habitante mais conhecido de Elba, Napoleão, foi exilado para aqui de maio de 1814 até fevereiro de 1815. Mas devemos dizer: podemos imaginar peor sítio para férias! Alem da sua residência o Palazzo dei Mulini, em Portoferraio, dispunha ele tambem a Villa San Martino. A sul encontra-se, ao alto, dominando o Golfo Stella, Capoliveri.

Der bekannteste Bewohner der Insel Elba war Napoleon, der vom Mai 1814 bis Februar 1815 in Verbannung lebte. Er residierte in der Villa dei Mulini im Hauptort Portoferraio und im Sommer in der einige Kilometer entfernten Villa San Martino, die heute ein Napoleon-Museum birgt. Im Süden liegt hoch über dem Stella-Golf das Städchen Capoliveri.

El habitante más famoso de Elba, Napoleón, fue deportado aquí de mayo de 1814 a febrero de 1815. Y hay que decir que un lugar de vacaciones peor es muy fácil de encontrar. Salvo su residencia Palazzo die Mulini en Portoferràio aún tenía una segunda casa Villa San Martini. En el sur, alzándose sobre el Golfo Stella, encontramos Capoliveri.

De bekendste bewoner van Elba, Napoleon wàs hier verbannen van mei 1814 tot februari 1815. En het moet gezegd worden een slechter vakantie-oord is denkbaar! Behalve zijn residentie Palazzo dei Mulini in Portoferràio had hij nog een buitenhuisje Villa San Martino. In het zuiden, boven de Golfo Stella vinden we Capoliveri.

Ο πιο γνωστός κάτοικος της Ελβα, ο Ναπολέων, εξορίστηκε εδώ σπό το Μάιο 1814-το Φεβρουάριο 1815. Υπάρχουν όμως χειρότεροι τόποι για να περνάει κανείς τις διακοπές του. Εκτός από την κατοικία του, το Παλάτσο ντέι Μουλίνι στο Πορτοφερράιο, είχε ο Ναπολέων, τη Βίλα Σαν Μαρτίνο. Στο Νότο, πάνω από την επιφάνεια του Γόλφο Στέλλα, βρίσκουμε το Καπολιβέρι.

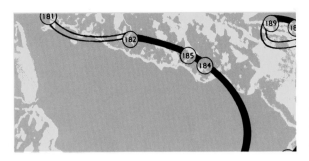

Prima dell'unità d'Italia, nel 1870, Roma apparteneva allo Stato Pontificio. La potenza secolare dei papi si ridusse in quell'anno all'attuale città del Vaticano. Il Campidoglio, il Foro Romano e il Colosseo sono solo alcuni dei celebri monumenti di Roma. In primo piano il monumento eretto per commemorare l'unità (1911).

Før Italiens samling i 1870 hørte Rom til Kirkestaten. Pavens verdslige magt blev i det år indskrænket til kun at omfatte den nuværende Vatikanby omkring St. Peterskirken. Capitol, Forum Romanum og Colosseum er kun nogle få af de mange seværdigheder som den evige stad har at byde på. I forgrunden enhedsmonumentet fra 1911.

Rom, die der Sage nach 753 v. Chr. gegründete Ewige Stadt, einst Mittelpunkt des Römischen Reiches, wurde nach langer Zugehörigkeit zum Kirchenstaat erst 1870 Hauptstadt des geeinten Italiens. Einen eigenen Staat bildet die Vatikanstadt um die Peterskirche – das Zentrum der katholischen Christenheit. Viel erinnert noch an die große alte Zeit der Römer, so das Forum Romanum und das Kolosseum. Im Vordergrund das 1911 zur Erinnerung an die Einigung errichtete Nationaldenkmal für Viktor Emanuel II.

In 1870, before the Unification of Italy, Rome formed part of the Papal State. In that year the power of the Pope was restricted to what is now known as the Vatican City, with St. Peter's Cathedral at its centre. The Capitol, the Forum Romanum and the Colosseum are some of the many architectural wonders in this ancient city. The monument celebrating the Unification of Italy, erected in 1911, stands in the foreground.

Antes de la unidad de Italia, en 1870, Roma pertenecía al Estado Eclesiástico. El poder mundano del Papa fue limitado ese año a lo que ahora es el Vaticano, alrededor de San Pedro. El Capitolio, el Foro Romano y el Coliseo son algunas de las muchas maravillas con las que cuenta Roma. En primer plano vemos el monumento de la unidad de 1911.

Antes de la unidad de Italia, en 1870, Roma appartenait à l'Etat pontifical. La puissance séculaire des papes fut limitée cette année-là à la ville actuelle du Vatican entourant St-Pierre. Le Capitole, le Forum Romanum et le Colisée ne sont que quelques-unes des nombreuses curiosités que compte la Ville éternelle. A l'avant-plan, le monument érigé (1911) pour commémorer l'unification.

Voor de éénwording van Italië, in 1870, hoorde Rome bij de Kerkelijke Staat. De pauselijke wereldmachtmacht werd in dat jaar begrensd tot het huidige Vaticaanstad rond de St. Pieter. Het Capitool, het Forum Romanum en het Collosseum zijn maar enkele van de vele bezienswaardigheden die de heilige stad Rome telt. Op de voorgrond het monument uit 1911 voor de eenwording.

Antes da unificação da Itália, em 1870, pertencia Roma à Santa Sé. O poder papal foi limitado nesse ano, dentro da cidade do Vaticano à volta da catedral de S. Pedro. O Capitólio, o Foro Romano e o Coliseu são uns quantos exemplos das curiosidades que existem em Roma. No primeiro plano o monumento de 1911 à unificação.

Πριν την ένωση της Ιταλίας, το 1870, η Ρώμη ανήκε στο κράτος της Εκκλησίας. Η τότε παγκόσμια εξουσία του Πάπα περιορίστηκε εκείνο το χρόνο στο σημερινό Βατικανό, γύρω από τον Άγιο Πέτρο. Αυτό όμως επισημοποιήθηκε το 1929. Το Καπιτόλ, το Φόρουμ Ρωμάνουμ και το Κολοσσαίο είναι μόνο λίγα από τα πολλά αξιοθέατα που προσφέρει η αιώνια πόλη της Ρώμης. Στο προσκήνιο βλέπεται το μνημείο της ένωσης από το 1911.

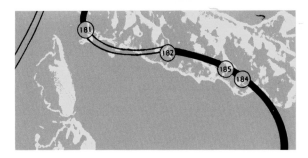

Con una veduta aerea si può dare uno sguardo all'interno del Vesuvio. C'è la possibilità di un'eruzione, come quella che fu fatale a Pompei nel '79? La scienza non lo può escludere, anche se l'ultima eruzione risale al marzo del 1944, quindi con un ciclo medio di 500 anni.

Fugleflugtsperspektivet giver os et kig ned i Vesuv. Er der fare for et udbrud som det, der ødelagde Pompei i år 79? Videnskaben udelukker det ikke helt, men det sidste udbrud fandt sted d. 20. marts 1944, med en cyklus på i gennemsnit 500 år! Se Neapel og dø lyder napolitanerens kendte motto. Der findes ingen by i Italien, der synes at være mere overbevist om sit eget værd end Napoli. Uanset om det drejer sig om fodbold eller pizza, der findes altid et napolitansk superlativ herfor.

La perspective à vol d'oiseau donne un coup d'œil dans le Vésuve. Y a-t-il des chances d'éruption, comme celle qui fut fatale à Pompei en 79? La science ne l'exclut pas totalement, mais la dernière manifestation remonte au 20 mars 1944, avec un cycle moyen de 500 ans. Voir Naples et puis mourir est la phrase que l'on entend le plus dans la bouche des Napolitains. Et aucune ville en Italie ne paraît plus convaincue de sa popre valeur que Naples. Qu'il s'agisse de football ou de pizza, il existe toujours un superlatif napolitain.

Ein Blick in den Krater des Vesuv. Im Jahre 79 wurde Pompeji durch einen gewaltigen Ausbruch des Vulkans verschüttet, aber um 1600 wiederentdeckt und seither großenteils ausgegraben – ein interessantes Zeugnis altrömischer Kultur.
Der Ausspruch 'Neapel sehen und sterben' zeugt vom ausgeprägten Selbstbewußtsein der Neapolitaner. Wir sehen hier die Hafenfront mit dem Castel Nuovo rechts vorn. Über 500 Kirchen und zahlreiche Klöster und Paläste finden sich in der um 550 v.Chr. von den Griechen gegründeten und 326 v.Chr. dem Römischen Reich einverleibten Hafenstadt.

Het vogelvluchtperspectief geeft ons een kijkje in de Vesuvius. Is er kans op een eruptie, zoals Pompeï in 79 fataal werd? De wetenschap wil het niet helemaal uitsluiten, maar de laatste uitbarsting was op 20 maart 1944, met een gemiddelde cyclus van 500 jaar!
Napels zien en dan sterven is het bekende motto van de Napolitaan. Geen stad in Italië die meer overtuigd lijkt van zijn eigenwaarde dan Napels. Of het nu over voetballen of pizza's gaat er is altijd een napolitaans superlatief.

Our bird's eye view enables us to look inside Vesuvius, the great volcano, that destroyed the city of Pompeii in 79 AD. Scientists do not exclude the possibility of another eruption, however Vesuvius is usually dormant in 500 year cycles and the last eruption was on 20th March 1944. "See Naples and then die", say its citizens. No other Italian city is so full of self-importance. Whether the subject is football or pizzas, the Neapolitan variety is always the best.

Esta vista panorâmica dá-nos uma mirada ao Vesúvio. Há possibilidade de uma erupção, como a que Pompeia sofreu em 79? Os cientistas não o excluem totalmente, mas a última erupção foi em 20 de março de 1944, com um ciclo médio de 500 anos! Ver Nápoles e morrer é a divisa dos napolitanos. Não há cidade na Itália que pareça mais convicta do seu próprio valor do que Nápoles. Quer se trate de futebol ou de pizzas há sempre um superlativo napolitano.

Una perspectiva a vista de pájaro nos da la posibilidad de echar una mirada al Vesubio. ¿Existe la posibilidad de una erupción, como la que destrozó Pompeya en el año 79? La ciencia no lo quiere excluir totalmente pero la última erupción fue el 20 de marzo de 1944, con una media de 500 años. Ver Nápoles y despues morir es un conocido dicho de los napolitanos. No hay otra ciudad en Italia que esté más convencida de su dignidad que Nápoles. Ya sea sobre fútbol o pizzas, en Nápoles siempre hay un superlativo.

Η πανοραμική άποψη μάς δίνει τη δυνατότητα να ρίξουμε μιά ματιά μέσα στο Βεσούβιο. Μπορεί να ξαναγίνει έκρηξη, όπως το 79 που καταστράφηκε η Πομπηία; Η επιστήμη δε θέλει να το αποκλείσει, αλλά η τελευταία έκρηξη ήταν στις 20 Μαρτίου 1944, με κύκλο πάνω κάτω 500 χρόνων.
Να δείς τη Νεάπολη και μετά να πεθάνεις, είναι το γνωστό ρητό της Νεάπολης. Δεν υπάρχει πόλη στην Ιταλία που να έχει περισσότερη αυτοεκτίμηση από τη Νεάπολη. Για το καθετί υπάρχει ναπολιτανική υπερβολή, είτε για ποδόσφαιρο είτε για πίτσες.

'Vedi Napoli e poi muori' è il motto famoso dei napoletani. Nessuna città in Italia è sicura del proprio valore quanto Napoli. Sia che si tratti di pizza o di football, vi è sempre qualcosa di superlativo nell'aggettivo napoletano.

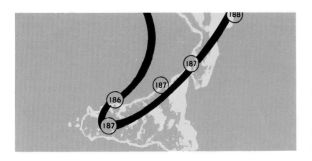

Palermo, capoluogo della Sicilia, ha conosciuto un passato burrascoso ed anche il suo presente è tutt'altro che tranquillo. Greci, Romani, Arabi, Normanni, Veneziani, Bizantini, Spagnoli e Francesi hanno successivamente occupato quest'isola e vi hanno lasciato le loro tracce. Sulla costa meridionale, sotto Palermo, troviamo le vestigia dei

Palermo, Siciliens hovedstad, har en bevæget fortid og nutiden er heller ikke altid uden problemer. Grækere, romere, arabere, normanner, venetianere, bysantinere, spaniere og franskmænd har besøgt øen og efterladt deres spor. På sydkysten, under Palermo, finder vi Selinunts græske tempelrester. Langs den nordlige kystvej finder vi i Cefalù en rigtig normannisk domkirke. I Messina er Messinastrædet smallest og Calabrien og det italienske fastland nærmest. Både bil og tog sættes over med færge, selvom der længe er blevet talt om en fast forbindelse over strædet.

Palermo, de capital de Sicilia, tiene un movido pasado pero también su presente no es siempre tranquilo. Griegos, romanos, árabes, normandos, venecianos, bizantinos, españoles y franceses: todos ellos han estado en esta isla y han dejado sus huellas. En la costa sur, bajo Palermo, encontramos restos del templo griego de Selinunt. En la costa norte hallamos Celafú una verdadera ciudad normanda. El lugar más estrecho del estrecho de Mesina es en Mesina misma y donde Calabria y la península más se acercan. Tanto el coche como el tren va en barco, aunque ya se habla desde hace mucho de una conexión fija de orilla a orilla.

Palerme, la capitale de la Sicile, a connu un passé agité et le présent n'est pas toujours très calme non plus. Grecs, Romains, Arabes, Normands, Vénitiens, Byzantins, Espagnols et Français se sont tous attaqués à cette île et y ont laissé des traces. Sur la côte méridionale, en-dessous de Palerme, nous trouvons les vestiges des temples grecs de Selinunt. Sur la côte septentrionale, Cefalu recèle un royaume normand bien conservé. A Messine, le détroit de Messine est le plus étroit et c'est là que la Calabre et le continent italien sont les plus rapprochés. Tant la voiture que le train vont sur le bateau, bien que l'on parle depuis longtemps d'une liaison terrestre des deux rives.

Palermo, de hoofdstad van Sicilië, heeft een roerig verleden en ook het heden is niet altijd even rimpelloos. Grieken, Romeinen, Arabieren, Noormannen, Venetianen, Byzantijnen, Spanjaarden en Fransen hebben allemaal dit eiland aangedaan en er hun sporen achtergelaten. Aan de zuidelijke kust, onder Palermo, vinden we de Griekse tempelresten van Selinunt. Langs de noordelijke kustweg vinden we in Cefalù een heuse Noormannendom. In Messina is de straat van Messina het smalst en Calabria en het Italiaanse vasteland het meest dichtbij. Zowel de auto als de trein gaan op de boot, hoewel over een vaste oeververbinding al heel lang gesproken worden.

Palermo, a capital da Sicília tem um passado turbulento e mesmo o presente nem sempre é sem problemas. Gregos, romanos, árabes, normandos, venezianos, bizantinos, espanhois e franceses todos estiveram nesta ilha e deixaram os seus vestígios. Na costa do sul, sob Palermo, encontramos os restantes do templo grego de Selinunt. Ao longo da estrada na costa do norte encontramos em Cefalù uma verdadeira catedral normanda. Em Messina está o estreito de Messina, e Calábria e o continente italiano mais próximos. Tanto o automóvel como o comboio vão num barco, embora já se fale há muito tempo numa ligação directa.

Το Παλέρμο, η πρωτεύουσα της Σικελίας, έχει ταραχώδες παρελθόν, αλλά και τώρα ακόμα δεν είναι πάντα ήρεμο. Έλληνες, Ρωμαίοι, Άραβες, Βίκιγκ, Βενετοί, Βυζαντινοί, Ισπανοί και Γάλλοι πέρασαν όλοι τους από το νησί αυτό και άφησαν εκεί τα ίχνη τους. Στη νότια ακτή, κάτω από το Παλέρμο υπάρχουν ελληνικοί ναοί του Σελινούντα. Δίπλα στον παράκτιο δρόμο στο Κεφαλού βρίσκουμε αληθινό ιερό των Βίκιγκ. Στη Μεσσήνη είναι ο Πορθμός πιο στενός και η Καλάβρια της στερεάς Ιταλίας πιο κοντά. Τα αυτοκίνητα όπως και τρένα μεταφέρονται με το πλοίο, αν και συζητείται εδώ και πολύ καιρό για ένα σταθερό συνδεσμό των δυο ακτών.

Jahrtausendelang stand Sizilien unter fremder Herrschaft. Auf phönikische und punische Seefahrer folgten griechische Kolonisatoren, dann die Karthager, Römer, Wandalen, Byzantiner, Araber, Normannen, Spanier und Franzosen. Sie alle haben auf der Insel ihre Spuren hinterlassen. Erst 1861 wurde Sizilien mit Italien vereint. Die Hauptstadt der Insel ist Palermo mit normannischem Dom und sarazenischnormannischen Schlössern. An die griechische Zeit erinnern die Tempelruinen von Selinunt an der Südküste. An der nördlichen Küstenstraße liegt Cefalù mit seiner sehenswerten Normannenkirche. An der nur 3,5 km breiten Meerenge zwischen Sizilien und dem süditalienischen Kalabrien liegt die von den Griechen gegründete Hafenstadt Messina, die einen regelmäßigen Fährverkehr mit dem Festland unterhält.

Palermo, the capital of Sicily, has had a tumultuous past, and even today life does not always run smoothly. Greeks, Romans, Arabs, Vikings, Venetians, Byzantines, Spaniards and French have all left their mark on the island. On the coast to the South of Palermo, are the ruins of the Greek temple of Selinunte. Along the Northern coastal road in Cefalu, there is a Norman cathedral, and in Messina, a Viking settlement. The strait of Messina is at its narrowest here, and cars and trains can cross by ferry at present, although there has been a lot of discussion about building a permanent connection.

templi greci di Selinunte. Sulla costa settentrionale, Cefalù racchiude una città normanna ben conservata. A Messina, lo stretto
braccio di mare avvicina l'isola al continente. Le automobili e i treni sono trasportati
con il traghetto, ma già da tempo si parla di
un collegamento terrestre fra le due rive.

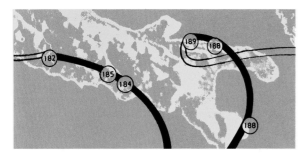

Castel del Monte rappresenta un'imponente eredità lasciata dall'imperatore Federico II che fece costruire questo castello ottagonale, simbolo della corona imperiale e dell'unità dell'Impero, nel 1240. Nel punto in cui la costa calabra ripiega verso l'entroterra, troviamo Capo Rizzuto. Zona dei Trulli è il nome di una vasta zona della Puglia che

Castel del Monte er et imponerende levn af sten fra kejser Frederik II, der i 1240 opførte dette ottekantede jagtslot, symbol på kejserskronen og rigsenheden.
Der, hvor Calabriens kystlinie ved støvlens fod bøjer indad, finder vi Capo Rizzuto.
Zone dei Trulli kaldes et stort område i Apulien efter de på denne egn meget talrige hvidkalkede huse med runde kuppeltage. Oprindelig fik husene kun lys ind gennem døren og røghullet i taget.

Die achteckige Hohenstaufenburg Castel del Monte ließ Kaiser Friedrich II. 1240 als Jagdsitz errichten; später diente sie auch den Königen aus dem Hause Anjou als Residenz. Am Rizzuto-Kap wendet sich die Küste der süditalienischen 'Stiefelspitze' landeinwärts.
Im Herzen Apuliens liegt die Murgia dei Trulli, das Gebiet der Trulli. So nennt man die aus Steinen aufgeschichteten, einräumigen runden Bauwerke, die von einem Kegeldach gekrönt werden. Ihre Ursprünge gehen in vorgriechische Zeit zurück; vielleicht sind sie Zeugnisse einer uralten Megalithkultur.

Castel del Monte is the impressive stonework legacy of Frederick II; he had this octagonal hunting lodge (the symbol of both the Emperor's Crown and State Unification) built in 1240. Capo Rizzuto is situated where the coastline of Calabria curves inwards at the foot of the boot. Zona dei Trulli is the name given to a large region in Apulia, where numerous small, white washed stone houses are topped with round dome-like roofs. Originally light entered through the doorway, while a hole in the roof provided an outlet for smoke.

Castel del Monte es una majestuosa herencia en piedra del emperador Federico II, que hizo construir exte castillo en 1240 como símbolo de la corona imperial y de la unidad del reino.
En el lugar en que la línea de la costa de Calabria, la punta de la bota, se tuerce hacia dentro, encontramos el Cabo Rizzuto. Con Zone dei Trulli se denomina una gran zona en Apulia refiriéndose a las casitas encaladas de blanco, con un techo en forma de cúpula redonda, que tanto abundan por aquí. Originariamente la luz sólo entraba por la puerta y el agujero para el humo en el techo.

Castel del Monte est un vestige impressionnant laissé par l'empereur Frédéric II qui fit construire ce château octogonal, symbole de la couronne impériale et de l'unité de l'empire, en 1240.
A l'endroit où la côte de Calabre, au pied de la botte s'infléchit vers l'intérieur, nous trouvons Capo Rizutto.
Zone dei Trulli est le nom que l'on donne à une large zone des Pouilles où de nombreuses petites maisons en pierres blanches sont dotées d'une coupole ronde. A l'origine, la seule lumière était celle qui entrait par la porte et la cheminée était un simple trou partiqué dans le toit.

Castel del Monte is een indrukwekkende stenen nalatenschap van Keizer Frederik II, die dit achthoekige jachtslot, symbool van de keizerskroon en rijkseenheid, in 1240 liet bouwen.
Waar de kustlijn van Calabria, de voet van de laars, naar binnen buigt, vinden we Capo Rizzuto.
Zone dei Trulli noemt men een groot gebied in Apulia naar de hier talrijk voorkomende witgekalkte stenen huisjes, die voorzien zijn van een rond koepeldak. Oorspronkelijk kwam het enige licht door de deur en het rookgat in het dak.

Apulia

prende nome dalle casette in pietra bianca con il tetto a forma di cono. In origine, la luce entrava solo dalla porta e il camino era un semplice buco fatto nel tetto.

Castel del Monte é uma impressionante herança em pedra do Imperador Frederico II, que mandou construir este castelo para a caça, em 1240, de forma octogonal, símbolo da coroa imperial e da unidade do reino.

No sítio onde a costa da Calábria, o pé da bota, se volta para dentro, encontra-se Capo Rizzuto.

Zone dei Trulli é o nome que se dá a uma região em Apulia, segundo as casinhas de pedra caiadas, que aqui existem em grande quantidade, e as quais têm por cima uma cúpula. Originalmente a luz entrava nelas somente pela porta e pelo buraco para o fumo.

Το Καστέλ ντελ Μοντε είναι η εντυπωσιακή πετρινή κληρονομιά του αυτοκράτορα Φρειδερίκου Β΄, που το 1240 έχτισε αυτό το οχτάγωνο κυνηγετικό περίπτερο, σύμβολο του αυτοκρατορικού θρόνου και ενιαίου κράτους.

Στις ακτές της Καλάβριας, όπου γυρίζει η πατούσα της μπότας προς τα μέσα, βρίσκεται το Κάπο Ριζούτο.

Ζώνη ντελ Τρούλι ονομάζεται μια μεγάλη περιοχή στην Απουλία εξαιτίας των πολυάριθμων ασπροβαμμένων μικρών σπιτιών που έχουν κυκλικό θόλο. Αρχικά έμπαινε το φως μόνο από την πόρτα και την καπνότρυπα της στέγης. Όλα τα τζάμια και καπνοδόχοι είναι μοντέρνες προσθέσεις.

15
ΕΛΛΑΣ
(Ellas)

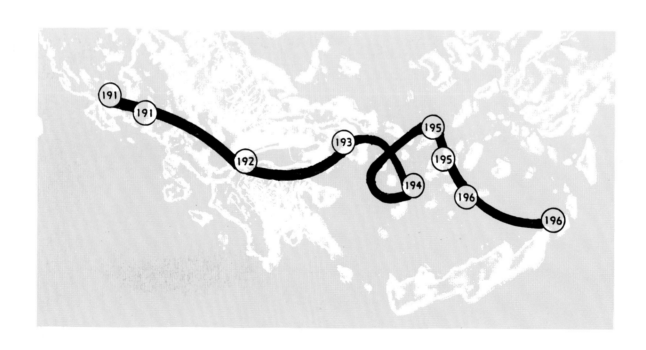

Το νησί Κέρκυρα με τη συνονόματη πόλη είναι από τη Δύση το πρώτο Ελληνικό λιμάνι. Αρχικά ιδρύθηκε από τους βενετούς σαν εμπορικός σταθμός και τώρα είναι προπαντώς αγαπητός τόπος διακοπών με το δικό του αεροδρόμιο. Στη στερεά Ελλάδα βρίσκεται η Ηγουμενίτσα που συνδέεται ακτοπλοϊκά με την Κέρκυρα. Πιο πέρα στην παραλία βρίσκεται η Πάργα, ένας αγαπητός τουριστικός τόπος, αλλά αυτά θα ακούσετε πολλές φορές στην Ελλάδα. Και εμείς θα λέγαμε: Σωστά.

Øen Korfu med byen af samme navn er fra vest Grækenlands første havn. Oprindeligt anlagt af venetianerne som handelspost, er den nu først og fremmest et elsket feriested med egen lufthavn. Fra fastlandet er der forbindelse til Korfu fra Igoumenitsa. På kysten ligger endvidere Parga et yndet turistmål, men sådanne historier vil de ofte komme til at høre i Grækenland. Og vi må sige med rette!

Wenn man sich auf dem Seeweg von Nordwesten Griechenland nähert, erreicht man als erstes die Insel Korfu mit ihrer gleichnamigen Hauptstadt. Ihre größte Zeit erlebte die beliebte Touristeninsel unter venezianischer Herrschaft (14.-18. Jahrhundert). Vom Festland aus erreicht man Korfu über Igumenitsa. An einer Bucht weiter südlich liegt Parga, eines der vielen beliebten Touristenziele, die man in Griechenland finden kann und die Besucher aus aller Welt anlocken.

The island of Corfu and its city of the same name is the first Greek port you reach when travelling to Greece by sea from the West. Originally established by the Venetians as a trading post, today it is a popular holiday resort having its own airport. Igoumenitsa links the mainland and the island of Corfu. Further down the coast lies the popular tourist resort of Parga.

La isla Corfu con la ciudad del mismo nombre es, viniendo del occidente, el primer puerto que encontramos de Grecia. Originariamente fue fundado por los venecianos como puesto comercial; ahora es, sobre todo, un visitado lugar veraniego con su propio aeropuerto. En tierra firme Egumenitsa es la conexión con Corfu. En la misma costa hallamos Parga, otro lugar veraniego muy visitado, aunque esta observación la oirá muchas veces en Grecia. ¡Y con razón!, pensamos.

L'île de Corfou, avec la ville du même nom, est le premier port grec que l'on voit en arrivant de l'ouest par la mer. Fondé à l'origine par les Vénitiens qui en firent un poste commercial, c'est avant tout aujourd'hui un lieu de vacances apprécié, qui possède son propre aérodrome. Sur le continent, Igoumenitsa assure la liaison avec Corfou. Plus loin sur la côte, on trouve Parga, une destination touristique de prédilection, mais vous entendrez plus souvent ce lieu commun en Grèce. Et à bon droit, pourrions-nous dire!

L'isola di Corfù, con la città omonima è il primo porto greco che si vede arrivando da ovest via mare. Fondato in origine dai Veneziani che ne fecero un centro commerciale esso è oggi un noto centro turistico dotato di un aerodromo. Sulla terraferma Igoumenitsa provvede al collegamento con Corfù. Sulla costa si trova anche Parga, un'altra nota località turistica, come si dice comunemente in Grecia. A buon diritto, del resto!

Het eiland Korfu met de gelijknamige stad is vanuit het westen over zee de eerste Griekse haven. Oorspronkelijk gesticht door de Venetianen als handelspost is het nu vooral een geliefde vakantiebestemming met ook een eigen vliegveld. Op het vasteland is Igoumenitsa de verbinding met Korfu. Verder aan de kust ligt Parga een geliefde toeristische bestemming maar dat verhaal zult u vaker horen in Griekenland. En terecht zouden we zo zeggen!

A ilha Corfu com a cidade do mesmo nome é o primeiro porto grego, quando se vem pelo mar, do ocidente. De início fundada pelos venezianos, como centro de comércio, é agora, em especial, procurada como centro de turismo, possuindo para esse fim um aeroporto. No continente forma Igoumenitsa o ponto de ligação com Corfu. Mas adeante, na costa, encontra-se Parga: outro centro turístico preferido. Mas esta informação é muito usual na Grécia. E com razão, a nosso ver!

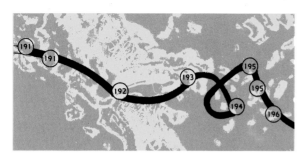

Η Πάτρα είναι η τρίτη πόλη της χώρας, μετά την Αθήνα και τη Θεσσαλονίκη και έχει τακτική θαλάσσια συγκοινωνία με τα Ιταλικά και Γιουγκοσλαβικά λιμάνια.

Το σύμβολο της Αθήνας και της Ελλάδας είναι η Ακρόπολη της Αθήνας. Σε ψηλούς στρατηγικούς λόφους χτίστηκαν στην αρχαία Ελλάδα αρχικά οχυρώματα. Αυτά

Efter Athen og Thessaloniki er Patras Grækenlands tredjestørste by med talrige skibsforbindelser til italienske og jugoslaviske havne. I det antikke Grækenland anlagdes oprindeligt fæstninger på strategisk beliggende højdedrag. Befæstningsværkerne blev efterhånden omdannet til templer. For Akropolis i Athen skete dette i år 450 f. kr. efter, at perserne i 480 f. kr. havde ødelagt det oprindelige Akropolis. Samlingen af templer er enestående, og højdepunktet er uden tvivl Parthenon.

Patras is the third major Greek city after Athens and Thessaloniki and has numerous ferry connections with Italian and Yugoslavian ports. In Ancient Greece, fortifications for defence were originally built on top of strategically positioned hillsides. Over the centuries these fortifications have gradually been replaced by temples and shrines. In 450 BC this happened to the Acropolis, the Romans having destroyed the original Acropolis in 480 BC. The collection of temples here are unique and the Parthenon is without doubt the most impressive.

Patras est la troisième ville du pays après Athènes et Thessalonique; la ville compte d'innombrables liaisons maritimes avec les ports italiens et yougoslaves. A l'origine, les forteresses de la Grèce antique étaient bâties sur des collines élevées, à la situation stratégique. Ces fortifications furent peu à peu remplacées par des temples. C'est ce qui se passa pour l'acropole où l'acropole originale fut dévastée par les Perses en 480 avant J.C. La série de temples réunie est unique, son point d'orgue étant sans aucun doute le Parthénon.

Patras is de derde stad van het land, na Athene en Thessaloniki, en het heeft talloze bootverbindingen met Italiaanse en Joegoslavische havens. Op hoge strategisch gelegen heuvels werden in antiek Griekenland oorspronkelijk versterkingen gebouwd. De fortificaties werden langzamerhand vervangen door heiligdommen. Bij de Akropolis in Athene vond dat plaats in 450 v. Chr. nadat de Perzen in 480 v. Chr. de oorspronkelijke Akropolis verwoest hadden. De verzameling tempels is uniek, en het hoogtepunt is zonder twijfel het Parthenon.

Die Hafenstadt Patras an der Nordküste des Peloponnes ist die drittgrößte Stadt Griechenlands. Die alten Griechen pflegten auf strategisch gelegenen Anhöhen Festungen zu errichten, zu deren Füßen sich Städte entwickelten. Aus diese Weise ist auch Athen entstanden, doch die Burg auf der Akropolis wurde nach ihrer Zerstörung durch die Perser (480 v.Chr.) durch Heiligtümer ersetzt. So entstand ein einzigartiger Tempelkomplex, der von dem wohl vollkommensten Bauwerk der Antike, dem Parthenon, gekrönt wird.

Patras es la tercera ciudad del país, después de Atenas y Tesalónica, y tiene multitud de conexiones marítimas con puertos italianos y yugoslavos. En montañas altas y estratégicas se construían las fortificaciones en la antigua grecia. Las fortificaciones fueron sustituidas poco a poco por santuarios. Esto ocurrió en la Acrópolis en el 450 a.C., después que los persas la hubieran destruido. La colección de templos es única y el punto culminante es, sin duda, el Partenón.

Patrasso è la terza città del Paese dopo Atene e Tessalonica: la città dispone di numerosi collegamenti marittimi con porti italiani e iugoslavi.
In origine, le fortezze della Grecia erano costruite su alte colline, in posizione strategica. Queste fortificazioni furono poco a poco sostituite de templi. Ciò accadde anche per l'acropoli in cui l'acropoli originaria fu distrutta dai Greci nel 480 a.C.. L'insieme dei templi é maestoso, ma il monumento più grandioso è senza dubbio il Partenone.

Patras é a terceira cidade do país, a seguir a Atenas e Tessaloniki, e tem inúmeras ligações por barco com portos italianos e jugoslavos. Os antigos gregos construiam as suas fortificações sobre montes altos, em pontos estratégicos. Os fortes foram a pouco e pouco substituídos por edifícios de carácter religioso. No caso de Acropolis, em Atenas, deu-se isto em 450 a.c., depois dos persas terem destruido o Acropolis original, em 480 a.c.. A colecção de templos é única no género, e o mais impressionante deles é, certamente, o Parthenon.

(Patras, Athinai)

τα οχυρωματικά έργα σιγά έγιναν ιερά. Αυτό έγινε με την Ακρόπολη της Αθήνας το 450 π.Χ, αφού οι Πέρσοι είχαν καταστρέψει την αρχική Ακρόπολη. Η συλλογή ναών είναι μοναδική και το αποκορύφωμα είναι χωρίς άλλο ο Παρθενώνας.

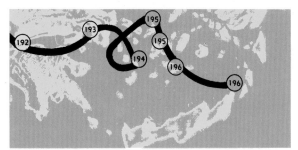
Η Αντίπαρος ανήκει στις Κυκλάδες. Οι Κυκλάδες είναι σκορπισμένες ανάμεσα στην Ελλάδα και τη Μικρασία και αποτελούσαν στα παλιά χρόνια ιδανικά λιμάνια προσφυγών για τη πρωτόγονη ναυτιλία· πηδούσε κανείς από νησί σε νησί. Σε ένα μικρό νησάκι, δεμένο με φράγμα με τη Νάξο, υπάρχει μια πελώρια πύλη (6 μ. ύψος και 4 μ. φάρδος), υπόλειμμα ενός ναού του Απόλλωνα από τον έκτο αιώνα προ Χριστού.

Στις Κυκλάδες ανήκει και η Μύκονος. Είναι πολυσύχναστος τόπος διακοπών και έχει μόλις 85τμ επιφάνεια. Το νησί είναι ορεινό και είναι γνωστό για τα άσπρα σπίτια του και για τους εκατοντάδες ανεμόμυλούς του.

with Naxos by a dam, is an enormous gate (6 m high and 4 m wide), remnant of an Apollo temple from the 6th century B.C.

The island of Mykonos is also to be found in this archipelago. Its small area – 85 km² – has not prevented it from becoming a much visited holiday resort. The landscape is mountainous, and the island is famous for its white houses and windmills.

La isla griega Antiparos forma parte del archipiélago de las Cicladas. Las Cicladas están desperdigadas entre Grecia y Asia Menor y en otras épocas fueron excelentes refugios de la navegación primitiva: 'saltaban' de isla a isla.

En una isla unida por un dique con Naxos, hay un enorme portón (6 m de altura y 4 m de ancho), un resto de un templo de Apolo del s. VI a.C.

Otras isla del archipiélago de las Cícladas es Miconos. Es un lugar de vacaciones muy visitado con una superficie de tan sólo 85 km². El relieve es montañoso y la isla es famosa por sus casas blancas y sus cientos de molinos de viento.

L'île de Mykonos fait partie de l'archipel des Cyclades. Les Cyclades sont dispersées entre la Grèce et l'Asia Mineure et formaient un refuge idéal pour la navigation antique qui faisait des 'sauts de puce' d'une île à l'autre.

L'île grecque de Naxos appartient à l'archipel des Cyclades, en Mer Egée. Sur la petite île, reliée à Naxos par une digue, se trouve un immense portail (6 m de haut sur 4 m de large), vestige du temple d'Apollon, érigé au 6ème siècle avant Jésus Christ.

L'île de Mykonos fait aussi partie de l'archipel des Cyclades. C'est un lieu de vacances très recherché alors que sa superficie est de 85 km² seulement. Le relief est montagneux et l'île est connue pour ses maisons blanches et ses centaines de moulins à vent.

Antiparos appartiene all'arcipelago delle Cicladi. Le Cicladi si trovano sparpagliate tra la Grecia e l'Asia Minore e costituivano in passato dei posti ideali di rifugio per la navigazione marittima primitiva: si 'saltava' da un'isola all'altra.

Su un'isoletta che è collegata a Naxos da una diga, si trova un tempio di Apollo del 6. secolo avanti Cristo.

All'arcipelago delle Cicladi appartiene anche l'isola di Mikonos. Questo è un posto turistico molto visitato ed è grande appena 82 km². Il paesaggio è montagnoso ed è nota per le sue case bianche e le centinaia di mulini a vento.

Antiparos behoort tot de Cycladen-archipel. De Cycladen liggen verspreid tussen Griekenland en Klein-Azië en vormden vroeger ideale vluchthavens voor de primitieve zeevaart: men 'sprong' van eiland tot eiland. Op een eilandje dat door een dam met Naxos is verbonden staat een enorme poort,

een restant van een Apollotempel uit de 6de eeuw voor Christus. Tot de archipel van de Cycladen behoort ook het eiland Mykonos. Het is een druk bezocht vakantie-oord en slechts 85 km² groot. Het reliëf is bergachtig en het eiland is bekend om zijn witte huizen en zijn honderden windmolens.

A ilha Antiparos pertence ao arquipélago das Cicladas. As Cicladas encontram-se entre a Grécia e a Asia Menor e eram antigamente refúgios ideais para a navegação primitiva: dava-se um 'salto' de ilha para ilha. Numa ilha que está ligada a Naxos, por meio de um dique, está um portal enorme; é um restante de um templo de Apolo, que data do século VI a.C.. Ao arquipélago das Cicladas pertence tambem a ilha de Miconos. Esta é um lugar de férias muito visitado e tem uma superfície de apenas 85 km². O relevo é montanhoso e a ilha é conhecida pelas suas casas brancas e pelas suas centenas de moínhos a vento.

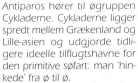

Antiparos hører til øgruppen Cykladerne. Cykladerne ligger spredt mellem Grækenland og Lille-asien og udgjorde tidligere ideelle tilflugtshavne for den primitive søfart: man 'hinkede' fra ø til ø.

På en lille ø, der er forbundet med Naxos via en dæmning, står der en enorm port, en levn fra et Apollotemplet fra det 6. århundrede f. kr.

Til øgruppen Cykladerne hører også øen Mykonos. Det er et meget besøgt feriested på kun 85 m². Øen er bjergagtig og kendt for sine hvide huse og hundredvis af vindmøller.

Zwischen Südgriechenland und der Türkei ragt die Inselkette der Kykladen aus dem Ägäischen Meer, ein Ferienparadies für sonnenhungrige Urlauber. Antiparos mit seiner mächtigen Tropfsteinhöhle liegt unweit der weltberühmten 'Marmorinsel' Paros.

Die größte Kykladeninsel ist Naxos. Auf einer Halbinsel vor dem gleichnamigen Hauptort erhebt sich die Türfassung eines um 530 v. Chr. begonnenen Apollo-Heiligtums.

Ein ungemein beliebtes Touristenziel ist die Felseninsel Mykonos mit ihren schneeweißen Häusern und den charakteristischen Windmühlen, die über das ganze Eiland verstreut sind.

Antiparos is an island in the Cyclades. The Cyclades are situated scattered between Greece and Asia Minor and once formed ideal harbours of refuge for the primitive navigation: they 'jumped' from an island to another.

On a little island, connected

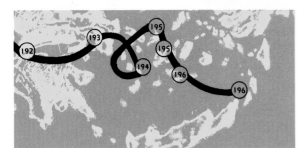

Σαντορίνη/Θήρα, Βάι
(Santorin/Thira, Vaion)

Το νησί Σαντορίνη, που λέγεται στα Ελληνικά επίσης θήρα, είναι αρχικά ηφαιστειογενές νησί που πλυμμηρίσε από τη θάλασσα. Στα χείλη του πρώην κράτηρα, ορθώνεται 300μ. από τη θαλασσα η πόλη Θήρα. Στο τέλος της πτήσης μας πάνω από την Ευρώπη φτάσαμε στην Κρήτη στην παραλία με το ξακουστό φοινικόδασο το βάι. Οι φοίνικες θα φύτρωναν από τα κουκούτσια των χουρμάδων που τα είχαν αφήσει οι Άραβες κατακτητές κατά την αποβίβασή τους, όπως λέει ένας θρύλος. Για μας πιο ωραία είναι η ιστορία ότι αυτή η μοναδική φυσική φοινικόφυτη παραλία της Ευρώπης είναι ο τόπος που ο ταύρος με την Ευρώπη στη ράχη του βγήκε από τη Θάλασσα και πάτησε τη στεριά της δικής μας ηπείρου.

Øen Santorin, der på græsk hedder Thira, er oprindeligt en vulkanø, der er oversvømmet af havet. I en højde af 300 m, stejlt over havet ligger byen Thira på kanten af det tidligere krater.
Ved afslutningen af vor flyvetur henover Europa er vi kommet til Kreta på Vaions berømte palmestrand. Historien fortæller, at palmerne voksede op af de dadelkerner som arbiske erobrer efterlod på stranden efter, at de var landet på øen. En endnu smukkere beskrivelse finder vi i sagnet om, at Europas eneste naturlige palmestrand er det sted, hvor tyren med Europa på ryggen kom i land fra havet.

Santorin, ein Archipel, das u.a. aus den Inseln Thera, Thirasia und Aspronisi besteht, ist nichts anderes als der Kraterrand eines versunkenen Vulkans. Geschaffen wurde diese bizarre Inselwelt durch einen mächtigen Vulkanausbruch im 2. vorchristlichen Jahrtausend. Die Stadt Thera liegt 300 m über dem Meer am fast senkrecht abfallenden Kraterrand. Unseren Europa-Rundflug beenden wir am Palmenstrand von Vaion. Der Sage nach sollen diese Palmen den Dattelkernen entsprossen sein, die einst arabische Eroberer zurückgelassen haben. Besser gefällt uns die Sage, wonach an dieser Stelle Zeus in Stiergestalt mit der von ihm entführten Königstochter Europa den Boden unseres Erdteils betreten haben soll.

The island of Santorini, the Greek name of which is Thira, was originally a volcanic island washed by the sea. The city of Thira is situated 300 metres almost vertically above the sea on the edge of the former crater.

At the end of our flight over Europe we have arrived at the famous palm beach of Vaion on the island of Crete. According to local legend, the palms are said to have grown from date seeds which were left on the beach by Arab conquerors who landed on the island. Another, possibly more romantic story, is that this natural palm beach is the place where Zeus in the form of a bull, carrying the maiden Europa on his back, first emerged from the sea and set foot on land.

La isla Santorín, que en griego se llama Tera, es originariamente una isla volcánica que ha sido inundada por el mar. En el borde del antiguo cráter del volcán a 300 sobre el nivel del mar se halla la ciudad Tera. Al final de nuestro vuelo sobre Europa llegamos a la famosa playa de palmeras de Vaion en Creta. Las palmeras habrían crecido a causa de los huesos de dátiles que los conquistadores árabes se habían dejado entre su carga, según dice un relato. Un relato más bonito es que en esta playa de palmeras natural, única en Europa, es donde el toro saliendo del mar llegó a tierra con Europa a sus espaldas.

L'île de Santorin dont le nom grec est Thira est, à l'origine, une île volcanique qui a été submergée par la mer. Au bord de l'ancien cratère, on trouve à 300 m au-dessus de la mer, la ville perchée de Thira. A la fin de notre survol de l'Europe, nous arrivons en Crète sur la célèbre plage aux palmiers de Vaion. Les palmiers auraient eu pour origine les noyaux de dattes qu'avaient laissés les conquérants arabes lors de leur arrivée ici, mais cela semble bien être une légende. Un récit plus joli nous semble être que cette seule plage de palmiers naturels d'Europe est l'endroit où le taureau a abordé le rivage avec Europe sur son dos.

L'isola di Santorini che in greco si chiama Thera è in origine un'isola vulcanica ed è stata sommersa dal mare. Sull'orlo del vecchio cratere, si trova, a 300 m. sul livello del mare, la città di Thera.

Alla fine del nostro volo sull'Europa, arriviamo a Creta sulla celebre spiaggia di palme di Vaion. La leggenda narra che le palme sarebbero originate dai noccioli di datteri che i conquistatori arabi avevano lasciato al momento della loro invasione.

Un'altra leggenda narra che quest'unica spiaggia di palme naturali d'Europa è il luogo in cui il toro è giunto a riva con Europa sulla schiena.

Het eiland Santorin dat in het Grieks Thíra heet is van oorsprong een vulkaaneiland dat door de zee is overspoeld. Op de rand van de voormalige krater ligt op 300 m steil boven zee de stad Thíra.

Aan het eind van onze vlucht over Europa zijn we in Kreta aangekomen op het beroemde palmenstrand van Vaion. De palmen zouden gegroeid zijn uit de dadelpitten die Arabische veroveraars bij hun landing achtergelaten hadden luidt een verhaal. Een mooier verhaal lijkt ons dat dit enige natuurlijke palmenstrand in Europa de plaats is waar de stier met Europa op zijn rug vanuit de zee aan land gekomen is.

A ilha Santorin, que em grego se chama Thira, é de origem vulcânica e foi inundada pelo mar. Na borda da cratera encontra-se, junto a um abismo, 300 m acima do mar, a cidade de Thira.

Ao fim do nossos voo pela Europa estamos em Creta, na famosa praia das palmeiras de Vaion. Segundo se conta, as palmeiras nasceram de caroços de tâmaras que os conquistadores árabes deitaram fora, por ocasião da sua invasão. Uma história interessante, parece-nos, é que esta única praia de palmeiras na Europa, por natureza, é o lugar onde o boi com a Europa às costas chegou à terra, vindo do mar.

Η θέα της παίζουσας πριγκίπισσας Ευρώπης στο σημερινό Λίβανο, έκανε το Δία να την ερωτευτεί κεραυνοβόλα. Πήρε τη μορφή ενός ωραίου ταύρου και ήξερε να παραπλανήσει την κοπέλα. Όταν αυτή κάθισε στη ράχη του, πήδηξε γρήγορα στη θάλασσα και κολυμπώντας έφυγε για να πατήσει πόδι στη γή της Κρήτης. Εκεί πήρε ξανά τη δική του μορφή. Η Ευρώπη έγινε ερωμένη του και του γέννησε δυο γιους, που απ᾽ αυτούς ο Κνωσός έκανε την Κρήτη να ακμάσει. Η Ευρώπη έδωσε το όνομά της στη νέα ήπειρο.

Ved synet af den legende kongedatter Europa, i det der nu hedder Libanon, blev Zeus på stedet forelsket. Zeus nærmede sig hende i form af en tyr. Europa satte sig på ryggen af dyret, der svømmede ud i havet og bragte hende til Kreta, her optrådte Zeus igen i sin oprindelige skikkelse. Europa blev Zeus elskede og skænkede ham to sønner, hvoraf Knossos skulle blive den, der fik Kreta til at blomstre. Europa gav sit navn til hendes nye verdensdel.

Im Gebiet des heutigen Libanon soll sich Zeus in die junge Königstochter Europa verliebt haben. Er nahm die Gestalt eines prächtigen Stieres an und bewog das Mädchen, sich auf seinen Rücken zu setzen. Dann sprang er schnell ins Meer und schwamm zur Insel Kreta, wo er wieder seine eigene Gestalt annahm. Europa wurde seine Geliebte und gebar ihm zwei Söhne, von denen Minos die Insel zu hoher Blüte brachte (minoische Kultur). Der Königstochter verdankt unser Erdteil seinen Namen Europa, wie die griechische Mythologie zu berichten weiß.

At the end of our flight over Europe we have arrived on the island of Crete, at the famous palm beach of Vaion. According to a local legend, these palms are said to have grown from date seeds which were left on the beach by Arab conquerors who landed on the island. Another, possibly more pleasant story, is that this palm beach – the only natural palm beach in Europe – is the place where Zeus in the form of a bull, carrying the maiden Europa on his back, first emerged from the sea and set foot on land.

Viendo a la doncella Europa como jugaba en lo que ahora se llama Líbano, hizo a Zeus enamorarse de ella. Este se transformó en un hermoso toro y supo seducir a la niña. Cuando ella se encontraba en su espalda corrió hacia el mar y se escapó nadando a la isla Creta. Ahí adoptó su figura normal. Europa fue la amante de Zeus y le dio dos hijos, de los cuales Knossos haría que Creta conociera tiempos de esplendor. Europa dio su nombre a su nuevo mundo.

Zeus tomba brusquement amoureux lorsqu'il vit jouer Europe, la fille du roi dans ce qui s'appelle aujourd'hui le Liban. Il prit la forme d'un magnifique taureau et sut séduire la jeune fille. Alors qu'elle s'était assise sur son dos, il plonga rapidement dans la mer et s'éloigna pour aborder à l'île de Crète. Là, il reprit sa forme réelle. Europe devint l'aimée de Zeus et lui donna deux fils, dont Cnossos qui allait faire de la Crète un royaume florissant. Europe donna son nom à sa nouvelle patrie.

Zeus si innamorò di Europa, la figlia del re, quando la vide giocare nel luogo che si chiama oggi Libano. Egli assunse la forma di un magnifico toro e riuscì a sedurre la ragazza. Mentre essa era seduta sulla sua schiena, egli si immerse in mare e si diresse verso l'isola di Creta dove riprese le sue vere sembianze. Europa divenne l'amante di Giove e gli diede due figli, uno dei quali, Cnosso, avrebbe dato grande prosperità a Creta. Europa diede il nome alla sua nuova patria.

De aanblik van de spelende koningsdochter Europa, in wat de Libanon heet, deed Zeus op' slag verliefd worden. Hij nam de gedaante aan van een prachtige stier en wist het meisje te verleiden. Toen zij op zijn rug zat sprong hij snel de zee in en zwom weg om bij het eiland Kreta weer aan land te komen. Daar nam hij zijn gestalte weer aan. Europa werd de Zeus' geliefde, schonk hem twee zonen, waarvan Knossos Kreta tot grote bloei zou brengen. Europa gaf haar naam aan het nieuwe werelddeel.

Quando Zeus viu a filha do rei, Europa, brincando no sítio onde hoje se encontra o Líbano, apaixonou-se logo por ela. Ele tomou a forma de um belo boi e conseguiu assim seduzi-la. Quando ela estava às costas dele, saltou ele para o mar e nadou até atingir a ilha de Creta, onde foi a terra. Lá tomou novamente a sua própria forma. Europa apaixonou-se por Zeus e deu-lhe dois filhos, dos quais Knossos deu um grande progresso a Creta. Europa ofereceu o seu nome ao seu novo continente.